The School of Freedom

Gilberto Highet, doctorum doctori
(1906–1978)
and to Dominique, always

The humanist wishes humanities to be taught, not as the history of superseded stages, but as the foundations of modern life.

Gilbert Highet [1]

The desire for education, as a way of life rather than as a means of livelihood or a mere intellectual exercise, is instinctive among English people and ready to reveal itself, under favourable conditions, at any moment.

Albert Mansbridge [2]

Disce ut doceas (Learn, that you may teach).

Alcuin of York [3]

---

[1] Quoted on the Columbia College website.

[2] Opening line of the preface to *University Tutorial Classes: a study in the development of higher education among working class men and women* (1913), p. vii.

[3] Sometimes claimed as the motto of the School of York; certainly an ideal Alcuin lived by, it is mentioned in his letters and was probably derived from the letters of St. Jerome.

The School of Freedom

**A Liberal Education Reader
from Plato to the Present Day**

Edited and Introduced by

Anthony O'Hear
and Marc Sidwell

imprint-academic.com

Published in the UK by Imprint Academic
PO Box 200, Exeter EX5 5YX, UK

Published in the USA by Imprint Academic
Philosophy Documentation Center
PO Box 7147, Charlottesville, VA 22906-7147, USA

ISBN 9 781845 401344

A CIP catalogue record for this book is available from the
British Library and US Library of Congress

Where possible, material has been taken from the public domain. The editors are grateful to the following copyright-holders, whose material is used with permission.

Translations of extracts from St. Augustine of Hippo's *De Magistro* and *Retractationes*, the works and letters of Alcuin, Ælfric's *Grammar*, St. Thomas Aquinas's *Quæstiones Disputatæ De Veritate*, John of Salisbury's *Metalogicon*, Richard Pace's *De Fructu Qui Ex Doctrina Percipitur* and the letters of St. Thomas More. All provided by Keith Sidwell (2008).

'An Experiment in Adult Education' by RH Tawney (1914). First published in *The Political Quarterly*, 2, May 1914. Reproduced with permission of Major General Charles Vyvyan as Executor of the RH Tawney Literary Estate.

Letter by Sir Winston Churchill to Sir Vincent Tewson (11 March 1953). Reproduced with permission of Curtis Brown Ltd, London on behalf of the Estate of Winston Churchill.

'A Place of Learning' by Michael Oakeshott (1974). By permission of Timothy Fuller, Editor of the Colorado College Studies, where the lecture was first published in Colorado College Studies 12, 1975, and of the Right Honourable Oliver Letwin MP on behalf of the Michael Oakeshott Literary Estate.

'Education, Value and the Sense of Awe' by Anthony O'Hear (1992; reprinted 2004). By permission of the author.

'The Seven Sleepers' by Mark Van Doren (1944). Copyrighted by Charles and John Van Doren as Executors of the Estate of Mark Van Doren and Used with Permission.

Translation of Goethe's 'Kennst du das Land?' Provided by Anthony O'Hear (2009)

Contents

Section 3: After Tradition

Section 4: Liberal Education *Redux*

Acknowledgements

This book has been several years in the journey from concept to publication. Thanks are due to all those who helped along the way, and to family and friends who were willing to hear of its progress and put up with its demands for so long. In particular, thank you to Ted Pappas and the Britannica blog for inviting us to join their Great Books forum, and also to both Michael Mosbacher and the Social Affairs Unit and Damian Thompson and the Catholic Herald for their early interest in the topic, and Thomas Aquinas College and Mark Henrie of the ISI for their assistance along the way. Elizabeth Sidwell's educational work remains an inspiration.

Profuse thanks to Dr Martin Stephen, High Master of St Paul's School, for providing his own take on this great and under-debated topic in his foreword, which offers an interesting essay on liberal education and its fortunes in the UK in its own right. As well as demonstrating that after 500 years the legacy of John Colet works its magic still, the High Master's foreword underlines what also emerges from the range of other pieces we include in this anthology; that what we are calling liberal education can accommodate differences of policy and emphasis, but that what matters and what unites all those who are animated by its generosity of spirit, marking them off from the dismal utilitarians and social engineers who dominate these days, is just that: the spirit, which it is the aim of this anthology to embody.

We would also like to thank the University of Buckingham, and particularly Terence Kealey its Vice Chancellor for providing for one of us an academic environment congenial to what this book stands for, and also several cohorts of Education students there, with whom many of the passages included here have been discussed (probably the only university Education department in the country where this could be done without apology or embarrassment). As always on educational matters, Chris Woodhead has been best friend and staunchest critic, while we hope that

Natasha, Jacob and Thea O'Hear still feel they have benefited from the spirit of a liberal education. Keith Sidwell's translations were invaluable — and here, as elsewhere, all errors are inevitably our own. We are also enormously grateful to the Estates of RH Tawney, Sir Winston Churchill, Mark Van Doren and Michael Oakeshott for permission to reprint extracts from these authors. Very special thanks must go to Imprint Academic for taking the project on.

Finally, a book so wide in its scope, ranging across two and a half millennia, can never do more than scratch the surface of any period and risks trespassing across the deeper knowledge of countless specialists. All we can hope is that this overview provides a reminder of the traditional meaning of a 'liberal education', encouraging deeper study and understanding.

The Strange Death of Liberal Education

Martin Stephen

(High Master, St Paul's School)

There is a basic problem with the concept of a liberal education, which is that for any state or parent-funded school pragmatism will be a bigger driver than liberalism. One definition of a liberal education is that it is an education that allows pupils to be exposed to the widest possible range of influences and opinions, seeking to develop the pupil's own judgement on those issues rather than impose or preach an Establishment view. A liberal education allows choices. A liberal education seeks to inculcate an aware-ness not just of why a thing works, but that it can be beautiful in its work-ing—a principle that applies to Maths as easily as English. A liberal education teaches passion for one's subject, a thirst for ideas rather than just facts, a hunger for food that feeds not just the mind but also the soul. A liberal education has time to gather flowers by the wayside. Unfortu-nately, this at times runs head-on into the basic need to educate children to earn a living and bang a hard core of basic skills in to them. A liberal edu-cation never ends, and the recipients carry on educating themselves long after any institution has had its way with them. Governments like boxes, with ticks in them. Like lacrosse, a liberal education is a game with no boundaries, but the urge of all but the most enlightened governments to slap border controls on at every opportunity condemns the two to a long-standing war.

Thomas Gradgrind used to symbolise the enemy of liberal education. The character in Charles Dickens's *Hard Times* famously wished to make education grindingly factual. In Gradgrind's world a horse was not a thing of beauty; it was a quadruped. The motivation behind such thinking in real as distinct from fictional society was the hard pragmatism of the Industrial Revolution. The huge wealth of the industrial revolution was not, with the exception of a very few cases, based on a liberal care for the individual and the cultivation of his or her imagination and finer sensibilities. Rather, it hinged for its success on cramming the maximum number of workers in to factories and back-to-back-housing that was a slum even as it was being built. The lasting irony of the Gradgrind approach was that it almost totally neglected science in favour of a concentration on the three R's, with a disastrous and lasting effect on this country's ability to produce or give credence to that most pragmatic of products, the engineer. That aside, the State educational system coming in to its own in the 1870's was pretty rough, tough and basic.

In an ideal world an independent sector of education would have, if not compensating, at least provided an alternative. In a dire example of why a market economy does not work in education, the independent sector instead sought to provide what its customers wanted. All too often, this was social acceptability. Thomas Arnold's 'Muscular Christianity' fed off two sources. In a country increasingly besotted by Empire and dependent on it for its wealth, the idea emerged that the role of top schools was to train people who would exercise moral leadership, a far cry from the mind-set of people such as Clive of India and those who grabbed the Empire who grasped the eternal truth that if you want an Empire your first priority is to control it, not to give it moral leadership. Moral leadership is a luxury that comes after you have acquired your Empire, and some would argue it is also the first step in losing it. It is much easier to have the secret police take Gandhi out the back and put a bullet in his head than it is to listen to him. Moral leadership also requires a very, and some would argue, too simple definition of what is good and what is bad. Such simplicity does not lend itself to a liberal anything, never mind an education. Added to the drive for moral leadership was the sad fact that for many people who had made money in the late-Victorian and Edwardian period one sent one's son to public school in order for him to undergo a form of social laundering, By following an outdated and tired curriculum consisting for the main only of the Classics, one was proving that one's heir need never work for a living. Ironically, the uselessness of the education was actually its main recommendation to many of those who purchased it.

Despite this inauspicious start, liberal education values have an annoying habit of not going away. When John Colet, Dean of St Paul's School, founded it in 1509 he announced that his school would be for the then-vast number of 153 pupils 'of all naciouns and countres indifferently', an extraordinary commitment for the time. It took some while—around 450 years—for the concept of a liberal education to make significant progress in the UK education system. Perhaps surprisingly, its heyday in the UK at least was in the late-1960's and 1970's. Grammar and Direct Grant schools may have offered a fairly unrelenting academic diet, but many of those subjects were taught for their own sake, by graduates, rather than being taught simply for examination success. The crucial importance of Art, Music and Drama spread even to the independent schools, and was accepted as a viable subject in the much-maligned comprehensive schools. That generation produced, among many others, the people who transformed the Royal Shakespeare Company and English comedy. One example is the Perse School in Cambridge, a highly academic school which nevertheless saw fit to introduce the Mummery tradition of English teaching, a quite extraordinary method that taught all English through the medium of classical drama. Sir Peter Hall was one of the people who benefited from it.

Contemporary education offers few such consolations. The most stringent testing and inspection regime of any industrialised country has come perilously close to resurrecting Thomas Gradgrind. Art, Music and Drama have been savagely slashed from school budgets. A key element in a liberal education, namely the elevation of tolerance and mutual respect in to a prime virtue, is threatened by faith schools and the polarisation of religious and ethnic groups.

Part of the sadness of the death of liberal education is that it has significant pragmatic justification. It is not just that the explosion of talent in the arts and in drama has earned this country significant amounts of money. The scientists produced by a liberal education have a capacity to be both innovative and inventive, to think outside the box, the envelope or whatever container contemporary slang uses to suggest someone whose thinking it not artificially contained and curtailed. It is no accident that the inventor of the world-wide web and the discoverers of the double helix were the product of just such a liberal education. The University of Cambridge, affording as it traditionally does its students the opportunity to change tack mid-stream in terms of what subject they study, is a flag-bearer for liberal education.

Liberals believe in the essential perfectibility of man. In education this is best expressed in trust — trust that children can make informed choices, trust that a teacher in the classroom does not have to have every sentence he or she speaks written out in advance, trust that not every good lesson has to tick all the boxes on the Inspector's clip-board. We are so far down the road of *Hard Times* that many of our politicians would not know what a liberal education was, never mind having the will to bring it back into our national culture. Perhaps a book such as this can at least make a gesture in the right direction. Who knows? It might even make a difference ....

Introduction

> We call those studies liberal, then, which are worthy of a free man:
> they are those through which virtue and wisdom are either practised
> or sought and by which the body and mind is disposed towards all the
> best things.[1]

Liberal education is not a theory. It is the tradition by which Western civilisation has preserved and enriched its inheritance for two and a half thousand years. While every civilisation persists by the instruction of the young in the ways of the past, only the Western tradition, centred upon freedom, devised a system that sought to make every human being their own master. This 'education for freedom' aimed to develop fully their capacities, that each might live well by the light of their own reason, enjoying, preserving and replenishing the treasures of their civilion: complete individuals, at home in their minds and bodies.

Yet liberal education is a term that has fallen from use in Britain, its traditional meaning now freely confused with its opposite.[2] An ahistorical view has taken hold, in which teeming theories of education exist in equal competition: all by and large recent, or at least post-Enlightenment in origin. This book is intended to correct that misapprehension, through the presentation of original source material from the high points in the liberal education tradition with particular focus on the British experience. For it is the great river of liberal learning that has carried reason, truth and individual freedom through the generations of the West. To use an image from *The Abolition of Man* by CS Lewis, the waters of liberal learning rise to irrigate deserts of ignorance; they solace the thirst of the mind unused. It is through a liberal education that most of our greatest geniuses have been encouraged to join the conversation begun in fifth-century Athens; it is the liberal education system against which others have always sought to react.

---

1   Pier Paolo Vergerio, *The Character and Studies Befitting a Free-Born Youth* (c. 1402–3).

2   See, for instance, 'Liberal education pioneer inspires new school plans', Kathleen Nutt, *The Times*, 30/7/06: 'It is the epitome of a liberal education, a school that allows pupils to skip classes, lay down their own rules and punish their classmates.'

When Rousseau, whose education began in reading Plutarch's *Lives*, wrote in Book II of his *Emile* that, '*La lecture est le fléau de l'enfance*' ['Reading is the curse of childhood'], he dreamt of throwing up a dam against the continued flow of liberal thought, not of a pedagogical system created *ex nihilo*.

Many have been tempted by Rousseau's vision since it was first articulated. While it seems perverse that anyone could choose a stagnant pond over the river of learning, such anxieties demonstrate the powerful originality of liberal education. For liberal education is a shocking idea. Where other societies used education to train men for a skill or bend them to the service of the state, the Athenians chose to set them free. No pedagogy has ever shown more faith in its charges; no generation of elders has ceded so much power to their successors.

What is Liberal Education?

I am your teacher; it is my task to educate you, to make you free.[3]

Again, liberal education is a practical tradition more than a pedagogical theory. It began and has continued to prove itself by action. That stands in contrast to Rousseau, who tested his theory on a fictional subject in *Emile*. Indeed, all education theory in the West can be said to begin as commentary upon the liberal classroom from a library desk. This distinction between the practical tradition and academe's theoretical response helps explain the current malaise of the liberal ideal, for liberal education's presence-in-the-world entails both historically contingent variations in practice that cross all schools in any one period and then constant adaptations toward local need and away from universal principles by each particular teacher. Liberal education is a working model, not a neat formula: it cannot be cut down to the size of an elegant policy paper. Yet it is by such intellectual standards that it is now judged and, as a consequence, found wanting.

Though liberal education is a broad church, there are core beliefs shared by all its followers. Liberal education begins by seeing education as shaping an individual student toward a human ideal. That ideal is characterised by personal freedom, guaranteed by self-mastery and the capacity for rational thought together with an educated sensibility in matters of value and the æsthetic. Liberal education is not vocational; it sees training and education as separate endeavours. Nevertheless, liberal education is concerned to produce individuals able to engage with the world politically, seeking to persuade others to the causes dictated by their reason. The Greek acceptance of an education for reasoned freedom was indeed predicated upon the rationality of the political life: if education for freedom

---

3   Epictetus, *Discourses*, II.19.29 (c.104–7 AD).

tended to produce introverts and solipsists who turned away from the public square, such an education and such a polity would be unsustainable. One thinks of the words Thucydides gave to Pericles:

> Here each individual is interested not only in his own affairs but in the affairs of the state as well: even those who are mostly occupied with their own business are extremely well-informed on general politics - this is a peculiarity of ours: we do not say that a man who takes no interest in politics is a man who minds his own business; we say that he has no business here at all.

Liberal education is, therefore, from the very start an education in active political independence—not by compulsion, but in its trust that reason will call its pupils to action. In the Roman tradition of Cicero and Quintilian, the ideal of the orator continued to emphasise the public duty of the educated individual. In the British tradition, from Alfred the Great to John Ruskin, the School of York to the Workers' Educational Association, liberal educators have always been engaged with their polity: seeking justice, demanding thoughtfulness, resisting their enemies.

To bring a child toward this ideal of free reason, liberal education relies upon what we might call the Three Cs: Curriculum, Canon and Character. Curriculum describes the essential knowledge and skills that must be learnt, usually codified as the seven liberal arts. Liberal education is unashamedly didactic and, moreover, didascalic[4]: it assumes that knowledge forms a whole, to be shared as far as possible by all, through one curriculum. Canon, memorably apostrophised by Matthew Arnold as 'the best that has been thought and said in the world', refers to our essential cultural treasures. Arnold's verbal and intellectual qualifiers centre the canon upon the great books, and remind us that the canon is not concerned only with imaginative works but also philosophical, political, historical and scientific classics. The commitment to a canon—although a canon permanently open to addition and piecemeal revision—shows liberal education's belief in civilisation as an ongoing conversation, to which new participants must be constantly introduced. Finally, in its attention to character, liberal education reveals its concern is not merely narrowly intellectual. As well as providing both instruction in essential subjects and introductions to great minds, liberal education seeks to work upon its charges in the name of freedom. This character education relies on the lessons of habit and particularly the moral power of instruction in certain kinds of music, dance and sport. It is a central tenet of liberal education

---

4   By extension from the *Didascalicon* of Hugh of St. Victor (written in the 1130s): concerned with teaching the full range of knowledge as an inter-related whole. Encyclopædic or cyclopædic might seem more appropriate terms, as their etymology speaks of 'the circle of knowledge', but these terms now carry a sense of exhaustive knowledge, more than a person could be naturally expected to master, misrepresenting the limited didactic ambitions of a liberal curriculum.

that personal freedom requires an internal locus of control, governed by reason but also graceful, effective and harmonious in action. A man unschooled in character could be well-read and able to reason wisely from his store of knowledge and yet be the slave of his passions, unfree to act as he thought he should.

Liberal Education aims at an ideal

> Clearly the content of education over the last two thousand years has altered significantly [...]. Nevertheless, the enterprise was informed, throughout this period, by conceptions of excellence, by the search for perfection, for the Idea in its highest form.[5]

As Bantock acknowledges, the ideal chosen by liberal educators has altered over the millennia, although it could not be said to be endlessly flexible: freedom and reason have always been integral. Today, it is this concept of a single human ideal almost as much as the nature of the ideal that marks out liberal education. This schooling is not student-centred. It has clear designs upon its charges: they are to be shaped to the liberal pattern.

Liberal education aims to teach every child how to become one, very special, kind of adult. In some of the earliest references to liberal education, Plato refers to the process as a physical moulding [πλάττειν] of the student (See *Republic* 377b; *Laws* 671c). Cicero expresses a similar idea in his *Pro Archia*: 'artibus quibus ætas puerilis ad humanitatem *informari* solet' ['those arts through which boys are normally moulded towards humanity']. The mediæval belief that bear cubs had to be 'licked into shape' by their parents, apparently popularised by the eleventh-century encyclopædia of Avicenna, provided a powerful metaphor for the abiding sense that child-rearing was a kind of soul sculpture.

The concept of pressing every child into the same mould cannot but seem oppressive. Our Romantic inheritance longs for emancipation, not prescription. Yet it remains the central paradox of liberal education that by aiming at such uniformity schools produce all the diversity of freedom. Three factors help explain the riddle.

First, the uniformity instilled by liberal education is at a deep level: it is concerned with matters of intellectual praxis and motivation, of the shared moral and cultural reference points that enrich debate between the liberally-educated, rather than the imposition of particular points of view. Liberally-educated individuals need not agree on the answers to the great questions of life; thinking for themselves, they are more likely to disagree than most. They will share a knowledge of what the great questions are, the classic responses that have been offered, and how to make (or with-

---

5   GH Bantock, 'Progressivism and the Content of Education' (1975).

hold in considered humility) their personal judgment on a controversy. Sharing so much, they will be able to discuss their differences of opinion in a civilised and humane, but still passionate, discourse.

Secondly, a liberal education sees freedom as dependent upon the use of reason. Since a child has by definition not yet reached the age of reason, freedom and childhood are irreconcilable. It is the responsibility of parents to exercise judgment on behalf of their growing children, and the most generous choice is to train the child's own reason in anticipation of his or her necessary freedom in majority. Thus from an honest, if unflattering, assessment of childhood's limits, the child is worked upon to transcend those limits and enter the adult world. Aristotle, in Book Ten of the *Nicomachean Ethics*, explains that, 'no one would choose to live with the intellect of a child throughout his life'. Vicesimus Knox, writing of the need for liberal educators to impose discipline in the eighteenth century, described childhood in stark terms.

> Human nature is, however, at every stage of life, prone to evil; particularly prone at a time when to inherent corruption are added, imbecility of understanding and want of experience.[6]

Out of the realistically critical assessment of childhood comes a commitment to education, a commitment made urgent by the sense of a time limit. The habit of learning should continue into adulthood, but the liberal arts themselves have traditionally been viewed as a transitional stage, since the training can only be imposed on a child and an adult needs such knowledge and skills at his or her fingertips. Petrarch, the father of Renaissance humanism, the movement that revived the study of Latin and Greek in the fourteenth and fifteenth centuries, wrote of the liberal arts that where we passed through with honour, we do not remain with praise, and, again, 'I do not condemn the liberal arts, but childish old people'.[7]

The ultimate justification for the imposition of the liberal ideal is the nature of that ideal—informed and reflective personal autonomy. It is indeed tyrannous to compel every child to worship a brutal dictator in the manner of fascist states. It is generosity itself to push every child toward taking responsibility for their own life. The liberal student learns by being moulded in the hands of a teacher. As an adult, he moulds himself, as Giovanni Pico Della Mirandola suggested in 1486, in his great 'Oration on the Dignity of Man'.

> [Y]ou may, as the free and proud shaper of your own being, fashion yourself in the form you may prefer.

6 From Knox's *Liberal Education* (1785); Quoted by GH Bantock in *The Minds and the Masses* (1984), p. 56.
7 A paraphrase of a quote by Robert E Proctor in *Defining the Humanities* (1998), p. 102 and a verbatim quote from the same source, p. 172.

The 'Three Cs'

(i) Curriculum

> Wisdom has builded her house, she hath hewn out her seven pillars.[8]

In mediæval universities, the *artes liberales* provided the core curriculum. There were seven 'liberal arts', codifying a tradition dating back to the ancient Greeks. The three foundational arts were known as the 'trivium'. The word connotes the junction of three roads; by implication a well-trodden thoroughfare. The roads of the trivium correspond to the three arts of language: grammar (the ability to read and express subtleties of meaning in words), dialectic (the process of reasoned and logical argument) and rhetoric (the art of communication and persuasion).

The trivial arts of language were supplemented by the four counting sciences of the 'quadrivium'. These were arithmetic (concerned with number), geometry (concerned with form), music (concerned with number and time) and astronomy (concerned with form, time and motion).[9]

Although since the Renaissance humanists there has been a tendency to read a liberal education as a study of the humanities, the quadrivium makes clear that the intent was originally wider, embracing the human capacity to understand the world through both language and number. That dual project seems to go back at least to Pythagoras in the sixth century BC, and to have come down through his influence into the doctrines of the Platonists. According to tradition, Plato had inscribed above the doorway to his Academy the phrase ΑΓΕΩΜΕΤΡΗΤΟΣ ΜΗΔΕΙΣ ΕΙΣΙΤΩ ['Let no one ignorant of geometry enter'].

The quartet of topics in the quadrivium can also be seen to move out from purely abstract numerical studies into geometry's lines, curves and shapes and the harmonies and rhythms of applied musical theory, before engaging with the nature of the heavens, a practical and ultimately scientific concern. It is also worthy of note that music, often treated as a frivolous supplement to the core curriculum today, is here a central plank, another reminder that liberal education is far from a restatement of obvious principles. In valuing music, liberal education once more rejects vocational utility for an education towards the full enjoyment of human potential.

Considered in the light of its origins, this curriculum can be understood as the skills and working knowledge of the world considered necessary for a citizen to be able to take control of his or her own life, to enjoy the full

---

8   Alcuin, quoting Proverbs 9.1 in a treatise on the trivium (8th century).

9   St. Augustine of Hippo gives the seventh art as philosophy. See his *Retractationes*, 1.6, in the section on 'Logos'.

resources of the human mind and also to serve as an active member of the educating polity—from the democracy of Athens and the Republic of Rome to the British parliamentary system. The arts of language and number remain the undeniable essence of a Western education, today more crudely articulated as the 'Three Rs'. And liberal education is also mindful of the importance, humanly speaking, of good taste in what one values in music and the other arts.

Keeping in step with the tradition, a liberal education for our older and more knowing civilisation must adapt and supplement the seven liberal arts. To the skills above, we will add our disciplines of essential knowledge: a sense of physical and temporal context through the narrative study of History and an emphasis on internalising the facts of Physical and, to a lesser extent, Human Geography. Classical and Modern Foreign Languages will be studied to permit access to great works of other times and cultures, including the indispensable writings of our Greek and Roman progenitors.

Statistics and economics are now essential additions to a liberal education in the science of number, without which much of our scientific and political discourse cannot be understood. The three master sciences of Biology, Chemistry and Physics in their descriptive/predictive as well as experimental aspects are natural replacements for Astronomy, itself no longer necessary for agriculture, navigation or divination. Finally as the student gains in maturity and experience, some initiation into the disciplines of Politics and Philosophy will be essential as introduction to the democratic conventions and intellectual arguments that each citizen will confront in adulthood.

In this re-imagining of the liberal curriculum, its three central characteristics are made plain: the liberal curriculum is not servile, it does not aim to prepare a student for a particular trade or profession; the liberal curriculum is didactic, it seeks to instil essential knowledge and skills in all students as a basis for contemplation, deliberative conversation and reasoned decision-making in adult life; the liberal curriculum is didascalic, it presents knowledge as an ordered whole in which certain disciplines take precedence over others and few, if any, subjects are optional.

(ii) Canon

> [C]ulture being a pursuit of our total perfection by means of getting to know, on all the matters which most concern us, the best which has been thought and said in the world, and, through this knowledge, turning a stream of fresh and free thought upon our stock notions and habits.[10]

---

10   Matthew Arnold, *Culture and Anarchy* (1882).

Alongside the curriculum of the seven liberal arts, there has always been a corollary emphasis on liberal education as the introduction to the greatest intellectual achievements of the student's forebears. This stresses direct engagement with original writings: Cæsar's *Gallic Wars*, for instance, rather than a textbook of classical civilisation. Face to face with genius, a pupil is inspired with the heights of human potential, instructed by the material itself and at the same time made aware of its historically-situated nature, and therefore the possibility of disagreement or disproof. This is knowledge presented as a living conversation, carried forward by individuals, one that the growing child is encouraged to join, not merely to observe. At Great Books colleges such as the twin campuses of St John's College in America, this tradition still provides the basis for a four years undergraduate course of unparalleled richness.

The canon of Great Books embraces literature, humanities and the sciences. It includes not only Shakespeare, Tolstoy and Dante, but also Newton and Darwin, Gibbon and Herodotus, Hobbes and Jefferson, Kant and Nietzsche, Adam Smith and Karl Marx. Liberal education, originating in Ancient Greece and carried into the Christian West via Rome, has also always placed a strong emphasis on the classical authors: not, as Gilbert Highet points out in *Man's Unconquerable Mind*, for their antiquarian interest, but because, in their powerful originality, 'they make us think'. The explosive power of the classical authors, with their emphasis on political liberty and the use of the intellect to establish right action, has sometimes led to their suppression. The British Parliament debated whether the Irish could be allowed to study such incendiary material. Freedom, human dignity and the power of reason are the lessons of the classics, as Hobbes knew all too well when he denounced them in his *Leviathan* and *Behemoth*. 'And as to rebellion in particular against monarchy; one of the most frequent causes of it, is the reading of the books of policy and histories of the ancient Greeks, and Romans.'[11]

The canon is notoriously subject to dispute and there will always be disagreement about the outlying contenders. However, we include in this collection an extract from David Hume's essay 'Of the Standard of Taste', in which he defends the canon and argues that greatness stands the test of time, necessitating a consistent canon. It should be remembered that even fifth-century Athens already had the example of Homer, whose genius had been accepted for centuries. In the Christian era, theologians were torn between the intellectual value they found in the pagan authors of antiquity and their faith. St. Augustine of Hippo adored the *Æneid* as a boy but as a theologian rejected 'empty romances' and regretted his lessons in

---

11   *Leviathan*, II, 29,14.

Virgil. In a letter from the fourth century, Jerome describes a nightmare in which on the Day of Judgment he is accused of being a Ciceronian and not a Christian. The Great Books have been feared as revolutionaries and as tempters. Yet they have moved the hearts of men and women in every station of life, from emperors to coal-miners. Their transformative power remains unabated and irresistible.

In their effect upon the reader, the books of the Western canon also present a philosophical dilemma. For there is a clear gap between the external, mandated content of a canon and the internal revolution these tools are intended to achieve. Can an educator ever close the gap between the words read and the lesson taken? As ever with liberal education, its practical and continued success is the best answer to the philosophical conundrum. Nevertheless, demonstrating the intellectual integrity and self-reflexive nature of liberal education, we have included an extract from the *De Magistro* of St. Augustine of Hippo, in which he attempts to solve this very question.

The development of a canon remains a central part of the project of liberal education. A canon is necessary first because the period of education is strictly limited and all works cannot be included. A canon also improves the conversation between liberally-educated minds: where there are points of common reference and knowledge it is easier to discuss a question in depth. Since selection is unavoidable, criticism — the search for the very best — becomes essential. The canon is made up of the necessary books: the finest displays of literary skill and the most original thoughts that challenge every generation of learners and remain their companions throughout their lives. As Charles Augustin Sainte-Beuve argues in 'What is A Classic?' the Great Books are always contemporary.

> A true classic, as I should like to hear it defined, is an author who has enriched the human mind, increased its treasure, and caused it to advance a step; who has discovered some moral and not equivocal truth, or revealed some eternal passion in that heart where all seemed known and discovered; who has expressed his thought, observation, or invention, in no matter what form, only provided it be broad and great, refined and sensible, sane and beautiful in itself; who has spoken to all in his own peculiar style, a style which is found to be also that of the whole world, a style new without neologism, new and old, easily contemporary with all time.

Robin Lane Fox, the academic and historian, has observed that reading Homer has been, 'one of the points of my life.'[12] CS Lewis thought that, 'to lose what I owe to Plato and Aristotle would be like the amputation of a

---

12   'Hooked on classics', Sally Kinnes, *Sunday Times*, 13/8/06.

limb.'[13] No one who has known the enrichment of life from great works of art, literature and philosophy would deny that this has made them a more fully formed and integrated human being. The human condition can only be grasped through the few, eternal works that penetrate our nature and demonstrate its permanence. Those trapped in the windowless room of the present can never truly know themselves or their own capacities. It is sometimes said, with a nod at culture-loving Nazis, that appreciation of the arts does not make men or women better. Great art does make a man more deeply himself. Liberal education is concerned with the canon for its own sake, for its value to each individual student, not for its social utility. Yet liberal education does place a value upon instruction towards virtue in other ways, as the next section will make clear.

(iii) Character

> This man is freed from servile bands
> Of hope to rise or fear to fall:
> Lord of himself, though not of lands,
> And having nothing, yet hath all.[14]

For the Athenians and their inheritors, education has always involved control of the body as well as the mind, a sense of harmonious action that could support the inward search for the true and the beautiful. To this end, a liberal education included not only music, but also dance and gymnastics — features of Plato's scheme for an ideal education, and still recognisable in the emphasis on musical performance and competitive sports at English public schools.

> Enough has been said to show that music has a power of forming the character, and should therefore be introduced into the education of the young.[15]

We are accustomed today to think of such pursuits as incidental rather than formative; the liberal educators have always granted them a central function, born of their understanding that character grows through practice and exposure to good influence rather than through the power of reason.

Character might be defined as practical wisdom, not merely knowing the good, but acting well: that which Aristotle designates as *'phronesis'* in the *Nicomachean Ethics*. As Aristotle also observed, we do not arrive at such mastery through reason but habit. Like any practical skill, such as building or playing a musical instrument, we begin by imitation of a master. Kant

---

13   In 'The Idea of an "English School"', *Rehabilitations and Other Essays* (1939), p. 64.
14   Sir Henry Wotton, 'The Character of a Happy Life' (17th century).
15   Aristotle, *Politics*, Book 8.

makes the same point in *On Education*: 'Discipline changes animal nature into human nature'. (I.3) More recently, RS Peters wrote in the 1960s of 'The Paradox of Moral Education', referencing Aristotle's observation that the palace of wisdom is reached through the courtyard of habit. This paradox is a special instance of the larger paradox of liberal education that we have already seen: under the pressure of adult strictures, the child moves toward freedom. It deserves a brief discussion in its own right.

Education for character is a proper part of liberal education because it identifies freedom with self-mastery. When we consider the classical virtues — prudence, justice, temperance and fortitude — they are all concerned not to impose prescriptive norms of conduct, but rather to subdue emotional responses such that the virtuous individual has greater rational control of his or her own life. Without prudence, we end in bankruptcy; without temperance, our greed will drive us to addiction and obesity; without fortitude we will be broken by fortune's slings and arrows; without justice, our conduct becomes arbitrary, breaking all the bonds of reciprocity and shared humanity that make the joys of human society possible. Through music and dance, gymnastic and sporting instruction, the liberally educated character will not only be more capable of the virtues of restraint, but becomes patterned with the easy and harmonious actions of the true gentleman, defined by Cardinal Newman as a person 'who never inflicts pain', which actions, Plato argues, also underpin the inner quest for truth, goodness and beauty.

The importance of character education through habitual training was stressed as early as Plato and Aristotle, and has remained a constant theme in the tradition. The Roman Stoics saw personal control as the only answer to the vicissitudes of fate. Christianity added faith, hope and charity to the virtues, and argued that self-mastery was now within the province of every soul. Petrarch's revival of the classical authors was born in large measure as he sought to control his own despair in a Europe devastated by plague. Today, character education remains a central topic in America's education debates. Senator John McCain published *Character is Destiny* in 2005, a collection of inspirational biographies illustrating the virtues, aimed at a school-age audience.[16]

Senator McCain's title captures another reason for the liberating qualities of character education: it believes that a child can choose to be a different kind of person. To believe in character education is to escape from the fatalism that follows inescapably on a pedagogy that lets every child live

---

16   Illustrating that such concerns are above all political lines, Gordon Brown published *Courage: 8 Portraits* in 2007, another collection of inspirational biographies emphasising the importance of character.

out their own moods. Senator McCain makes the point well in his introduction.

> It is your character, and your character alone, that will make your life happy or unhappy. That is all that really passes for destiny. And you choose it.

An education for character, as always in liberal education, begins in compulsion and habitual repetition but moves toward free choice. A canon of art and music, a given set of physical disciplines on the sports pitch or in dance and gymnastics, all tend to instil grace and freedom within and without. In this sense, its early strictures are no paradox at all, but rather the equivalent of the universally mandated scales and arpeggios that ultimately permit every musician to play the melody of his or her choice.

It must be added that it is of course possible to be of good moral character without an education. Yet the gifted still have lessons to learn. One of the persisting arguments between Christianity and liberal education is whether it would be better to be ignorant and pious or well-educated and of bad character. The film *Forrest Gump* made popular entertainment out of its celebration of the Holy Fool. Liberal education strives instead for both strength of character and wisdom, arguing that to rely on natural goodness of character either ignores the crooked timber of humanity or at least discriminates against those of us without such inborn grace. Further, goodness without the refinements of a liberal education will lack the power and delicacy of judgment that Newman identified in the gentleman and which a Gump could never compass.

> His benefits may be considered as parallel to what are called comforts or conveniences in arrangements of a personal nature: like an easy chair or a good fire, which do their part in dispelling cold and fatigue, though nature provides both means of rest and animal heat without them.

An education in character should complete and accentuate what may be present by nature. It also seeks to reform that which nature has flawed, giving one more indication of the characteristic generosity of the liberal education project. If not always achieving its goals, the ends toward which it moves ensure that more children enter adulthood in possession of a good character than a Romantic faith in their goodness would manage alone.

Liberal Education for all?

> It is a complaint without foundation that, 'to very few people is granted the faculty of comprehending what is imparted to them, and that most, through dullness of understanding, lose their labour and

their time'. On the contrary, you will find the greater number of men both ready in conceiving and quick in learning, since such quickness is natural to man.[17]

Liberal education begins as an extension of an aristocratic, leisured tradition of education to all Athenian citizens, in recognition of their democratic rights and responsibilities. That inception contains the defining generosity and optimism of the tradition. Robert Maynard Hutchins, one of the major American spokesmen for liberal education's revival in the twentieth century, used to say that, 'the best education for the best is the best education for all'. Every man and woman, says the liberal educator, deserves to be educated toward the management of their own lives.

Precisely because it has never been vocational, the absence of women from the world of work was never seen as a reason to refuse their liberal education. Consequently, sex equality has always been at the heart of the tradition. Plato mandates the same education for both sexes in his *Republic*. When St. Thomas More recreated the Academy within his household it was so that his daughters could be properly educated. In *The Taming of the Shrew*, Shakespeare expresses the sentiment through the father of Katherine and Bianca.

Baptista:
> Schoolmasters will I keep within my house
> Fit to instruct her youth. If you, Hortensio,
> Or, Signor Gremio, you know any such,
> Prefer them hither; for to cunning men
> I will be very kind, and liberal
> To mine own children in good bringing up.[18]

Liberal education is not just concerned with equality between the sexes, but across all classes, backgrounds and political persuasions. Such optimism opposes the contemporary doctrine of 'relevance', which would set readings in the light of a student's social background and presumed level of competence. Refusing such a prejudicial assessment of what any child can master, liberal education allows all students access to the very best.

Many sources attest to the benefits of this open-minded approach. Perhaps the most famous example is that of Kate McMullen, the illegitimate child of an alcoholic mother, born into poverty in North East England, who left school at thirteen and went into domestic service before ultimately reinventing herself as Catherine Cookson, Britain's most widely read novelist. Always possessed of a sense that she could rise in society, McMullen acknowledged that her achievement of that dream was due in no small part to the encouragement and stimulus she found in the eigh-

---

17   Quintilian, *Institutio Oratoria*, I.1.1 (c. AD 92).
18   I.1.94-99.

teenth-century letters of Lord Chesterfield to his bastard son, encouraging his self-improvement.

> He helped me enormously, my life's really been Lord Chesterfield ver-
> sus my Grand-da. Then I went to the public library and read all sorts of
> things, Erasmus and John Donne and Chaucer. At first I thought Eras-
> mus made that "Erathmic Soap" they used to advertise, but I soon
> learnt better.[19]

Borrowing volumes from South Shields library, a workhouse laundress discovered the world of humane learning. It was a route-map not just to fame and fortune, but to a fuller human life. With a former Lord Lieutenant of Ireland as her guide, Kate McMullen could begin her transformation into Catherine Cookson.

Jonathan Rose has made a wide study of reading habits among the working classes in nineteenth-century and early twentieth-century Britain, finding many analogous stories. Striking examples populate his 2004 article for *City Journal*, 'The Classics in the Slums'. JR Clynes (b. 1869) rose from the textile mills of Oldham to deputy leader of the House of Commons, taking his political lessons from Shakespeare's *Twelfth Night* and *Julius Cæsar*. Joseph Keating shovelled waste in a mine and studied Greek philosophy by night. He was not alone: deep below the surface he heard a co-worker quoting Pope to ease his mind. Many workers encountered the classics to their lasting benefit, thanks to an education system that still paid tribute to the canon and also due to copyright laws that made classic works cheaper than the latest writing.

More recently, Earl Shorris has brought liberal education to the modern American underclass through his Clemente Course in the Humanities. Beginning in New York, demanding only the ability to read a tabloid newspaper, Shorris introduced the poor and marginalised to Socrates, logic and a range of college-level humanities modules. The course has been taken up nationally and internationally with considerable success, demonstrating the continuing power of a liberal education to reach those far enough from aristocracy as to constitute its antonym.

The point was proved from the 1880s into the first quarter of the twentieth century in Britain with the University Settlement and Educational Settlement movements, from which Toynbee Hall remains the most famous instance. Latterly inspired by Quakerism and generally taking a more socially conservative standpoint than Shorris, strong on religious education, fellowship and service, the settlements brought the university-educated to live among the poor, providing a liberal education and putting their own liberal education to use. Choosing to transfer their natural civic

---

19   From an interview with John Mortimer.

duties onto deprived neighbourhoods, the settlements brought liberal education and fresh hope to the ash heap of Victorian society. The Mary Ward Centre in London continues to offer Adult Education courses in the home of the Passmore Edwards Settlement, which she founded after the runaway success of her novel *Robert Elsmere* (1888), the tale of a heterodox East End settlement.

However, evidence that some of the poor have benefited from a liberal education is not to prove that it can easily be given to all. The conflict between the generous ambitions of liberal education and the challenges of modern, mass education remains imperfectly resolved. In Britain it was hoped by some that a comprehensive system of schooling would preserve all that was valuable in grammar school education for those children who received it and make it available to more children. That did not happen, and we discuss an article by GH Bantock from the 1970s, in which he attempts to explain what was lost in these well-meaning plans. In the next section of this essay, we examine the historical role of Christianity in widening access to liberal education, and the complications this entails.

If liberal education does not offer a simple answer to the question of how to introduce every child to liberal learning, nevertheless it offers an attitude of optimism in the debate. To the liberal educator, class is no more important than sex: the individual is measured by their capacity to receive liberal instruction, and there is a natural presumption of capacity. Equally, in its combination of a conservative account of human nature with a view of politics as open to progress and change through rational debate and individual action, liberal education manages to stand not merely above class but also above political allegiances. Both the Right and Left can find common cause in a system of education that prepares the citizen to choose wisely. From the neoconservatism of Leo Strauss, who saw liberal education as the 'counterpoison to mass culture' to the cultural relativism of Earl Shorris, liberal education remains the cause of thoughtful individuals, whatever their affiliation or background.

Controversies of Liberal Education

(i) Christianity and Liberal Education

> A person who is a good and a true Christian should realize that truth belongs to his lord, wherever it is found, gathering and acknowledging it even in pagan literature but rejecting superstitious vanities.[20]

Christianity preserved and extended the liberal education tradition after the fall of Rome. The monastic schools kept liberal learning alive in the

---

20 St. Augustine of Hippo, *De Doctrina Christiana* (AD 426/427).

Dark Ages. The mediæval universities began in scholasticism and then accepted the new learning of the Renaissance humanists, but in both phases offered a liberal arts education for the priesthood and not merely a vocational course in theology. Hastings Rashdall, in his seminal 1936 history, *The Universities of Europe in the Middle Ages*, writes that, 'the pursuit of knowledge became an end in itself: a disinterested intellectual enthusiasm became an element of the Churchman's ideal'. Throughout the twentieth century and into our own day, it has been true that many of the strongest proponents of liberal education have evinced a strong, if not always orthodox, faith. From spokesmen such as Cardinal Newman and CS Lewis, to practitioners from Albert Mansbridge of the Workers' Educational Association to Alexander Lindsay, the founder of Keele University, to the growing Christian Classical School and Catholic College movements in America today, Christian faith features strongly in the liberal education movement, even as state education has tended towards secular forms.

It must be stressed that liberal education is by no means an exclusively Christian concern. Beginning in pagan Greece and Rome, liberal education has been taken up by atheistic social reformers, Jewish intellectuals like Leo Strauss and a secular thinker like Michael Oakeshott. Liberal education is valued by all those who see individual freedom based upon the exercise of human reason as a primary good, and who recognise in the Western canon a community of human experience and insight that stretches across millennia.

It is also evident that Christianity in some moods is antagonistic to liberal education. Not every Catholic found the pronouncements of Cardinal Newman to their taste. St. Jerome and St. Augustine of Hippo were both torn between their appreciation of certain pagan authors and their faith in the all-sufficiency of Holy Writ. In his *Confessions*, I.13–14, it is clear that Augustine hated the Greek lessons of his own schooldays, and latterly repented of his relish for Virgil's *Æneid*. In *De Doctrina Christiana* he admits pagan learning (not pagan fiction) to Christian study, but only in order to advance biblical exegesis. Today, the theory of evolution keeps evangelical Protestants committed to the literal truth of the Bible from joining the scientific mainstream. Patrick Henry College and the Logos School are significant American instances of the liberal education tradition being carried forward by those who provide an exceptionally high standard of education but also teach evolution as an error of thought.

Christianity may not be a necessary component of every variety of liberal education. Nevertheless, despite tensions, it will continue to be a powerful force in the preservation and spread of the tradition. This is because Christianity, while offering salvation through faith rather than intellect, nevertheless, born of the Hebraic tradition, also gives a high status to reason and to individual self-mastery in God's service. St. Thomas Aquinas, the *Doctor Communis* or Universal Doctor of the Catholic Church, brought Christian theology and Aristotelian logic into harmony. In the 1998 encyclical, *Fides et Ratio*, Pope John Paul II declared that, 'Faith and reason are like two wings on which the human spirit rises to the contemplation of truth.'

Perhaps most significant of all, it is the universal ambition of the Christian Church, seeking to bring every human soul to the free worship of God, that helped remake liberal education as a practical mass project. The Athenians may have extended liberal education to all citizens, but their franchise was far from universal and Aristotle saw some humans as natural slaves. For the Roman Stoics, the freedom brought through education was only theoretically available to all. Epictetus saw his task as giving freedom to able students, not perfecting a general human capacity. The good human life required the very highest levels of intellectual self-mastery; all could try, but few would succeed. Cicero goes so far as to write in *De Re Publica* (I.28)

> [T]hough others may be called men, none are really so but those who are perfected in the arts appropriate to humanity.

Christianity transformed these limiting interpretations. Offering universal salvation through special grace, the Church taught that while fallen humanity could never hope to escape its sinfulness on earth, every human being was born with free will and could become a better person with the help of the triune God and their own God-given reason. As we saw in relation to character education, this can sometimes lead to a claim that education towards freedom is now unnecessary. At its best however, such faith goes hand in hand with the injunction to as much education as natural capacity, aided by the Holy Spirit, will receive. CS Lewis gives a stern rebuke on this subject.

> The proper motto is not 'Be good, sweet maid and let who can be clever,' but 'Be good, sweet maid, and don't forget that this involves being as clever as you can'.[21]

Lewis expresses the traditional view. Liberal education, coming to Britain and the post-Roman world through the Christian Church, confirmed its universal optimism and its human value by alliance with religious faith.

The ideal of universal education is no longer a purely Christian province, yet as we have seen in the British experiment with comprehensivisation, mass liberal education shorn of a Christian context can easily run aground on the shoals of individual difference. Leo Strauss

---

21   *Mere Christianity* (1952), Book III, Chapter 2.

conceived of reviving the pre-Christian tradition, at the price of educating only a few, as he makes clear in his lecture of 1959, 'What is Liberal Education?'.

> Liberal education is the necessary endeavor to found an aristocracy within democratic mass society. Liberal education reminds those members of a mass democracy who have ears to hear, of human greatness.

It is a feature of our current educational predicament that the intellectual mainstream finds both a Straussian elite and a wide-reaching Christian pedagogy intolerant. A mass secular liberal education remains to be formulated, although Mortimer Adler's *The Paideia Proposal* (1982) could be considered a first attempt. Adler himself, it should be noted, converted to Christianity in 1983 and was received into the Catholic Church in 1999.

The importance of Christianity to liberal education is longstanding, continuing and cannot be gainsaid. Yet the two co-exist uneasily and the relationship must be constantly reaffirmed and re-examined if it is not to suffer deformation. Christianity's universal love of humankind demands that it extend the education it helped to forge to all persons, whatever their background, in the hope of their free choice of salvation. Liberal education demands that Christians prefer St. Anselm of Canterbury's '*Credo ut intelligam*' to Tertullian's apocryphal '*Credo quia absurdum*' [actually '*certum est, quia impossibile*'].[22] Never entirely reconciled, the Christian faith and liberal education are bound together by history and a commitment to truth and reason. They must continue to work out their differences in the twenty-first century, to the benefit of all.

(ii) Science and Liberal Education

> [I]f I had to live my life again, I would have made a rule to read some poetry and listen to some music at least once every week; for perhaps the parts of my brain now atrophied would thus have been kept active through use. The loss of these tastes is a loss of happiness, and may possibly be injurious to the intellect, and more probably to the moral character, by enfeebling the emotional part of our nature.[23]

Darwin acknowledged that his great scientific work had been achieved at the cost of a *déformation professionnelle*: he had lost his appreciation of the humanities. Recognising that science, for all its remarkable achievements, may if over-emphasised imbalance the study of other liberal arts, liberal

22 '*Credo ut intelligam*': 'I believe in order to understand' [*Proslogion* I; derived from the writings of St. Augustine of Hippo]; '*Credo quia absurdum*': 'I believe because it is absurd'; '*certum est, quia impossibile*': 'It is certain, because it is impossible' [James Moffatt suggests the influence of Aristotle's *Rhetoric* II.23.21 (1400a5), on the unlikelihood of certain statements increasing their credibility].
23 Charles Darwin, *The Autobiography of Charles Darwin* (1876).

education has tended to be cautious in the status given to the sciences in its curriculum. This caution has shifted over the centuries: Aristotle and Cardinal Newman both emphasised science more than Petrarch and Matthew Arnold. Both the editors of this volume would certainly wish to assert the value of a religiously neutral science to any liberal curriculum. Yet since the Enlightenment science has staked a new claim: calling the heart of education for its own. That status is one liberal educators have always been loath to concede. This collection references two pairs of lectures: the notorious Snow-Leavis dispute and also a conversation between Darwin's Bulldog, Thomas Huxley, and Matthew Arnold. Both Arnold and Leavis resist the claims of science to centrality, without refusing its importance in education.

This second-order position for science within the liberal curriculum is entirely consistent with its didascalic nature, as outlined earlier. Liberal learning situates its disciplines in relation to one another. Some are valuable, without being of central importance. Leonardo Bruni, the leading Renaissance humanist, explained the point in terms of mathematics.

> For there are certain disciplines in which just as it is not fitting to be entirely uninstructed, so too there is nothing glorious in ascending to their heights — for example, geometry and arithmetic, in which, if one were to continue to consume a great deal of time, prying into their subtleties and obscurities, I would pull him up and drag him away.[24]

Science provides important information about the behaviour of the physical world, essential facts to be learned and a method of investigation to be grasped and followed. However, much of science being concerned with means rather than ends, much of science education will be directed to the achievement of our goals, rather than the setting of them. And even where science is conceived as the disinterested enquiry into the ultimate processes of the universe and of nature, it will do this in a way which prescinds from human meanings, concerns and goals, treating the world as it would be even if we were not there. By contrast, the humanities, concerned with knowing the human condition and judging right human action, remain at the centre of a true liberal education. Sir Richard Livingstone made the point robustly in his *A Defence of a Classical Education*, written in 1916.

> While supporting any attempt to improve the teaching of science where it is deficient, and to bring more science where it is needed in national life, we shall remember that an education based on physical science would not only leave the mind unflexible, unsympathetic, unimaginative, undeveloped, but would ignore what is more important than the cosmos itself. Our motto was written 2500 years ago on

---

24   Quoted in Proctor (1998), p.9.

the walls of the temple of Apollo at Delphi, Γνῶθι σεαυτόν, 'Know Thyself'.

In fact, in rejecting the Baconian view of science as primarily a means to remake the world for man's desiring and viewing science as first and foremost a means to grasp the world more fully, liberal education separates science from engineering, and draws it into the circle of liberal knowledge. Rather than Baconian over-reaching, this is science through the eyes of Aristotle. Following the first line of the *Metaphysics*, it says 'all men desire to know', and not that Man is the world's master. This could be felt as a demotion, for both science and Man, but it is a more secure place for science in a world of ecological concern. Today, the transforming power of science is viewed with increasing suspicion. Placed within the liberal framework, science still reaches out upon the world, but with less pride and from a standpoint in the order of knowledge that a rejection of certain technologies cannot shake.

Liberal Education and the Future

what we have loved,
Others will love and we will teach them how[25]

The Spanish Jesuit, Juan Bonifacio, wrote in 1576 that '*Puerilis institutio est renovatio mundi*' ['the education of children is the renewal of the world'].[26] Liberal education is the means by which the West renews itself in every generation. Often unremarked, liberal education has been the background of Western success for more than twenty centuries. At times of intellectual ferment such as the rise of Christianity, the rediscovery of classical learning and more recently the rise of science we find liberal education at the centre of the debate, struggling to react to change without losing contact with its original principles. At times of crisis, liberal education is reasserted by the West's defenders. So Alfred the Great was translating Boethius even as he struggled with the Danish barbarians, Sir Richard Livingstone first spoke up for a classical education in the midst of World War I, while Dorothy L Sayers, TS Eliot and CS Lewis defended the tradition during and immediately after the West's existential struggle with Nazism.

It is no surprise that the great revival of liberal education in the twentieth century occurred in the United States of America, a nation founded on liberty. It would be tragic if Britain, having played a central role in the preservation of liberal learning across many centuries, should reject this most precious inheritance. Now it is American students who know Mil-

---

25 William Wordsworth, 'The Prelude', Book 14 (1799–1805).
26 Quoted by John Paul Russo in *The Future Without a Past* (2005), p. 83.

ton's *Areopagitica* better than Milton's own countrymen, and country-women. It is American parents who have taken a lecture given in Oxford by Dorothy Sayers and turned *The Lost Tools of Learning* into a new system of schooling. In Britain, everyone knows our ancient grammar schools had to go, but few appreciate the golden thread broken in that decision.

However, the recent general amnesia in Britain over liberal education has given rise to several significant philosophical efforts to justify the tradition to modernity. We collect two contributions from recent decades. Liberal education remains a practical tradition, but it will only reclaim its place in the classroom if it can persuade the sceptical intellects of the twenty-first century to respect its merit on paper.

We believe that merit cannot be ignored. Liberal education exists in a condition of eternal urgency; it knows that it has a brief time in which to act, and a great responsibility to discharge. The ancient Greeks understood that children are always strangers in the land unless we bring them into the secrets of their inheritance. Their phrase οι νεοι, 'the new ones', implies both childishness and an ignorance of tradition.[27] Carrying in their language the reminder that civilisation must be instilled in every generation, the Greeks devoted themselves as no other culture to the task of education, of, in their word, *paideia*.

We must learn once more that the classical texts are not important because they are old, but because they are the beginning of an exceptional civilisation, with the power to open our minds as nothing else can. We must remember that to leave our children to find their own sense in the world is to reject them, to leave them aliens in their own country. Teaching our children to be free, we will rediscover the confidence and the means by which anyone of any background, as Isocrates promised, can share the conversation of reason, culture and self-mastery that first took place around the hearth-fires of Athens.

ΛΙΜΗΝ ΠΕΦΥΚΕ ΠΑΣΙ ΠΑΙΔΕΙΑ ΒΡΟΤΟΙΣ

Paideia, said the Greek dramatist Menander, three hundred years before the birth of Christ, 'is a haven for all mankind'.[28] This is the continuing message of the liberal education tradition. Now, in an hour where mankind is in need of havens and of unifying ideals, it is vital to remember how we came to those heights of civilisation we now occupy. Tolstoy used to say that without Greek, there is no education. Without our ancient school of freedom, Britain, and the West at large, will find it ever harder to pass forward the torch of liberty.

---

27 See *The Clouds* by Aristophanes, 1059.

28 Menander, *Monostichoi* (*Maxims*) 2 and 312; Quoted in *Paideia*, trans. Highet (1943), p. ix.

Further Reading

I. The Classical Tradition

Paideia: The Ideals of Greek Culture, Werner Jaeger, trans. Gilbert Highet (1944).

The Classical Tradition: Greek and Roman Influences on European Literature, Gilbert Highet (1949).

The Classical Heritage and its Beneficiaries, RR Bolgar (1954).

Greek Ways: How the Greeks Created Western Civilization, Bruce Thornton (2000).

Climbing Parnassus: A New Apologia for Greek and Latin, Tracy Lee Simmons (2002).

Amo, Amas, Amat and All That, Harry Mount (2006; published in the US as *Carpe Diem: Put a Little Latin in Your Life*, 2007).

It's All Greek to Me, Charlotte Higgins (2008).

[See also *Iris Magazine*, a classics magazine designed for secondary students published by the Iris Project, which promotes classical education in the UK's state schools.]

II. The Great Books

The Western Canon: The Books and School of the Ages, Harold Bloom (1994).

Great Books: My Adventures with Homer, Rousseau, Woolf and Other Indestructible Writers of the Western World, David Denby (1996).

The Great Canon Controversy: the Battle of the Books in Higher Education, William Casement (1996).

The New Lifetime Reading Plan: The Classical Guide to World Literature, Revised and Expanded, Clifton Fadiman and John S Major (1999; Fadiman's original *Lifetime Reading Plan* was published in 1960).

The Great Books: From The Iliad *and* The Odyssey *to Goethe's* Faust: *a journey through 2,500 years of the West's classic literature*, Anthony O'Hear (2007; ISI Books, 2009).

A Great Idea at the Time: The Rise, Fall and Curious Afterlife of the Great Books, Alex Beam (2008).

Racing Odysseus: A College President Becomes a Freshman Again, Roger H Martin (2008).

The Whole Five Feet: What the Great Books Taught Me About Life, Death and Pretty Much Everything Else, Christopher R Beha (2009).

[The Harvard Classics can be found online at Bartleby.]

III. Liberal Education, in History, Practice and Theory

How to Read a Book: The Art of Getting a Liberal Education, Mortimer Jerome Adler (1940; substantially revised with Charles Van Doren in 1972)

Liberal Education, Mark Van Doren (1943)

Education for Freedom, Robert Maynard Hutchins (1943)

The Abolition of Man: Or, Reflections on education with special reference to the teaching of English in the upper forms of schools, CS Lewis (1943)

The Great Conversation (1952;1990) [*Great Books of the Western World*, I]

Escape from Scepticism: Liberal Education as if Truth Mattered, Christopher Derrick (1977)

The Paideia Proposal: An Educational Manifesto, Mortimer J Adler, on behalf of the members of the Paideia Group (1982)

Orators and Philosophers: A History of the Idea of Liberal Education, Bruce Kimball (1986; 1995)

The Closing of the American Mind, Allan Bloom (1987)

Cultural Literacy: What Every American Needs to Know, ED Hirsch (1987)

Education's Great Amnesia: Reconsidering the Humanities from Petrarch to Freud: with a Curriculum for Today's Students, Robert E Proctor (1988; reprinted in a second edition as *Defining the Humanities: How Rediscovering a Tradition Can Improve Our Schools*, 1998)

Another Sort of Learning: Selected Contrary Essays on How Finally to Acquire an Education While Still in College or Anywhere Else, James V Schall (1988)

Recovering the Lost Tools of Learning: An Approach to Distinctively Christian Education, Douglas Wilson (1991)

Cultivating Humanity: A Classical Defense of Reform in Liberal Education, Martha C Nussbaum (1997)

Who Killed Homer?: The Demise of Classical Education and the Recovery of Greek Wisdom, Victor Davis Hanson and John Heath (1998)

The Well-Trained Mind: A Guide to Classical Education at Home, Susan Wise Bauer and Jessie Wise (1999)

Liberal Anxieties and Liberal Education, Alan Ryan (1999)

A Student's Guide to the Core Curriculum, Mark Henrie (2000)

A Student's Guide to Liberal Learning, James V Schall (2000)

Riches for the Poor: The Clemente Course in the Humanities, Earl Shorris (2000)

Radical Visions: Stringfellow Barr, Scott Buchanan, and Their Efforts on behalf of Education and Politics in the Twentieth Century, Charles A Nelson (2001)

The Greatest Minds and Ideas of All Time, Will Durant, Compiled and Edited by John Little (2003)

The Future Without a Past: The Humanities in a Technological Society, John Paul Russo (2005)

The Great Tradition, ed. Richard M Gamble (2007)

The Illumination of Merton Browne, JM Shaw (2007)

Bringing Knowledge Back In: From social constructivism to social realism in the sociology of education, Michael FD Young (2007)

Real Education: Four Simple Truths for Bringing America's Schools Back to Reality, Charles Murray (2008)

IV. The Trivium

The Trivium Integrated with College Composition, Sister Miriam Joseph (1937; revised by Marguerite McGlinn as *The Trivium: The Liberal Arts of Grammar, Logic and Rhetoric* in 2002)

Classical Rhetoric for the Modern Student, Edward PJ Corbett and Robert J Connors (Fourth edition, 1998)

Rediscover Grammar, David Crystal (Second edition, 2004)

Socratic Logic: A Logic Text Using Socratic Method, Platonic Questions, and Aristotelian Principles, Peter Kreeft (Second edition, 2005)

V. Lectures, Essays and Articles

'What is Liberal Education?', Leo Strauss, June 1959.

'Liberal Education and Responsibility', Leo Strauss, March 1960.

[Both lectures are collected in Strauss's *Liberalism Ancient and Modern* (1968).]

Michael Oakeshott, 'Education: The Engagement and its Frustration' (1971). [Reprinted in *Education and the Development of Reason*, ed. Dearden, Hearst and Peters (1972) and in *The Voice of Liberal Learning*, ed. Timothy Fuller (1989; 2001).]

Roger Scruton, 'Modern Philosophy and the Neglect of Æsthetics' (1987).

[*Times Literary Supplement*, 5/6/87; *The Philosopher on Dover Beach* (1990).]

'The Necessity of the Classics', Louise Cowan, *Intercollegiate Review*, 37:1, Fall 2001, 3-11.

'Whither the Great Books?', William Casement, *Academic Questions*, Fall 2002, 36-47. [Lists Great Books courses in the US]

'The Pursuit of Excellence', Anthony O'Hear (1992). Reprinted in *Values, Education and the Human World*, ed. John Haldane, Imprint Academic (2004).

'The Classics in the Slums', Jonathan Rose, *City Journal*, Autumn 2004.

'The New Classical Schooling', Peter J Leithart, *Intercollegiate Review*, 43:1, Spring 2008, 3-12.

'Academic Freedom and the Liberal Arts', Robert P George, *The American Spectator*, September 2008, 28-36.

'The Humanities Move Off Campus', Victor David Hanson, *City Journal*, Autumn 2008, vol. 18, no. 4.

SECTION ONE
Origins

*Liberal education was born alongside the democratic freedoms of Athens. Centuries later, the Romans turned to Greece in order to cultivate their highest selves. As Horace observed (*Epistulæ, *II.2, 156-7)* 'Græcia capta ferum victorem cepit et artes intulit agresti Latio' *[Greece, though captured, captured her savage conqueror and brought the arts into rustic Latium]. Cicero and the Stoics were instrumental in reviving the liberal education tradition for the Empire. With the spread of Christianity and the conversion of Constantine, liberal education encountered a fresh opportunity, and a fresh challenge: the Greek concept of Logos became identified with God Himself, but the power of revelation could claim to have supplanted reason. Despite his schoolboy disdain for Greek, his abiding disquiet at the study of artistic fictions (reminiscent of Plato) and his disgust before pagan claims to intellectual adequacy without Christian faith, St. Augustine ultimately asserted the value, although not the necessity or sufficiency, of the pagan authors. Today, anti-intellectual strains of Christianity endure, but the papacy values* 'fides et ratio': *reason and faith. The Christian faith was spread by reasoned advocacy in the name of a God who was Reason itself. Liberal education would persist in Europe after the fall of Rome by way of the Church.*

Chapter I

Greece: Paideia

Liberal education begins in Greece, where it was known as παιδεια or *paideia* (pronounced "pye–day–ah"). Today the word survives in English as part of the compound word 'encyclopædia', which literally refers to a complete circle of knowledge. *Paideia* itself described a suite of different skills and knowledge, both physical (gymnastic and musical skill; virtuous and graceful bodily habits), mental (logical, reasoned thought; knowledge of the mathematical arts; instruction in classic authors) and interpersonal (the skilled and grammatical use of language, particularly in order to discuss a subject publicly and persuade others of the correct course of action through rhetoric). These were considered not the attributes required for any particular career (the concern of slaves), but the sign of an excellent, fully-realised human being, thinking and deciding for himself or herself (Plato's *Republic* recommends educating both men and women as Guardians) by way of the arts of language and number. Those so educated were also being prepared to argue toward the truth with other citizens on great questions of policy as part of the world's first democracy: thus *paideia* was an education for both personal and political freedom. The democracy of Athens became the great centre of liberal education, and Isocrates boasts by 380 BC that his city has become an inspiration to all of Greece. But in his suggestion that this education erased accidents of birth, creating a community among all those so educated, whatever their personal background, Isocrates points further, to the adoption of *paideia* by Rome and the Christian Church, and ultimately as the foundation stone of Western culture.

(a) Cimon: An Athenian without a Liberal Education

The earliest known reference to liberal education is by Stesimbrotos of Thasos, c.450 BC. While the original text by Stesimbrotos has been lost, his words come down to us through Plutarch's Lives of the Noble Greeks and Romans, *com-*

posed at the beginning of the second century AD.[1] Stesimbrotos emphasises the verbal fluency encouraged by Greek education, but contrasts it with the plain virtue of the untutored Cimon, showing a self-awareness of liberal education's limits and a tension between refined skill and simple goodness – two themes that would prove persistent as the tradition developed.

Stesimbrotus Thasian, who was about Cimons time, wryteth, that Cimon never learned musike, nor any other of the liberall sciences accustomably taught to young noble men's sonnes of Greece, & that he had no sharpe wit, nor good grace of speaking, a vertue proper unto children borne in the country of Attica: how beit that he was of a noble minde, and plaine, without dissimulacion, so that he rather lived Peloponnesian like, then like an Athenian.

(b) Isocrates:
The Glory of Athens is an Education Open to the World

Isocrates was apparently ten years in the composition of his Panegyricus, *a speech intended for performance at one of the great Greek festivals (perhaps the games at Olympia, where all Greeks came together under a sacred truce every four years). Finished around 380 BC, the* Panegyricus *offers a far more confident celebration of a liberal education than Stesimbrotus offered a century earlier. Unsurprisingly from one of the great teachers of oratory of the day, Isocrates concentrates on education in the verbal arts. While the speech is a claim for the right of Athens to lead all Greece, Isocrates stresses the liberal tradition as open to all, and widely recognised as beneficial to all. He suggests it provides a counterforce to claims to power based on money or martial courage, offering a better touchstone of fitness to rule. While rendered suspect by Plato's attacks on empty sophists, Isocrates too saw the ideal orator as someone not only gifted with verbal fluency, but virtuous and possessed of deep understanding. In 390 BC, he had already written* Against the Sophists, *an attack on those who taught only skill with words, and on lawyers who used their skill for 'making the worse appear the better cause'. In all this he was highly influential on both Cicero and Quintilian and so the transmission of liberal education to Rome.*

Practical philosophy, moreover, which helped to discover and establish all these institutions, which at once educated us for action and softened our

1   This translation is by Thomas North (1579). A copy was consulted by William Shakespeare in the composition of *Julius Cæsar*. North dedicated his translation to Queen Elizabeth I, herself a highly-educated woman (see also Roger Ascham's account of her education in Part II). North felt justified in praising his Queen's classical learning with these words 'For, most gracious Sovereigne, though this booke be no booke for your Majesties selfe, who [...] can better understand it in Greeke, than any man can make it Englishe...' The connections between Stesimbrotus, Plutarch, and the glories of Elizabethan England are an apt reminder, from the very beginning, of the timeless inspiration and enduring power of the liberal arts.

mutual intercourse, which distinguished calamities due to ignorance from those which spring from necessity, and taught us to avoid the former and nobly to endure the latter, was introduced by Athens; she also paid honour to eloquence, which all men desire, and begrudge to those who are skilled in it: for she was aware that this is the only distinguishing characteristic which we of all creatures possess, and that by this we have won our position of superiority to all the rest of them; she saw that in other spheres of action men's fortunes are so capricious that often in them the wise fail and the foolish succeed, and that the proper and skilful use of language is beyond the reach of men of poor capacity, but is the function of a soul of sound wisdom, and that those who are considered clever or stupid differ from each other mainly in this respect; she saw, besides, that men who have received a liberal education from the very first are not to be known by courage, or wealth, or such-like advantages, but are most clearly recognised by their speech, and that this is the surest token which is manifested of the education of each one of us, and that those who make good use of language are not only influential in their own states, but also held in honour among other people. So far has Athens left the rest of mankind behind in thought and expression that her pupils have become the teachers of the world, and she has made the name of Hellas distinctive no longer of race but of intellect, and the title of Hellene a badge of education rather than of common descent.

(c) Plato: How to Educate an Ideal Leader

Plato (427–347 BC) offers a comprehensive account of what a liberal education could mean in practice and what it might aim to achieve. In Protagoras, *he succinctly defines liberal education's non-vocational nature and expresses the concern, shared by Isocrates, that a teacher may not live up to the true liberal ideal. In* Republic, *Plato sets out his ideal course of study: the curriculum that would prepare the Guardians of his Republic; an education open to both men and women. The curriculum is strong on the science of number as well as the dialectical skill favoured by Isocrates. While arithmetic, geometry and astronomy are in part useful, at the same time, Plato stresses that it is their intellectual purity that will prepare the students for dialectic, and the contemplation of the good and the absolute. Plato also emphasises that such an education must be physical as much as intellectual, although always to spiritual ends, encouraging grace and fluency and virtuous habits through music and gymnastic, which help to create an inner harmony as the basis of character, on which mathematical studies and dialectic can build. If democracy appears to be distrusted by Plato, it is because he sees the dangers attendant on training inexperienced and unformed minds to think for themselves and recognises, in line with the tradition, that it is only through personal disci-*

pline that personal liberation can be achieved. Plato also points out that liberal learning requires pupils to respect their teachers for knowing more than they do, this is the basis for their status and for the pupil's willing cooperation in didactic exercises to transfer that knowledge and skill. Teachers are not facilitators or pupils' equals but masters, and the corruption of this relationship renders instruction impossible: the world is turned upside down and the old imitate and flatter the ignorance of the young. Yet Plato still affirms that an education for liberty cannot be compelled. Finally, in Laws, *Plato stresses the centrality of virtue to education, and broaches the subject, taken up by Aristotle, that education begins in habit rather than reasoned understanding, as a child is taught to like the good and dislike the bad.*

Protagoras

What will Protagoras make of you, if you go to see him?

He answered, with a blush upon his face (for the day was just beginning to dawn, so that I could see him): Unless this differs in some way from the former instances, I suppose that he will make a Sophist of me.

By the gods, I said, and are you not ashamed at having to appear before the Hellenes in the character of a Sophist?

Indeed, Socrates, to confess the truth, I am.

But you should not assume, Hippocrates, that the instruction of Protagoras is of this nature: may you not learn of him in the same way that you learned the arts of the grammarian, or musician, or trainer, not with the view of making any of them a profession, but only as a part of education, and because a private gentleman and freeman ought to know them?

Just so, he said; and that, in my opinion, is a far truer account of the teaching of Protagoras.

I said: I wonder whether you know what you are doing?

And what am I doing?

You are going to commit your soul to the care of a man whom you call a Sophist. And yet I hardly think that you know what a Sophist is; and if not, then you do not even know to whom you are committing your soul and whether the thing to which you commit yourself be good or evil.

The Republic

Book II

And may we not say confidently of man also, that he who is likely to be gentle to his friends and acquaintances, must by nature be a lover of wisdom and knowledge?

That we may safely affirm.

Then he who is to be a really good and noble guardian of the State will require to unite in himself philosophy and spirit and swiftness and strength?

Undoubtedly.

Then we have found the desired natures; and now that we have found them, how are they to be reared and educated? Is not this an enquiry which may be expected to throw light on the greater enquiry which is our final end — How do justice and injustice grow up in States? for we do not want either to omit what is to the point or to draw out the argument to an inconvenient length.

Adeimantus thought that the enquiry would be of great service to us.

Then, I said, my dear friend, the task must not be given up, even if somewhat long.

Certainly not.

Come then, and let us pass a leisure hour in story-telling, and our story shall be the education of our heroes.

By all means.

And what shall be their education? Can we find a better than the traditional sort? — and this has two divisions, gymnastic for the body, and music for the soul.

True.

Book III

But there is no difficulty in seeing that grace or the absence of grace is an effect of good or bad rhythm.

None at all.

And also that good and bad rhythm naturally assimilate to a good and bad style; and that harmony and discord in like manner follow style; for our principle is that rhythm and harmony are regulated by the words, and not the words by them.

Just so, he said, they should follow the words.

And will not the words and the character of the style depend on the temper of the soul?

Yes.

And everything else on the style?

Yes.

Then beauty of style and harmony and grace and good rhythm depend on simplicity,—I mean the true simplicity of a rightly and nobly ordered mind and character, not that other simplicity which is only an euphemism for folly?

Very true, he replied.

And if our youth are to do their work in life, must they not make these graces and harmonies their perpetual aim?

[...]

And therefore, I said, Glaucon, musical training is a more potent instrument than any other, because rhythm and harmony find their way into the inward places of the soul, on which they mightily fasten, imparting grace, and making the soul of him who is rightly educated graceful, or of him who is ill-educated ungraceful; and also because he who has received this true education of the inner being will most shrewdly perceive omissions or faults in art and nature, and with a true taste, while he praises and rejoices over and receives into his soul the good, and becomes noble and good, he will justly blame and hate the bad, now in the days of his youth, even before he is able to know the reason why; and when reason comes he will recognise and salute the friend with whom his education has made him long familiar.

[...]

Thus much of music, which makes a fair ending; for what should be the end of music if not the love of beauty?

I agree, he said.

After music comes gymnastic, in which our youth are next to be trained.

Certainly.

Gymnastic as well as music should begin in early years; the training in it should be careful and should continue through life. Now my belief is, — and this is a matter upon which I should like to have your opinion in confirmation of my own, but my own belief is, — not that the good body by any bodily excellence improves the soul, but, on the contrary, that the good soul, by her own excellence, improves the body as far as this may be possible. What do you say?

Yes, I agree.

Then, to the mind when adequately trained, we shall be right in handing over the more particular care of the body; and in order to avoid prolixity we will now only give the general outlines of the subject.

Very good.

That they must abstain from intoxication has been already remarked by us; for of all persons a guardian should be the last to get drunk and not know where in the world he is.

Yes, he said; that a guardian should require another guardian to take care of him is ridiculous indeed.

[...]

The very exercises and toils which he undergoes are intended to stimulate the spirited element of his nature, and not to increase his strength; he will not, like common athletes, use exercise and regimen to develop his muscles.

Very right, he said.

Neither are the two arts of music and gymnastic really designed, as is often supposed, the one for the training of the soul, the other for the training of the body.

What then is the real object of them?

I believe, I said, that the teachers of both have in view chiefly the improvement of the soul.

How can that be? he asked.

Did you never observe, I said, the effect on the mind itself of exclusive devotion to gymnastic, or the opposite effect of an exclusive devotion to music?

In what way shown? he said.

The one producing a temper of hardness and ferocity, the other of softness and effeminacy, I replied.

Yes, he said, I am quite aware that the mere athlete becomes too much of a savage, and that the mere musician is melted and softened beyond what is good for him.

Yet surely, I said, this ferocity only comes from spirit, which, if rightly educated, would give courage, but, if too much intensified, is liable to become hard and brutal.

That I quite think.

On the other hand the philosopher will have the quality of gentleness. And this also, when too much indulged, will turn to softness, but, if educated rightly, will be gentle and moderate.

True.

And in our opinion the guardians ought to have both these qualities?

Assuredly.

And both should be in harmony?

Beyond question.

[...]

And so in gymnastics, if a man takes violent exercise and is a great feeder, and the reverse of a great student of music and philosophy, at first the high condition of his body fills him with pride and spirit, and he becomes twice the man that he was.

Certainly.

And what happens? If he do nothing else, and holds no converse with the Muses, does not even that intelligence which there may be in him, having no taste of any sort of learning or enquiry or thought or culture, grow feeble and dull and blind, his mind never waking up or receiving nourishment, and his senses not being purged of their mists?

True, he said.

And he ends by becoming a hater of philosophy, uncivilized, never using the weapon of persuasion, — he is like a wild beast, all violence and fierceness, and knows no other way of dealing; and he lives in all ignorance and evil conditions, and has no sense of propriety and grace.

That is quite true, he said.

And as there are two principles of human nature, one the spirited and the other the philosophical, some God, as I should say, has given mankind two arts answering to them (and only indirectly to the soul and body), in order that these two principles (like the strings of an instrument) may be relaxed or drawn tighter until they are duly harmonized.

That appears to be the intention.

And he who mingles music with gymnastic in the fairest proportions, and best attempers them to the soul, may be rightly called the true musician and harmonist in a far higher sense than the tuner of the strings.

You are quite right, Socrates.

Book VII

And now shall we consider in what way such guardians will be produced, and how they are to be brought from darkness to light, — as some are said to have ascended from the world below to the gods?

By all means, he replied.

[...]

There were two parts in our former scheme of education, were there not?

Just so.

There was gymnastic which presided over the growth and decay of the body, and may therefore be regarded as having to do with generation and corruption?

True.

Then that is not the knowledge which we are seeking to discover?

No.

But what do you say of music, what also entered to a certain extent into our former scheme?

Music, he said, as you will remember, was the counterpart of gymnastic, and trained the guardians by the influences of habit, by harmony making them harmonious, by rhythm rhythmical, but not giving them science; and the words, whether fabulous or possibly true, had kindred elements of rhythm and harmony in them. But in music there was nothing which tended to that good which you are now seeking.

You are most accurate, I said, in your recollection; in music there certainly was nothing of the kind. But what branch of knowledge is there, my dear Glaucon, which is of the desired nature; since all the useful arts were reckoned mean by us?

Undoubtedly; and yet if music and gymnastic are excluded, and the arts are also excluded, what remains?

Well, I said, there may be nothing left of our special subjects; and then we shall have to take something which is not special, but of universal application.

What may that be?

A something which all arts and sciences and intelligences use in common, and which every one first has to learn among the elements of education.

What is that?

The little matter of distinguishing one, two, and three — in a word, number and calculation: — do not all arts and sciences necessarily partake of them?

Yes.

[...]

I should like to know whether you have the same notion which I have of this study?

What is your notion?

It appears to me to be a study of the kind which we are seeking, and which leads naturally to reflection, but never to have been rightly used; for the true use of it is simply to draw the soul towards being.

[...]

Then this is knowledge of the kind for which we are seeking, having a double use, military and philosophical; for the man of war must learn the art of number or he will not know how to array his troops, and the philosopher also, because he has to rise out of the sea of change and lay hold of true being, and therefore he must be an arithmetician.

That is true.

And our guardian is both warrior and philosopher?

Certainly.

Then this is a kind of knowledge which legislation may fitly prescribe; and we must endeavour to persuade those who are to be the principal men of our State to go and learn arithmetic, not as amateurs, but they must carry on the study until they see the nature of numbers with the mind only; nor again, like merchants or retail-traders, with a view to buying or selling, but for the sake of their military use, and of the soul herself; and because this will be the easiest way for her to pass from becoming to truth and being.

[...]

And have you further observed, that those who have a natural talent for calculation are generally quick at every other kind of knowledge; and even the dull, if they have had an arithmetical training, although they may derive no other advantage from it, always become much quicker than they would otherwise have been.

Very true, he said.

And indeed, you will not easily find a more difficult study, and not many as difficult.

You will not.

And, for all these reasons, arithmetic is a kind of knowledge in which the best natures should be trained, and which must not be given up.

I agree.

Let this then be made one of our subjects of education. And next, shall we enquire whether the kindred science also concerns us?

You mean geometry?

Exactly so.

[...]

[T]he knowledge at which geometry aims is knowledge of the eternal, and not of aught perishing and transient.

That, he replied, may be readily allowed, and is true.

Then, my noble friend, geometry will draw the soul towards truth, and create the spirit of philosophy, and raise up that which is now unhappily allowed to fall down.

Nothing will be more likely to have such an effect.

Then nothing should be more sternly laid down than that the inhabitants of your fair city should by all means learn geometry. Moreover the science has indirect effects, which are not small.

Of what kind? he said.

There are the military advantages of which you spoke, I said; and in all departments of knowledge, as experience proves, any one who has studied geometry is infinitely quicker of apprehension than one who has not.

Yes indeed, he said, there is an infinite difference between them.

Then shall we propose this as a second branch of knowledge which our youth will study?

Let us do so, he replied.

And suppose we make astronomy the third — what do you say?

I am strongly inclined to it, he said; the observation of the seasons and of months and years is as essential to the general as it is to the farmer or sailor.

I am amused, I said, at your fear of the world, which makes you guard against the appearance of insisting upon useless studies; and I quite admit the difficulty of believing that in every man there is an eye of the soul which, when by other pursuits lost and dimmed, is by these purified and re-illumined; and is more precious far than ten thousand bodily eyes, for by it alone is truth seen.

[...]

[B]ut you are speaking, Socrates, of a vast work.

What do you mean? I said; the prelude or what? Do you not know that all this is but the prelude to the actual strain which we have to learn? For you surely would not regard the skilled mathematician as a dialectician?

Assuredly not, he said; I have hardly ever known a mathematician who was capable of reasoning.

But do you imagine that men who are unable to give and take a reason will have the knowledge which we require of them?

Neither can this be supposed.

And so, Glaucon, I said, we have at last arrived at the hymn of dialectic. This is that strain which is of the intellect only, but which the faculty of sight will nevertheless be found to imitate; for sight, as you may remember, was imagined by us after a while to behold the real animals and stars, and last of all the sun himself. And so with dialectic; when a person starts on the discovery of the absolute by the light of reason only, and without any assistance of sense, and perseveres until by pure intelligence he arrives at the perception of the absolute good, he at last finds himself at the end of the intellectual world, as in the case of sight at the end of the visible.

[...]

Then dialectic, and dialectic alone, goes directly to the first principle and is the only science which does away with hypotheses in order to make her ground secure; the eye of the soul, which is literally buried in an outlandish slough, is by her gentle aid lifted upwards; and she uses as handmaids and helpers in the work of conversion, the sciences which we have been discussing. Custom terms them sciences, but they ought to have some other name, implying greater clearness than opinion and less clearness than science: and this, in our previous sketch, was called understanding. But why should we dispute about names when we have realities of such importance to consider?

[...]

Until the person is able to abstract and define rationally the idea of good, and unless he can run the gauntlet of all objections, and is ready to disprove them, not by appeals to opinion, but to absolute truth, never faltering at any step of the argument — unless he can do all this, you would say that he knows neither the idea of good nor any other good; he apprehends only a shadow, if anything at all, which is given by opinion and not by science; — dreaming and slumbering in this life, before he is well awake here, he arrives at the world below, and has his final quietus.

In all that I should most certainly agree with you.

And surely you would not have the children of your ideal State, whom you are nurturing and educating — if the ideal ever becomes a reality — you would not allow the future rulers to be like posts, having no reason in them, and yet to be set in authority over the highest matters?

Certainly not.

Then you will make a law that they shall have such an education as will enable them to attain the greatest skill in asking and answering questions?

Yes, he said, you and I together will make it.

Dialectic, then, as you will agree, is the coping-stone of the sciences, and is set over them; no other science can be placed higher — the nature of knowledge can no further go?

I agree, he said.

[...]

And, therefore, calculation and geometry and all the other elements of instruction, which are a preparation for dialectic, should be presented to the mind in childhood; not, however, under any notion of forcing our system of education.

Why not?

Because a freeman ought not to be a slave in the acquisition of knowledge of any kind. Bodily exercise, when compulsory, does no harm to the body; but knowledge which is acquired under compulsion obtains no hold on the mind.

Very true.

Then, my good friend, I said, do not use compulsion, but let early education be a sort of amusement; you will then be better able to find out the natural bent.

That is a very rational notion, he said.

[...]

[A]nd those who have most of this comprehension, and who are most
steadfast in their learning, and in their military and other appointed
duties, when they have arrived at the age of thirty will have to be chosen
by you out of the select class, and elevated to higher honour; and you will
have to prove them by the help of dialectic, in order to learn which of them
is able to give up the use of sight and the other senses, and in company
with truth to attain absolute being: And here, my friend, great caution is
required.

Why great caution?

Do you not remark, I said, how great is the evil which dialectic has
introduced?

What evil? he said.

The students of the art are filled with lawlessness.

[...]

[Y]ou know that there are certain principles about justice and honour,
which were taught us in childhood, and under their parental authority we
have been brought up, obeying and honouring them.

That is true.

There are also opposite maxims and habits of pleasure which flatter and
attract the soul, but do not influence those of us who have any sense of
right, and they continue to obey and honour the maxims of their fathers.

True.

Now, when a man is in this state, and the questioning spirit asks what is
fair or honourable, and he answers as the legislator has taught him, and
then arguments many and diverse refute his words, until he is driven into
believing that nothing is honourable any more than dishonourable, or just
and good any more than the reverse, and so of all the notions which he
most valued, do you think that he will still honour and obey them as
before?

Impossible.

And when he ceases to think them honourable and natural as heretofore, and he fails to discover the true, can he be expected to pursue any life other than that which flatters his desires?

He cannot.

And from being a keeper of the law he is converted into a breaker of it?

Unquestionably.

Now all this is very natural in students of philosophy such as I have described, and also, as I was just now saying, most excusable.

Yes, he said; and, I may add, pitiable.

Therefore, that your feelings may not be moved to pity about our citizens who are now thirty years of age, every care must be taken in introducing them to dialectic.

[...]

You are a sculptor, Socrates, and have made statues of our governors faultless in beauty.

Yes, I said, Glaucon, and of our governesses too; for you must not suppose that what I have been saying applies to men only and not to women as far as their natures can go.

There you are right, he said, since we have made them to share in all things like the men.

Well, I said, and you would agree (would you not?) that what has been said about the State and the government is not a mere dream, and although difficult not impossible, but only possible in the way which has been supposed; that is to say, when the true philosopher kings are born in a State, one or more of them, despising the honours of this present world which they deem mean and worthless, esteeming above all things right and the honour that springs from right, and regarding justice as the greatest and most necessary of all things, whose ministers they are, and whose principles will be exalted by them when they set in order their own city?

How will they proceed?

They will begin by sending out into the country all the inhabitants of the city who are more than ten years old, and will take possession of their children, who will be unaffected by the habits of their parents; these they will train in their own habits and laws, I mean in the laws which we have given them: and in this way the State and constitution of which we were speaking will soonest and most easily attain happiness, and the nation which has such a constitution will gain most.

Yes, that will be the best way. And I think, Socrates, that you have very well described how, if ever, such a constitution might come into being.

Enough then of the perfect State, and of the man who bears its image—there is no difficulty in seeing how we shall describe him.

There is no difficulty, he replied; and I agree with you in thinking that nothing more need be said.

Book VIII

Have you not observed how, in a democracy, many persons, although they have been sentenced to death or exile, just stay where they are and walk about the world—the gentleman parades like a hero, and nobody sees or cares?

Yes, he replied, many and many a one.

See too, I said, the forgiving spirit of democracy, and the "don't care" about trifles, and the disregard which she shows of all the fine principles which we solemnly laid down at the foundation of the city—as when we said that, except in the case of some rarely gifted nature, there never will be a good man who has not from his childhood been used to play amid things of beauty and make of them a joy and a study—how grandly does she trample all these fine notions of ours under her feet, never giving a thought to the pursuits which make a statesman, and promoting to honour any one who professes to be the people's friend.

Yes, she is of a noble spirit.

These and other kindred characteristics are proper to democracy, which is a charming form of government, full of variety and disorder, and dispensing a sort of equality to equals and unequals alike.

We know her well.

[...]

Are not necessary pleasures those of which we cannot get rid, and of which the satisfaction is a benefit to us? And they are rightly called so, because we are framed by nature to desire both what is beneficial and what is necessary, and cannot help it.

True.

We are not wrong therefore in calling them necessary?

We are not.

And the desires of which a man may get rid, if he takes pains from his youth upwards — of which the presence, moreover, does no good, and in some cases the reverse of good — shall we not be right in saying that all these are unnecessary?

Yes, certainly.

Suppose we select an example of either kind, in order that we may have a general notion of them?

Very good.

Will not the desire of eating, that is, of simple food and condiments, in so far as they are required for health and strength, be of the necessary class?

That is what I should suppose.

The pleasure of eating is necessary in two ways; it does us good and it is essential to the continuance of life?

Yes.

But the condiments are only necessary in so far as they are good for health?

Certainly.

And the desire which goes beyond this, of more delicate food, or other luxuries, which might generally be got rid of, if controlled and trained in youth, and is hurtful to the body, and hurtful to the soul in the pursuit of wisdom and virtue, may be rightly called unnecessary?

Very true.

[...]

And so the young man passes out of his original nature, which was trained in the school of necessity, into the freedom and libertinism of useless and unnecessary pleasures.

Yes, he said, the change in him is visible enough.

[...]

Yes, I said, he lives from day to day indulging the appetite of the hour; and sometimes he is lapped in drink and strains of the flute; then he becomes a water-drinker, and tries to get thin; then he takes a turn at gymnastics; sometimes idling and neglecting everything, then once more living the life of a philosopher; often he is busy with politics, and starts to his feet and says and does whatever comes into his head; and, if he is emulous of any one who is a warrior, off he is in that direction, or of men of business, once more in that. His life has neither law nor order; and this distracted existence he terms joy and bliss and freedom; and so he goes on.

[...]

In such a state of society the master fears and flatters his scholars, and the scholars despise their masters and tutors; young and old are all alike; and the young man is on a level with the old, and is ready to compete with him in word or deed; and old men condescend to the young and are full of pleasantry and gaiety; they are loth to be thought morose and authoritative, and therefore they adopt the manners of the young.

[...]

The excess of liberty, whether in States or individuals, seems only to pass into excess of slavery.

Laws

An Athenian:
> At the outset of the discussion, let me define the nature and power of education; for this is the way by which our argument must travel onwards to the God Dionysus.

Cleinias, a Cretan:
> Let us proceed, if you please.

A: Well, then, if I tell you what are my notions of education, will you consider whether they satisfy you?

C: Let us hear.

A: According to my view, any one who would be good at anything must practise that thing from his youth upwards, both in sport and earnest, in its several branches: for example, he who is to be a good builder, should play at building children's houses; he who is to be a good husbandman, at tilling the ground; and those who have the care of their education should provide them when young with mimic tools. They should learn beforehand the knowledge which they will afterwards require for their art. For example, the future carpenter should learn to measure or apply the line in play; and the future warrior should learn riding, or some other exercise, for amusement, and the teacher should endeavour to direct the children's inclinations and pleasures, by the help of amusements, to their final aim in life. The most important part of education is right training in the nursery. The soul of the child in his play should be guided to the love of that sort of excellence in which when he grows up to manhood he will have to be perfected. Do you agree with me thus far?

C: Certainly.

A: Then let us not leave the meaning of education ambiguous or
    ill-defined. At present, when we speak in terms of praise or blame
    about the bringing-up of each person, we call one man educated and
    another uneducated, although the uneducated man may be some-
    times very well educated for the calling of a retail trader, or of a cap-
    tain of a ship, and the like. For we are not speaking of education in
    this narrower sense, but of that other education in virtue from youth
    upwards, which makes a man eagerly pursue the ideal perfection of
    citizenship, and teaches him how rightly to rule and how to obey.
    This is the only education which, upon our view, deserves the name;
    that other sort of training, which aims at the acquisition of wealth or
    bodily strength, or mere cunning apart from intelligence and justice,
    is mean and illiberal, and is not worthy to be called education at all.
    But let us not quarrel with one another about a word, provided that
    the proposition which has just been granted hold good: to wit, that
    those who are rightly educated generally become good men. Neither
    must we cast a slight upon education, which is the first and fairest
    thing that the best of men can ever have, and which, though liable to
    take a wrong direction, is capable of reformation. And this work of
    reformation is the great business of every man while he lives.

    [...]

A: Let me once more recall our doctrine of right education; which, if I am
    not mistaken, depends on the due regulation of convivial intercourse.

C: You talk rather grandly.

A: Pleasure and pain I maintain to be the first perceptions of children,
    and I say that they are the forms under which virtue and vice are orig-
    inally present to them. As to wisdom and true and fixed opinions,
    happy is the man who acquires them, even when declining in years;
    and we may say that he who possesses them, and the blessings which
    are contained in them, is a perfect man. Now I mean by education
    that training which is given by suitable habits to the first instincts of
    virtue in children;—when pleasure, and friendship, and pain, and
    hatred, are rightly implanted in souls not yet capable of understand-
    ing the nature of them, and who find them, after they have attained
    reason, to be in harmony with her. This harmony of the soul, taken as
    a whole, is virtue; but the particular training in respect of pleasure
    and pain, which leads you always to hate what you ought to hate, and
    love what you ought to love from the beginning of life to the end, may
    be separated off; and, in my view, will be rightly called education.

(d) Aristotle: Liberal Education Accords with Human Nature

*Aristotle (384-322 BC) approached the subject of education as both a natural sci-
entist, interested in the teachings proper to the true nature of humankind, and as a*

supreme philosopher, devoted to the dialectical investigation so celebrated by Plato. Importantly, he stressed the need for phronesis, *or 'practical wisdom' — the ability not merely to discern the good and the true, but to act upon that knowledge. Aristotle is at pains to distinguish between "mere cunning" and true "mental cleverness": the agile mind of a sophist may possess cunning, but lacks virtue. This demonstrates the importance of virtue in the ancient conception of education, and the possibility, in this understanding, of becoming intellectually brilliant but in a very real sense remaining uneducated, lacking the virtue that underpins practical wisdom. For Aristotle, the aim of early education will be very much to instil habits of virtue, leading to a love of the good, on which reason may build; for without such love, the intellect, when it comes to reason about conduct, could just as well argue in favour of the vicious and the weak, as in favour of the good. For Aristotle freedom consists essentially in the enjoyment of pursuits where knowledge, beauty and goodness are celebrated for their own sakes, and not for narrowly utilitarian purposes. With Plato, he observes that physical habit, and not reason, is a crucial instructor in such matters, but affirms that unthinking correct actions are not equivalent to mindful virtue. Aristotle celebrates the use of the intellect as the centre of the good life and his own work, like Plato's, eventually became an essential component of the education of future generations, particularly in the art of philosophical logic. However, for many centuries his works were untranslated and effectively silent. More than any other author, his rediscovery, via the translation movement in Islamic Spain, helped to revive the mediæval intellect. These translations would form the basis of the scholastic movement in Europe's first universities, and, through St. Thomas Aquinas, would provide the patterns of thought by which faith and reason would be decisively and permanently knitted together within Catholic christendom.*

Metaphysics

All men by nature are actuated with the desire of knowledge, and an indication of this is the love of the senses; for even, irrespective of their utility, are they loved for their own sakes; and preeminently above the rest, the sense of sight. For not only for practical purposes, but also when not intent on doing anything, we choose the power of vision in preference, so to say, to all the rest of the senses. And a cause of this is the following, — that this one of the senses particularly enables us to apprehend whatever knowledge it is the inlet of, and that it makes many distinctive qualities manifest.

Nicomachean Ethics

Book II

It is necessary, however, to consider as an indication of habits the pleasure or pain which is attendant on actions. For he who abstains from corporeal pleasures, and is delighted in so doing, is a temperate man; but he who is grieved when he abstains from them is intemperate. And he, indeed, who endures dreadful things, and is delighted with his endurance, or feels no pain from it, is a brave man; but he who feels pain from the endurance of them, is a timid man. For ethical virtue is conversant with pleasures and pains. For we act basely through the influence of pleasure; but we abstain from beautiful conduct through the influence of pain. Hence, it is necessary, as Plato says, to be so educated in a certain respect immediately after our youth, that we may be delighted and pained with things from which it is requisite to feel pleasure or pain; for this is right education.

Book VI

There is [...] a certain power which is called "mental cleverness". But this is a power of such a kind, that by its assistance those things may be performed and obtained, which contribute to noble and just action. The purpose is beautiful, and this power is laudable; if the purpose is bad, this power becomes "mere cunning": on which account, also, we say that men who possess practical wisdom are "clever of mind", and not "merely cunning". Practical wisdom, however, is not "mental cleverness", though it does not subsist without it [...] it is impossible for anyone to be wise in practice, unless he is first virtuous.

[...]

[I]t is said, that all the virtues are practical wisdoms. And Socrates, indeed, investigated partly with rectitude, and partly with error. For because he thought that all the virtues are practical wisdoms he erred; but it is well said by him, that the virtues are not without practical wisdom. But as an indication of this, all men now, when they define virtue, add to the definition habit, and that they energise according to right reason. And right reason is that which subsists according to practical wisdom. All men, therefore, appear in a certain respect to prophesy, that a habit of this kind, which subsists according to practical wisdom, is virtue. It is necessary, however, to change, in a small degree, the definition; for not only a habit according to right reason, but also a habit in conjunction with right reason, is virtue.

[...]

Hence, it is evident, from what has been said, that it is not possible to be a good man properly, without practical wisdom; nor a prudent man without ethical virtue.

[...]

For all the virtues are present, at the same time that practical wisdom, which is one virtue, is present. But it is evident, that though practical wisdom were not a practical thing, it would be necessary, because it is the virtue of a part of the soul, and because deliberate choice will not be right without practical wisdom, nor without virtue; for one of these is the end, but the other causes us to do things which contribute to the end.

Book X

But a happy life appears to be conformable to virtue; and this is a worthy life, and does not consist in amusements.

[...]

[T]he energy of intellect, which is contemplative, appears to excel other energies in ardor, and to desire no other end besides itself; if also it possesses a proper pleasure, which increases its energy, and has, in addition to this, self-sufficiency, leisure and unwearied power, so far as the condition of human nature will permit, with whatever else is attributed to the blessed, and appears to subsist according to this energy;—if such be the case this will be the perfect felicity of man when it receives a perfect length of life: for nothing belonging to felicity is imperfect. Such a life, however, will be more excellent than that which is merely human; for man will not thus live so far as he is man, but so far as he contains in himself something divine.

[...]

[F]or that which is intimately allied to any nature is most excellent and pleasant to that nature; and hence, a life according to intellect will be most excellent and pleasant to man, since this part is most eminently man. This life, therefore, is also most happy.

Politics

It is evident, then, that there is a sort of education in which parents should train their sons, not as being useful or necessary, but because it is liberal or noble. Whether this is of one kind only, or of more than one, and if so, what they are, and how they are to be imparted, must hereafter be determined. Thus much we are now in a position to say that the ancients witness to us; for their opinion may be gathered from the fact that music is one of the received and traditional branches of education. Further, it is clear that children should be instructed in some useful things, — for example, in reading and writing, — not only for their usefulness, but also because many other sorts of knowledge are acquired through them. With a like view they may be taught drawing, not to prevent their making mistakes in their own purchases, or in order that they may not be imposed upon in the buying or selling of articles, but rather because it makes them judges of the beauty of the human form. To be always seeking after the useful does not become free and exalted souls. Now it is clear that in education habit must go before reason, and the body before the mind; and therefore boys should be handed over to the trainer, who creates in them the proper habit of body, and to the wrestling-master, who teaches them their exercises.

Chapter II

Rome: Humanitas

When liberal education was taken up from Greece by the Roman Empire, the qualities it taught became known as *humanitas*, from where we derive the term 'humanities' today. Here, Rome brought its own influences to the Greek ideal: by focusing on the idea of educating 'the good human being', which is the approximate meaning of *humanitas*, liberal education gained a more austere, virtue-centred emphasis than the ancient Greeks had supplied (although they had, as the previous section shows, been concerned with issues of educating for virtue). Under Rome, the liberal arts met the philosophy of Stoicism, which cultivated a life free of emotional incontinence, ruled by reason and self-restraint rather than sudden fears and enthusiasms, tightly-disciplined even to the point of choosing the moment of one's own death in the face of dishonour. The Greek education for inner fullness and intelligent discussion developed a focus on self-mastery and action in the world, while never losing its appreciation of inner development by reading well and deeply, all in the service of developing the kind of humane compassion that did not always accompany *imperium* (formal power over others) in the harsh world of ancient Rome. But as Seneca points out, education is no certain road to virtue of this kind, at best only preparing the way. These tensions prefigure both the rise of Christianity in the Roman world, offering new answers to these challenges, and the ambivalent relationship that would as a consequence develop between all-sufficient faith and Greek reason.

(a) Cicero: The Liberally Educated Politician

While the liberal education tradition passed down from Greece to Rome, it was by no means inevitable, and the figure of Marcus Tullius Cicero (106-43 BC) was crucial in that transition. His enthusiasm for restoring the lost Greek learning is a passion visible both in his dogged investigation leading to the rediscovery of the tomb of Archimedes and in his advice to his son to learn both Latin and Greek in De Officiis *(On Duties). For Cicero, the ultimate end of philosophy and learning is to be serviceable to the interest and good of mankind. To the classical mind, this did not conflict with learning for its own sake: full human development required one to wrestle with intellectual disciplines on their own terms, but also was seen to lead naturally into moral service and political action. The Greek concept of 'logos' meant both the inner thought and its expression in the world. Cicero's dialogue, Hortensius, (now lost) would inspire St. Augustine to take up philosophy seriously and embark on his journey toward Christ. Cicero himself, a brilliant orator and by profession a lawyer, later a great figure of the Roman state, exemplified the civilised man of action, drawing on his liberal education in the service of Rome and as retreat from its hurly-burly, as when he travelled to his villa in Tusculum with philosophically-minded friends and spent days discussing the great questions of life, some of which discussions are recorded in the* Tusculanæ Disputationes. *Cicero proved that Rome was not merely continuing but enriching the tradition of Greece with its own special concern for law and its rhetorically-charged, republican politics. For Cicero, Aristotle's contention that human beings were political animals meant that the clash of beliefs in the* polis, *not pure contemplation, was essential for the good life. He rewrote the oratorical textbooks with* De Oratore, *and in his oration for Archias the poet Cicero gave one of Western civilisation's great defences of the liberal arts, as important for its call for their continual renewal by great work as for its celebration of the Greek tradition of learning.*

De Oratore

For this purpose, I shall not repeat any string of precepts which we learned when we were children at school, and just come from under the nurse's care; no, I mean to give you the arguments which I heard formerly urged in a debate among some friends, men of the greatest eloquence and eminence in Rome. Not that I despise the principles which the Greek professors and teachers of eloquence have left us; but since they are well known, and in everybody's hands, and impossible to receive any ornament or explanation from my interpretation, you will pardon me, my dear brother, if, in my opinion, the authority of such of our own countrymen as all Rome allows to be finished orators, is to be preferred to that of the Greeks.

Tusculanæ Disputationes

I will present you with an humble and obscure mathematician of the same city, called Archimedes, who lived many years after: whose tomb, overgrown with shrubs and briars, I in my quæstorship discovered, when the Syracusians knew nothing of it, and even denied that there was any such thing remaining: for I remembered some verses, which I had been informed were engraved on his monument. These set forth that on the top of it there was placed a sphere with a cylinder. When I had carefully examined all the monuments (for there are a great many) at the gate Achradinæ, I observed a small column standing out a little above the briars, with the figure of a sphere and a cylinder upon it; whereupon I immediately said to the Syracusians, for there were some of their principal magistrates there, that I imagined that was what I was inquiring for. Several men being sent in with scythes, cleared the way, and made an opening for us. When we could get at it, and were come near to the front base of it, I found the inscription, though the latter parts of all the verses were effaced almost half away. Thus one of the noblest cities of Greece, and once, likewise, the most learned, had known nothing of the monument of its most ingenious citizen, if it had not been discovered to them by a native of Arpinum.

Pro Archia Poeta

You ask us, O Gratius, why we are so exceedingly attached to this man. Because he supplies us with food whereby our mind is refreshed after this noise in the forum, and with rest for our ears after they have been wearied with bad language. Do you think it possible that we could find a supply for our daily speeches, when discussing such a variety of matters, unless we were to cultivate our minds by the study of literature; or that our minds could bear being kept so constantly on the stretch if we did not relax them by that same study? But I confess that I am devoted to those studies, let others be ashamed of them if they have buried themselves in books without being able to produce anything out of them for the common advantage or anything which may bear the eyes of men and the light. But why need I be ashamed, who for many years have lived in such a manner as never to allow my own love of tranquillity to deny me to the necessity or advantage of another or my fondness for pleasure to distract, or even sleep to delay my attention to such claims?

Who then can reproach me or who has any right to be angry with me, if I allow myself as much time for the cultivation of these studies as some take for the performance of their own business, or for celebrating days of festival and games, or for other pleasures, or even for the rest and refreshment of mind and body, or as others devote to early banquets, to playing at dice, or at ball? And this ought to be permitted to me, because by these studies my power of speaking and those faculties are improved, which, as far as they do exist in me, have never been denied to my friends when they have been in peril. And if that ability appears to any one to be but moderate, at all events I know whence I derive those principles which are of the greatest value.

[...]

Some one will ask, "What? were those identical great men, whose virtues have been recorded in books, accomplished in all that learning which you are extolling so highly?" It is difficult to assert this of all of them; but still I know what answer I can make to that question: I admit that many men have existed of admirable disposition and virtue, who, without learning, by the almost divine instinct of their own mere nature, have been, of their own accord, as it were, moderate and wise men. I even add this, that very often nature without learning has had more to do with leading men to credit and to virtue, than learning when not assisted by a good natural disposition. And I also contend, that when to an excellent and admirable natural disposition there is added a certain system and training of education, then from that combination arises an extraordinary perfection of character; such as is seen in that god-like man, whom our fathers saw in their time, Africanus; and in Caius Lælius and Lucius Furius, most virtuous and moderate men; and in that most excellent man, the most learned man of his time, Marcus Cato the elder; and all these men, if they had been to derive no assistance from literature in the cultivation and practice of virtue, would never have applied themselves to the study of it. Though, even if there were no such great advantage to be reaped from it, and if it were only pleasure that is sought from these studies, still I imagine you would consider it a most reasonable and liberal employment of the mind: for other occupations are not suited to every time, nor to every age or place; but these studies are the food of youth, the delight of old age; the ornament of prosperity, the refuge and comfort of adversity; a delight at home, and no hindrance abroad; they are companions by night, and in travel, and in the country.

[...]

Do we all who are occupied in the affairs of the state, and who are surrounded by such perils and dangers in life, appear to be so narrow-minded, as, though to the last moment of our lives we have never passed one tranquil or easy moment, to think that everything will perish at the same time as ourselves? Ought we not, when many most illustrious men have with great care collected and left behind them statues and images, representations not of their minds but of their bodies, much more to desire to leave behind us a copy of our counsels and of our virtues, wrought and elaborated by the greatest genius? I thought, at the very moment of performing them, that I was scattering and disseminating all the deeds which I was performing, all over the world for the eternal recollection of nations. And whether that delight is to be denied to my soul after death, or whether, as the wisest men have thought, it will affect some portion of my spirit, at all events, I am at present delighted with some such idea and hope.

De Officiis

Book I

My Dear Son Marcus,

Though after a year's study under Cratippus, and that at such a place as Athens, you ought to have abundantly furnished yourself with knowledge in the doctrines and rules of philosophy; having had the advantage of so eminent a master to supply you with learning, and a city that affords you such excellent examples; yet I should think it convenient for you (which is a method I took for my own improvement) always to mingle some Latin with your Greek, in the studies of eloquence, as well as philosophy, that you may be equally perfect in both those ways of writing, and make yourself master of either language: for the furtherance of which, I am apt to imagine, I have done no inconsiderable service to our countrymen; so that not only those who do not understand Greek, but even the learned themselves will confess, that by reading my works, they have mended their styles, and somewhat improved their reason and judgments.

[...]

First, then, if the duties of justice, or preserving the community, and those of prudence, or the knowledge of truth, should come into competition one with another; the former, I think, should take place of the latter, as being more consonant to the dictates of nature, which may easily be proved by this following argument. Suppose a wise man to be in such a place as afforded him all the conveniences of life, and all the opportunities of leisure in abundance, so that he might study and contemplate every thing that was any ways worthy his knowledge or contemplation; yet were he wholly deprived of all company, and had nobody ever come near him to be seen, he would quickly be tired, and grow weary of his life. Again, the principal of all the virtues is that sort of wisdom which comprehends the knowledge of things both divine and human; that is, the society and relation of men with the gods, and with one another. If then this, as most certainly it is, be the greatest virtue, it follows, that duties which flow from society must as certainly be the greatest; for the deepest knowledge and contemplation of nature is but a very lame and imperfect business, unless it proceed and tend forward to action. Now the occasions wherein it can show itself best consist in maintaining the interest of men, and of consequence belong to the society of mankind: whence it follows that the maintaining of this should in reason take place before learning and knowledge. Nor is this any more than what all good men show they judge to be true by their actions and practices: for who is there so wholly addicted to contemplation and the study of nature, as that, if his country should fall into danger, while he was in one of his noblest researches, he would not immediately throw all aside, and run to its relief with all possible speed; nay, though he thought he might number the stars, or take the just dimensions of the whole world? And the same would he do in the case of any danger to a friend or a parent. From all which things it undeniably appears that the duties of knowledge and searching after truth are obliged to give way to the duties of justice, which consist in upholding society among men; than which there is nothing for which we should be more concerned.

Nay, those very men, who have spent their whole lives in philosophy and learning, have yet always endeavoured, as much as they could, to be serviceable to the interest and good of mankind: for many brave men, and very useful members of their several states, have in great part been made such by their institutions. Thus Epaminondas, the famous Theban, was indebted for his education to Lysis, the Pythagorean; Dion of Syracuse, for his to Plato; and the same may be said of a great many others: even I myself, whatsoever service I have done the republic—if, at least, it may be said that I have done it any service, must wholly ascribe it to that learning and those instructions I received from my masters. Neither is their teaching and instructing others determined to the time of their living here; but they continue to do it even after they are dead, by the learned discourses which they leave behind them: for there is no one point they have left unhandled, relating either to the laws, customs, or discipline of the commonwealth; so that they seem to have sacrificed their leisure and opportunities of study to the benefit of those who are engaged in business; and thus we see how those men themselves, whose lives have been spent in the pursuit of wisdom, have nevertheless endeavoured by their learning and prudence to be some way profitable to the community of mankind. And for this one reason, persuasive speaking, if joined with prudence, is a greater accomplishment than the acutest thinking, if destitute of eloquence: for thinking is terminated in itself alone, but speaking reaches out to the benefit of those with whom we are joined in the same society. Now, as bees do not therefore unite themselves together, that so they may the better prepare their combs, but therefore prepare their combs, because they do by nature unite themselves together; so men, and much more, being creatures that naturally love society, in consequence of that, seek how they may find methods of living happily in it. Hence it follows, that the knowledge of things, unless it is accompanied with that sort of virtue which consists in defending and preserving of men, i.e. in the maintenance of human society, is but a barren and fruitless accomplishment; and even greatness of soul, without a regard to this society and conjunction, is very little better than savageness and barbarity. Thus we may see, that the getting of knowledge is a duty of much less concern and moment than the preserving this society and union amongst men. It is a very false notion that hath been advanced by some people, that necessity alone was the motive to this society, which we have so often mentioned; and that men would never have associated together, but that they were not able, in a solitary life, to furnish themselves with the necessaries of nature; and that every great and exalted genius, would Providence supply him with food and the other conveniences of life, would withdraw from all business and intercourse with mankind, and give himself wholly to study and contemplation. This is not so; for he would avoid solitude, endeavour to find a companion in his studies, and always be desirous of teaching and learning, of hearing and speaking; from all which things it is abundantly evident that the duties belonging to human society should in reason take place before those which relate to inactive knowledge.

Book II

For what is there, O ye gods, more desirable than Wisdom? What more excellent and lovely in itself? What more useful and becoming for a man? Or what more worthy of his reasonable nature? Now those who are busied in the pursuit of this are called philosophers, and the word philosophy signifies no more, if you would take it literally, than a certain desire and love for wisdom: and wisdom is defined by the old philosophers, the knowledge of things both divine and human, together with the causes on which they depend; the study of which whosoever finds fault with, I confess I cannot perceive what it is he would commend; for what study is there that brings so much quiet and satisfaction to the mind, if these are the things which we propose to ourselves, as theirs, who are always searching out something which may contribute to the welfare and happiness of their lives? Or if it be virtue and constancy that we desire, either this is the method of obtaining them, or else there is not any to be found in the world.

[…]

The whole work and exercise of virtue in general consists in some one of these three things: the first is a knowledge, in all we undertake, of what is agreeable to truth and sincerity; what is becoming and suitable to every one's character; what will be the consequence of such or such actions; what are the materials out of which things are made, and what the causes that first brought them into being: the second, a restraining the violent motions and passions of the soul, and bringing the irregular inclinations of the appetite under the power and government of reason: the third is a skilfulness of address in our carriage, and a winning demeanor toward the rest of men, with whom we are joined in one common society; that so by their help we may be supplied in abundance with all those things which our natures stand in need of; and by the same may be enabled, should any injury be offered us, to keep ourselves secure from the violence of it; and not only so, but to revenge ourselves also on the guilty person, and inflict such punishments as are according to the rules of humanity and justice.

(b) Seneca: Liberal Arts need Stoic Virtues

Seneca the Younger (4 BC–AD 65) is the first author in this collection to span the transition from the pre-Christian to the Christian era in the West, and it is appropriate that he serves in some ways as a precursor to the critique that early Christians offer to the liberal arts in the next section. In his letters to Lucilius, Seneca commends the liberal arts, but his emphasis is on self-discipline, rather than promiscuous learning. His emphasis on a life of action as well as contemplation in De Otio *(On Leisure) is close to Cicero; he also adds a remarkable pæan to scientific investigation that presages the direction of much of our cosmological investigations since his time. Seneca goes further in warning that liberal science is insufficient without the Stoic philosophy that protects a man against emotional weakness amid the winds of fate and chance. In this, he in some respects only echoes the strong concern with virtue that had long been an important aspect of the liberal education ideal. However, in questioning the adequacy of the unprepared but intellectually brilliant soul, Seneca takes the critique to a new level, and anticipates the Christian concern that an understanding of things of this world, however complete, will never fully satisfy the human spirit.*

Epistulæ Morales Ad Lucilium

Letter II

I am happy, Lucilius, in conceiving great hopes of you, both from what you write, and from what I hear of you: it seems, you are no wanderer, nor apt to disquiet yourself in vain with change of place; a restlessness which generally springs from some malady in the mind. The chief testimony, I apprehend, of a mind truly calm and composed, is, that it is consistent with, and can enjoy itself.

Be pleased likewise to consider that the reading many authors, and books of all sorts, betrays a vague and unsteady disposition. You must attach yourself to some in particular, and thoroughly digest what you read, if you would entrust the faithful memory with anything of use. He that is everywhere, is nowhere. They who spend their time in travelling, meet indeed with many an host, but few friends. This is necessarily the case of those, who apply not familiarly to any one study, but run over everything cursorily and in haste.

[...]

Variety of books distracts the mind; when you cannot read, therefore, all that you have; it is enough to have only what you can read. But you will say, you have a mind sometimes to amuse yourself, with one book and sometimes with another: it is a sign, my friend, of a nice and squeamish stomach, to be tasting many viands, which, as they are various and of different qualities, rather corrupt than nourish. Read therefore always the most approved authors, and if you are pleased at any time to taste others, by way of amusement, still return to those as your principal study. Be continually treasuring up something to arm you against poverty, something against the fear of death and other the like evils, incident to man. And when you have read sufficiently, make a reserve of some particular sentiment for that day's meditation.

Letter LXXXVIII

You desire, Lucilius, to know my opinion concerning the Liberal Sciences: I cannot say that I greatly admire any one of them, nor reckon any of them among what I call good, especially when pursued merely for lucre. They are arts, meritorious, and useful indeed, so far as they prepare, and do not detain and cramp, the genius. For no longer are they to be indulged and dwelt upon, than while the mind is not capable of any thing greater: they are the rudiments, but not the whole exercise of man. They are called liberal, you know, because they become a free man, and are full worthy the application of a gentleman.

But there is only one study or science that is truly liberal, viz. that which gives freedom indeed. And what is that, but the study of wisdom, sublime, strong, and manly?

[...]

For what pretence, I pray you, have those morning sots, who fatten the body, but starve the mind, to be called professors of liberal arts? Can gluttony and drunkeness be thought a liberal study fit for youth, whom our ancestors were wont to exercise always in an erect attitude, in throwing darts, toning the pike, breaking their horses, or handling their arms? They taught their children nothing that was to be learned in an easy and lolling posture. But after all, neither these arts nor the former teach and nourish virtue. For what avails it a man to manage a horse, and break him to the bit, if still he himself is carried away by his unbridled passions? What advantages it a man to overcome many in wrestling and boxing, if in the meantime he is overcome himself by anger? What then, are the liberal sciences of no advantage to us? Yes, certainly, of great advantage, in all other respects, save in regard to virtue.

For low as the mechanic arts are, which are wholly manual, they are most useful instruments, and of great service in life, though they belong not to virtue. Why then do we instruct children in the liberal sciences? Not because they instil virtue, but because they prepare the mind for the reception of it. As the first principles of literature (so called by the ancients) by which children were taught their ABC, teach not the liberal arts, but only prepare them for instruction therein; so the liberal arts carry not the mind directly to virtue, but only expand, and make it fit for it.

[...]

But when you affirm, it is said, that without the liberal sciences a man cannot reach virtue; how can you deny that they contribute to virtue? Why, because neither without food can a man arrive at virtue, and yet food belongs not to virtue. Timber of itself contributes nothing to a ship, though without timber a ship cannot be built. There is no reason, I say, to think, that a thing should be made by that, without which it cannot be made. It may indeed be said, that without the liberal arts a man may arrive at virtue: for though virtue be a thing to be learned, yet it is not learned merely by these sciences. And why should I not think that a man may become a wise man, though he knows not his letters; since wisdom consists not in the knowledge of letters? It is conversant about things, not about words; and I know not whether that may not prove the more faithful memory, which depends upon its own intrinsic strength.

Wisdom is very powerful and extensive; it requires a large space to range in; it must study all things both divine and human; things past, and to come; transitory, and eternal; and even Time itself.

De Otio

We have a habit of saying that the highest good is to live according to nature: now nature has produced us for both purposes, for contemplation and for action. Let us now prove what we said before: nay, who will not think this proved if he bethinks himself how great a passion he has for discovering the unknown? How vehemently his curiosity is roused by every kind of romantic tale. Some men make long voyages and undergo the toils of journeying to distant lands for no reward except that of discovering something hidden and remote. This is what draws people to public shows,

and causes them to pry into everything that is closed, to puzzle out everything that is secret, to clear up points of antiquity, and to listen to tales of
the customs of savage nations. Nature has bestowed upon us an inquiring
disposition, and being well aware of her own skill and beauty, has produced us to be spectators of her vast works, because she would lose all the
fruits of her labour if she were to exhibit such vast and noble works of such
complex construction, so bright and beautiful in so many ways, to solitude
alone. That you may be sure that she wishes to be gazed upon, not merely
looked at, see what a place she has assigned to us: she has placed us in the
middle of herself and given us a prospect all around. She has not only set
man erect upon his feet, but also with a view to making it easy for him to
watch the heavens, she has raised his head on high and connected it with a
pliant neck, in order that he might follow the course of the stars from their
rising to their setting, and move his face round with the whole heaven.
Moreover, by carrying six constellations across the sky by day, and six by
night, she displays every part of herself in such a manner that by what she
brings before man's eyes she renders him eager to see the rest also. For we
have not beheld all things, nor yet the true extent of them, but our eyesight
does but open to itself the right path for research, and lay the foundation,
from which our speculations may pass from what is obvious to what is less
well known, and find out something more ancient than the world itself,
from whence those stars came forth: inquire what was the condition of the
universe before each of its elements were separated from the general mass:
on what principle its confused and blended parts were divided: who
assigned their places to things, whether it was by their own nature that
what was heavy sunk downwards, and what was light flew upwards, or
whether besides the stress and weight of bodies some higher power gave
laws to each of them: whether that greatest proof that the spirit of man is
divine is true, the theory, namely, that some parts and as it were sparks of
the stars have fallen down upon earth and stuck there in a foreign substance. Our thought bursts through the battlements of heaven, and is not
satisfied with knowing only what is shown to us: "I investigate", it says,
"that which lies without the world, whether it is a bottomless abyss, or
whether it also is confined within boundaries of its own: what the appearance of the things outside may be, whether they be shapeless and vague,
extending equally in every direction, or whether they also are arranged in
a certain kind of order: whether they are connected with this world of ours,
or are widely separated from it and welter about in empty space: whether
they consist of distinct atoms, of which everything that is and that is to be,
is made, or whether their substance is uninterrupted and all of it capable of
change: whether the elements are naturally opposed to one another, or

whether they are not at variance, but work towards the same end by different means." Since man was born for such speculations as these, consider
how short a time he has been given for them, even supposing that he
makes good his claims to the whole of it, allows no part of it to be wrested
from him through good nature, or to slip away from him through careless-
ness; though he watches over all his hours with most miserly care, though
he live to the extreme confines of human existence, and though misfortune
take nothing away from what Nature has bestowed upon him, even then
man is too mortal for the comprehension of immortality. I live according to
Nature, therefore, if I give myself entirely up to her, and if I admire and
reverence her. Nature, however, intended me to do both, to practise both
contemplation and action: and I do both, because even contemplation is
not devoid of action.

"But," say you, "it makes a difference whether you adopt the contemplative life for the sake of your own pleasure, demanding nothing from it
save unbroken contemplation without any result: for such a life is a sweet
one and has attractions of its own." To this I answer you: it makes just as
much difference in what spirit you lead the life of a public man, whether
you are never at rest, and never set apart any time during which you may
turn your eyes away from the things of earth to those of Heaven. It is by no
means desirable that one should merely strive to accumulate property
without any love of virtue, or do nothing but hard work without any cultivation of the intellect, for these things ought to be combined and blended
together; and, similarly, virtue placed in leisure without action is but an
incomplete and feeble good thing, because she never displays what she
has learned. Who can deny that she ought to test her progress in actual
work, and not merely think what ought to be done, but also sometimes use
her hands as well as her head, and bring her conceptions into actual being?

(c) Quintilian: Learning is Natural to Humankind

*Quintilian (c. AD 35-100), a professional orator from the Iberian peninsula and
the teacher of Pliny the Younger, was a significant means of transmission for the
classical tradition of rhetoric into mediæval and Renaissance Europe. Quintilian
himself drew on a tradition that he traced back to Isocrates. His twelve-volume*
Institutio Oratoria *details both the training of an orator and his broader liberal
education and is justly considered the culmination of the Roman tradition. His
work had a long influence, even Martin Luther counting Quintilian as among his
favourite authors, although this fame had declined by the nineteenth century.
Quintilian is notable for his belief that almost anyone could benefit from education, a universal theme at odds with the traditional classical view, but, again, at*

home in a Christian era. He stresses the importance of virtue, the need to read the
best authors and denies that a single method offers a royal road to liberal learning.

Institutio Oratoria

Preface

Now, according to my definition, no man can be a complete orator unless
he is a good man: I therefore require, that he should be not only all-accom-
plished in eloquence, but possessed of every moral virtue.

Book I

A father, the moment he becomes so, ought to entertain the greatest hopes
of his son; he will therefore the more early watch over his improvement.
For it is a mistaken complaint, that very few people are naturally endowed
with quick apprehension; and that most persons lose the fruits of all their
application and study, through a natural defect of understanding. The
case is the very reverse, because we find mankind in general to be quick in
apprehension, and susceptible of instruction. This is the characteristic of
the human race; and as birds are provided by nature with a propensity to
fly, horses to run, and wild beasts to be savage; so the working and the
sagacity of the brain is peculiar to man; and hence it is, that his mind is
supposed to be of divine original. Now, the dull and the indocile are in no
other sense the productions of nature, than are monstrous shapes, and
extraordinary objects, which are very rare. To prove this, we have known
many boys, who had the most promising appearances, all which vanished
as they grew up: a plain evidence it was not their nature, but care, that was
deficient. I readily admit, that the capacity of one man may be better than
that of another; some make great, others less, proficiency; but, we never
knew a man whom study did not somewhat improve. Whoever is sensible
of this, as soon as he becomes a father, ought to employ the most diligent
attention to the education of the future orator.

[...]

When a boy is able to read and write, he is immediately put under the care
of a professor of classical learning. It makes no difference here whether the
language he is to study be Greek or Latin; though I am of opinion he
should begin with Greek. Both are to be studied in the same manner. Now
this profession is divided at first into two branches; correctness of style,
and the explication of the poets; a division which is of greater importance
than it appears at first to be. For, in order to write well, we are supposed to
speak well, and we must read the poets correctly before we can explain
them, and all must be guided by critical judgment. In this respect the

ancient professors were so rigorous, that they took upon them not only to censure particular passages, and to remove supposititious books as a spurious brood intruding into a family; but they made an arrangement of authors, allotting to some an ordinary and to others an extraordinary degree of merit. Neither is it enough that a professor has read the poets; he ought to canvass every species of writing; not only on account of the narrative, but the words, which often derive their force from the author who uses them. Without some knowledge of music, a professor cannot be accomplished, as he will have occasion to treat of measures and numbers; and without astronomy he cannot understand the poets, who (to give only one instance) so often mark the seasons by the rising and setting of the heavenly bodies. We see, almost in all poems, a vast number of passages relating to the most abstruse points of natural philosophy; besides, Empedocles amongst the Greeks, and Varro and Lucretius amongst the Latins, have laid down systems of philosophy in verse; therefore, a professor must not be ignorant of that kind of learning. He must likewise possess no common degree of eloquence in order to express himself with propriety and perspicuity upon all the several points I have here mentioned. It is therefore intolerably impertinent in some, to treat this as a dry, trifling profession; for unless the future orator lays his foundation deep in the liberal arts, all the superstructure he shall afterwards raise upon it, must tumble to the ground. In short, this profession is to the young a necessary, and to the old an agreeable, assistant in retired study; and is perhaps the only branch of learning that has in it more of the solid than of the showy.

Book II

I would not have young gentlemen think that they are sufficiently instructed in this art, if they have got by heart one of the little books of rhetoric that are generally handed about, and imagine themselves as safe with them, as if they were fortified with the very bulwarks of eloquence. The art of speaking well requires close application, extensive practice, repeated trials, deep sagacity, and a ready invention. Rules, however, may assist it, provided they point out the direct road, without confining the learner to a single track, from which, should anyone think it unlawful to depart, he must be contented to make as leisurely a progress as a dancer does upon a slack rope. For this reason we often, for a nearer cut, strike off from the high road, which perhaps has been the work of an army, and when our direct way is barred up by bridges broken down with the force of torrents, we are obliged to go round; and if the door is in flames, we must get out at the window.

Chapter III

Christianity: Logos

With the first verse of his Gospel, St. John the Evangelist made a remarkable claim for the unity of the Greek tradition with Christianity: 'In the beginning was the λογος, and the λογος was with God, and the λογος was God'. λογος (or '*Logos*') expressed the ancient Greek concept of the inward thought and its outward expression: both intellect and oratory. Closely related to the outward and inward aspects of the liberal education tradition, it also helped to express both the sustaining rationality of the divine order and the outward-inward Mystery of the Incarnation. The New Testament, wholly written in Koine Greek, made it impossible for the Church Fathers to ignore the Hellenic intellectual tradition, but it would be twelve centuries before St. Thomas Aquinas would definitively unite rediscovered Aristotelian logic with Christian dogma. Nevertheless, the Church proved a crucial influence on the tradition, introducing the Hebraic/Abrahaminic conceptions of love, human dignity and justice, together with a Gospel of universal Grace. Bolgar (1954) also argues that Augustine, together with Cappella and Cassiodorus, helped to imagine a new model of the classical world's liberal education, taking what had been designed to prepare public speakers, the future orators of democratic republics, and inventing a new form centred on the private intellect and accurate habits of inward thought, emphasising the other face of the coin of *Logos*. For Augustine, the seven liberal arts included philosophy in place of astronomy: favouring incorporeal over corporeal contemplation. While not influential on Augustine's contemporaries, this approach would prove ideally suited to the monasticism of the Middle Ages. By drawing liberal education inward, Christianity would preserve it, but ultimately risked accusations of irrelevance: Scholasticism became accused of debating logical riddles of theology at the expense of contemplating the world; a fault the revival of the "new" Greek learning and the fresh classicism of the Renaissance would redress. Christianity preserved and enriched the tradition, while limiting its ambition through the belief that intellectual sophistication and wise action could never be either necessary or sufficient for salvation. That last answered some of the questions raised by the Roman concept of *humanitas*, while presenting a new risk of the devout seeing no need for such an education. That issue remains, but John Paul II's encyclical of 1998, *Fides et Ratio*, asserted that 'faith and reason are like two wings on which the human spirit rises to the contemplation of truth', and when Pope Benedict XVI lectured in Regensburg on 12 September 2006, he spoke of "the intrinsic necessity of a rapprochement between Biblical faith and Greek inquiry" and stated that "John thus [by using the word '*Logos*'] spoke the final word on the biblical concept of God".

(a) St. Jerome: Christian or Ciceronian?

For the brilliant men who formed the early Church, their faith and their intellect presented them with a great dilemma: their minds relished the great books of the pagan authors; their faith assured them that God alone could offer salvation. St. Jerome epitomises this dilemma in his letter to Eustochium (AD 384). The great ascetic recalls his torment as a young man who adored Cicero, but felt the call of Christ. Ultimately, St. Jerome turned his back on Cicero, but the difficulty of that choice was a sign that the Church would not find it easy to reject these treasures from the pre-Christian past. It would be St. Augustine of Hippo, despite his own reservations, who began to point the way to an accommodation.

A Letter to Eustochium

How can Horace go with the psalter, Virgil with the gospels, Cicero with the apostle? Is not a brother made to stumble if he sees you sitting at meat in an idol's temple? Although 'unto the pure all things are pure' and 'nothing is to be refused if it be received with thanksgiving', still we ought not to drink the cup of Christ, and, at the same time, the cup of devils. Let me relate to you the story of my own miserable experience.

Many years ago, when for the kingdom of heaven's sake I had cut myself off from home, parents, sister, relations, and—harder still—from the dainty food to which I had been accustomed; and when I was on my way to Jerusalem to wage my warfare, I still could not bring myself to forgo the library which I had formed for myself at Rome with great care and toil. And so, miserable man that I was, I would fast only that I might afterwards read Cicero. After many nights spent in vigil, after floods of tears called from my inmost heart, after the recollection of my past sins, I would once more take up Plautus. And when at times I returned to my right mind, and began to read the prophets, their style seemed rude and repellent. I failed to see the light with my blinded eyes; but I attributed the fault not to them, but to the sun. While the old serpent was thus making me his plaything, about the middle of Lent a deep-seated fever fell upon my weakened body, and while it destroyed my rest completely — the story seems hardly credible — it so wasted my unhappy frame that scarcely anything was left of me but skin and bone.

Meantime preparations for my funeral went on; my body grew gradually colder, and the warmth of life lingered only in my throbbing breast. Suddenly I was caught up in the spirit and dragged before the judgment seat of the Judge; and here the light was so bright, and those who stood around were so radiant, that I cast myself upon the ground and did not dare to look up. Asked who and what I was I replied: "I am a Christian." But He who presided said: "Thou liest, thou art a follower of Cicero and not of Christ. For 'where thy treasure is, there will thy heart be also.'"[1] Instantly I became dumb, and amid the strokes of the lash — for He had ordered me to be scourged — I was tortured more severely still by the fire of conscience, considering with myself that verse, 'In the grave who shall give thee thanks?' Yet for all that I began to cry and to bewail myself, saying: "Have mercy upon me, O Lord: have mercy upon me." Amid the sound of the scourges this cry still made itself heard. At last the bystanders, falling down before the knees of Him who presided, prayed that He would have pity on my youth, and that He would give me space to repent of my error. He might still, they urged, inflict torture on me, should I ever again read the works of the Gentiles. Under the stress of that awful moment I should have been ready to make even still larger promises than these. Accordingly I made oath and called upon His name, saying: "Lord, if ever again I possess worldly books, or if ever again I read such, I have denied Thee."

Dismissed, then, on taking this oath, I returned to the upper world, and, to the surprise of all, I opened upon them eyes so drenched with tears that my distress served to convince even the incredulous. And that this was no sleep nor idle dream, such as those by which we are often mocked, I call to witness the tribunal before which I lay, and the terrible judgment which I feared. May it never, hereafter, be my lot to fall under such an inquisition! I profess that my shoulders were black and blue, that I felt the bruises long after I awoke from my sleep, and that thenceforth I read the books of God with a zeal greater than I had previously given to the books of men.

---

1   It is interesting to compare this to the legendary dream motivating the Abbasid translation movement, which eventually restored a knowledge of Aristotle to European learning. One night in ninth-century Baghdad, according to the *Fihrist* of Ibn al-Nadim, Caliph al-Ma'mun saw a white man with a broad forehead sitting on his bed. The man told him that he was Aristotle and that what is good is according to reason, asserting the compatibility of Greek reason with Islamic revelation, and therefore legitimating the study of books other than the Qu'ran.

(b) St. Augustine of Hippo:
Pagan Learning Informs the Reading of Scripture

Even more than St. Jerome, St. Augustine of Hippo (AD 354-430) was a man of formidable intellect. In De Magistro *(On the Teacher), he enquires into the nature of teaching, a taste of his philosophical subtlety and interest in the central questions that attended the liberal education tradition. He wrestles with the Socratic paradox of education discussed in Plato's* Meno: *in the end the learner has to see for himself the truth and validity of what is taught, but unless he already in a sense knew this, how could he perform this act of recognition? For Socrates, all learning must be a kind of remembering, an idea that captures the active, inward understanding of learning that influenced classical thought on education. For the same reason, in* Phædrus *(274-5), Plato's Socrates tells the story of the king of Egypt inveighing against writing, as causing men to rely on external marks, rather than taking things into their own souls. For Augustine, teachers oversee a meeting of minds between pupils and 'the learned' — the great minds of the past. Nevertheless, like Jerome, Augustine came to regret his youthful delight at the classics: in his case, for his fondness of the stories in Virgil's Æneid. Augustine's* Confessiones *make clear how ashamed he felt for the form of his early education. Certainly Augustine appreciates profoundly the limitations in what a good liberal education can offer. But he was also possessed of far too power-ful a mind to lay it aside easily. He resisted expelling the pagan authors. In* De Doctrina Christiana, *Augustine lays out a path for employing pagan knowledge in the service of Christian understanding. If not yet the full celebration of liberal learning that was to come, here the path of Christian acceptance is clear. Augus-tine's employment of Neoplatonism in his theology was an intimation of the full synthesis between Aristotelian and Christian thought that St. Thomas Aquinas would make some eight centuries later. For the philosophically-minded Augus-tine, the seven liberal arts included philosophy in place of astronomy, as he makes plain toward the end of his life when reconsidering his earlier works in* Retractationes.

De Magistro

Surely teachers do not claim that it is their own thoughts, rather than the actual teachings which they consider that they transmit through their speech, that are received and assimilated? For who is so stupidly curious as to send his child to school in order to learn what the teacher thinks? But when they have explained in words those teachings which they claim to teach, both those of virtue and wisdom, then those who are called pupils think over within themselves whether they have been told the truth, look-ing according to their strength at that truth which is, so to speak, inside them. Then indeed do they learn. And when they have internally discovered that what was said is true, they applaud, not realising that it is not the teachers that they praise, but rather the learned, if indeed the teachers actually know what they are saying. Men are in error, however, in calling "teachers" those who are not, because usually there is no delay between the moment of speaking and the moment of understanding. And since they learn inwardly soon after the expostulation of the speaker, externally they think they have learned from the one who has expostulated.

Confessiones

Book I

But why did I so much hate the Greek, which I studied as a boy? I do not yet fully know. For the Latin I loved; not what my first masters, but what the so-called grammarians taught me. For those first lessons, reading, writing, and arithmetic, I thought as great a burden and penalty as any Greek. And yet whence was this too, but from the sin and vanity of this life, because I was flesh, and a breath that passeth away and cometh not again? For those first lessons were better certainly, because more certain; by them I obtained, and still retain, the power of reading what I find written, and myself writing what I will; whereas in the others, I was forced to learn the wanderings of one Æneas, forgetful of my own, and to weep for dead Dido, because she killed herself for love; the while, with dry eyes, I endured my miserable self dying among these things, far from Thee, O God my life.

For what more miserable than a miserable being who commiserates not himself; weeping the death of Dido for love to Æneas, but weeping not his own death for want of love to Thee, O God. Thou light of my heart, Thou bread of my inmost soul, Thou Power who givest vigour to my mind, who quickenest my thoughts, I loved Thee not. I committed fornication against Thee, and all around me thus fornicating there echoed "Well done! Well done!" for the friendship of this world is fornication against Thee; and "Well done! Well done!" echoes on till one is ashamed not to be thus a man. And all this I wept not, I who wept for Dido slain, and "seeking by the sword a stroke and wound extreme," myself seeking the while a worse extreme, the extremest and lowest of Thy creatures, having forsaken Thee, earth passing into the earth. And if forbid to read all this, I was grieved that I might not read what grieved me. Madness like this is thought a higher and a richer learning, than that by which I learned to read and write.

[…]

Bear with me, my God, while I say somewhat of my wit, Thy gift, and on what dotages I wasted it. For a task was set me, troublesome enough to my soul, upon terms of praise or shame, and fear of stripes, to speak the words of Juno, as she raged and mourned that she could not

> 'This Trojan prince from Latium turn.'

Which words I had heard that Juno never uttered; but we were forced to go astray in the footsteps of these poetic fictions, and to say in prose much what he expressed in verse. And his speaking was most applauded, in whom the passions of rage and grief were most preeminent, and clothed in the most fitting language, maintaining the dignity of the character. What is it to me, O my true life, my God, that my declamation was applauded above so many of my own age and class? Is not all this smoke and wind? And was there nothing else whereon to exercise my wit and tongue? Thy praises, Lord, Thy praises might have stayed the yet tender shoot of my heart by the prop of Thy Scriptures; so had it not trailed away amid these empty trifles, a defiled prey for the fowls of the air. For in more ways than one do men sacrifice to the rebellious angels.

[...]

Behold, O Lord God, yea, behold patiently as Thou art wont, how carefully the sons of men observe the covenanted rules of letters and syllables received from those who spake before them, neglecting the eternal covenant of everlasting salvation received from Thee.

[...]

In quest of the fame of eloquence, a man standing before a human judge, surrounded by a human throng, declaiming against his enemy with fiercest hatred, will take heed most watchfully, lest, by an error of the tongue, he murder the word "human-being;" but takes no heed, lest, through the fury of his spirit, he murder the real human being.

Book III

Among such as these, in that unsettled age of mine, learned I books of eloquence, wherein I desired to be eminent, out of a damnable and vainglorious end, a joy in human vanity. In the ordinary course of study, I fell upon a certain book of Cicero, whose speech almost all admire, not so his heart. This book of his contains an exhortation to philosophy, and is called *Hortensius*. But this book altered my affections, and turned my prayers to Thyself, O Lord; and made me have other purposes and desires. Every vain hope at once became worthless to me; and I longed with an incredibly burning desire for an immortality of wisdom, and began now to arise, that

I might return to Thee. For not to sharpen my tongue, (which thing I seemed to be purchasing with my mother's allowances, in that my nineteenth year, my father being dead two years before,) not to sharpen my tongue did I employ that book; nor did it infuse into me its style, but its matter.

How did I burn then, my God, how did I burn to re-mount from earthly things to Thee, nor knew I what Thou wouldest do with me? For with Thee is wisdom. But the love of wisdom is in Greek called "philosophy," with which that book inflamed me. Some there be that seduce through philosophy, under a great, and smooth, and honourable name colouring and disguising their own errors: and almost all who in that and former ages were such, are in that book censured and set forth: there also is made plain that wholesome advice of Thy Spirit, by Thy good and devout servant; Beware lest any man spoil you through philosophy and vain deceit, after the tradition of men, after the rudiments of the world, and not after Christ. For in Him dwelleth all the fulness of the Godhead bodily. And since at that time (Thou, O light of my heart, knowest) Apostolic Scripture was not known to me, I was delighted with that exhortation, so far only, that I was thereby strongly roused, and kindled, and inflamed to love, and seek, and obtain, and hold, and embrace not this or that sect, but wisdom itself whatever it were; and this alone checked me thus enkindled, that the name of Christ was not in it. For this name, according to Thy mercy, O Lord, this name of my Saviour Thy Son, had my tender heart, even with my mother's milk, devoutly drunk in, and deeply treasured; and whatsoever was without that name, though never so learned, polished, or true, took not entire hold of me.

Book IV

And what did it profit me, that scarce twenty years old, a book of Aristotle, which they call the ten Predicaments,[2] falling into my hands, (on whose very name I hung, as on something great and divine, so often as my rhetoric master of Carthage, and others, accounted learned, mouthed it with cheeks bursting with pride,) I read and understood it unaided? And on my conferring with others, who said that they scarcely understood it with very able tutors, not only orally explaining it, but drawing many things in sand, they could tell me no more of it than I had learned, reading it by myself. And the book appeared to me to speak very clearly of substances, such as "man," and of their qualities, as the figure of a man, of what sort it is; and stature, how many feet high; and his relationship, whose brother he is; or where placed; or when born; or whether he stands or sits; or be shod

---

2   Also known as *Categories*.

or armed; or does, or suffers anything; and all the innumerable things which might be ranged under these nine Predicaments, of which I have given some specimens, or under that chief Predicament of Substance.

[...]

And what did it profit me, that all the books I could procure of the so-called liberal arts, I, the vile slave of vile affections, read by myself, and understood? And I delighted in them, but knew not whence came all, that therein was true or certain. For I had my back to the light, and my face to the things enlightened; whence my face, with which I discerned the things enlightened, itself was not enlightened. Whatever was written, either on rhetoric, or logic, geometry, music, and arithmetic, by myself without much difficulty or any instructor, I understood, Thou knowest, O Lord my God; because both quickness of understanding, and acuteness in discerning, is Thy gift: yet did I not thence sacrifice to Thee. So then it served not to my use, but rather to my perdition, since I went about to get so good a portion of my substance into my own keeping; and I kept not my strength for Thee, but wandered from Thee into a far country, to spend it upon harlotries. For what profited me good abilities, not employed to good uses? For I felt not that those arts were attained with great difficulty, even by the studious and talented, until I attempted to explain them to such; when he most excelled in them, who followed me not altogether slowly.

[...]

What profited me then my nimble wit in those sciences and all those most knotty volumes, unravelled by me, without aid from human instruction; seeing I erred so foully, and with such sacrilegious shamefulness, in the doctrine of piety? Or what hindrance was a far slower wit to Thy little ones, since they departed not far from Thee, that in the nest of Thy Church they might securely be fledged, and nourish the wings of charity, by the food of a sound faith.

De Doctrina Christiana

Book II

Ignorance of things, too, renders figurative expressions obscure, as when we do not know the nature of the animals, or minerals, or plants, which are frequently referred to in Scripture by way of comparison. The fact so well known about the serpent, for example, that to protect its head it will present its whole body to its assailants — how much light it throws upon the meaning of our Lord's command, that we should be wise as serpents; that is to say, that for the sake of our head, which is Christ, we should willingly offer our body to the persecutors, lest the Christian faith should, as it were, be destroyed in us, if to save the body we deny our God!

[...]

Ignorance of numbers, too, prevents us from understanding things that are set down in Scripture in a figurative and mystical way. A candid mind, if I may so speak, cannot but be anxious, for example, to ascertain what is meant by the fact that Moses and Elijah, and our Lord Himself, all fasted for forty days.

[...]

[W]e ought not to give up music because of the superstition of the heathen, if we can derive anything from it that is of use for the understanding of Holy Scripture; nor does it follow that we must busy ourselves with their theatrical trumpery because we enter upon an investigation about harps and other instruments, that may help us to lay hold upon spiritual things. For we ought not to refuse to learn letters because they say that Mercury discovered them; nor because they have dedicated temples to Justice and Virtue, and prefer to worship in the form of stones things that ought to have their place in the heart, ought we on that account to forsake justice and virtue. Nay, but let every good and true Christian understand that wherever truth may be found, it belongs to his Master; and while he recognizes and acknowledges the truth, even in their religious literature, let him reject the figments of superstition, and let him grieve over and avoid men who, "when they knew God, glorified him not as God, neither were thankful; but became vain in their imaginations, and their foolish heart was darkened. Professing themselves to be wise, they became fools, and changed the glory of the incorruptible God into an image made like to corruptible man, and to birds, and four-footed beasts, and creeping things."

[...]

For it is one thing to say: If you bruise down this herb and drink it, it will remove the pain from your stomach; and another to say: If you hang this herb round your neck, it will remove the pain from your stomach. In the former case the wholesome mixture is approved of, in the latter the superstitious charm is condemned; although indeed, where incantations and invocations and marks are not used, it is frequently doubtful whether the thing that is tied or fixed in any way to the body to cure it, acts by a natural virtue, in which case it may be freely used; or acts by a sort of charm, in which case it becomes the Christian to avoid it the more carefully, the more efficacious it may seem to be. But when the reason why a thing is of virtue does not appear, the intention with which it is used is of great importance, at least in healing or in tempering bodies, whether in medicine or in agriculture.

[...]

Again, the science of definition, of division, and of partition, although it is frequently applied to falsities, is not itself false, nor framed by man's device, but is evolved from the reason of things. For although poets have applied it to their fictions, and false philosophers, or even heretics — that is, false Christians — to their erroneous doctrines, that is no reason why it should be false, for example, that neither in definition, nor in division, nor in partition, is anything to be included that does not pertain to the matter in hand, nor anything to be omitted that does. This is true, even though the things to be defined or divided are not true.

[...]

Moreover, if those who are called philosophers, and especially the Platonists, have said aught that is true and in harmony with our faith, we are not only not to shrink from it, but to claim it for our own use from those who have unlawful possession of it. For, as the Egyptians had not only the idols and heavy burdens which the people of Israel hated and fled from, but also vessels and ornaments of gold and silver, and garments, which the same people when going out of Egypt appropriated to themselves, designing them for a better use, not doing this on their own authority, but by the command of God, the Egyptians themselves, in their ignorance, providing them with things which they themselves, were not making a good use of; in the same way all branches of heathen learning have not only false and superstitious fancies and heavy burdens of unnecessary toil, which every one of us, when going out under the leadership of Christ from the fellowship of the heathen, ought to abhor and avoid; but they contain also liberal instruction which is better adapted to the use of the truth, and some most excellent precepts of morality; and some truths in regard even to the worship of the One God are found among them. Now these are, so to speak, their gold and silver, which they did not create themselves, but dug out of the mines of God's providence which are everywhere scattered abroad, and are perversely and unlawfully prostituting to the worship of devils. These, therefore, the Christian, when he separates himself in spirit from the miserable fellowship of these men, ought to take away from them, and to devote to their proper use in preaching the gospel. Their garments, also, — that is, human institutions such as are adapted to that intercourse with men which is indispensable in this life, — we must take and turn to a Christian use.

And what else have many good and faithful men among our brethren done? Do we not see with what a quantity of gold and silver and garments Cyprian, that most persuasive teacher and most blessed martyr, was loaded when he came out of Egypt? How much Lactantius brought with him? And Victorinus, and Optatus, and Hilary, not to speak of living men! How much Greeks out of number have borrowed! And prior to all these, that most faithful servant of God, Moses, had done the same thing; for of him it is written that he was learned in all the wisdom of the Egyptians. And to none of all these would heathen superstition (especially in those times when, kicking against the yoke of Christ, it was persecuting the Christians) have ever furnished branches of knowledge it held useful, if it had suspected they were about to turn them to the use of worshipping the One God, and thereby overturning the vain worship of idols. But they gave their gold and their silver and their garments to the people of God as they were going out of Egypt, not knowing how the things they gave would be turned to the service of Christ. For what was done at the time of the exodus was no doubt a type prefiguring what happens now. And this I say without prejudice to any other interpretation that may be as good, or better.

Retractationes

1,6: About The Books of Disciplines

About the same time as I was waiting to receive baptism in Milan, I also attempted to compose *The Books of Disciplines* asking questions of those who were with me and did not shrink from studies of this sort. I was desirous of either arriving at or leading others towards the incorporeal via the corporeal by some sure steps, as it were. But of these I was only able to complete the book *On Grammar*, which I later lost from my bookcase, and the six volumes *On Music* as far as that part called 'Rhythm'. But those same six books, I did write after my baptism and my return from Italy to Africa. Indeed, I had only started that discipline in Milan. Of the other five disciplines which I had likewise begun there — dialectic, rhetoric, geometry, arithmetic, philosophy — only selected passages remained, which I also lost however, but I think that some people still have copies.

SECTION TWO
The British Tradition

For eight centuries, Britain has been centrally involved in the preservation and revival of liberal education. Britain was not always a lone defender of the tradition: the role of the Church meant that for many centuries this was a pan-European effort, with Italy also playing an especially important part. In particular, the founding of the great universities of Paris and Bologna, the marriage of reason and faith by St. Aquinas and the Petrarchan Renaissance were all unique and irreplaceable contributions. Yet from the influence of Alcuin of York on the Carolingian Empire and its inheritors (our modern formation of the letters of the alphabet and system of punctuation still owe a great deal to Alcuin's reforms), to the unparalleled literary quality of the British Renaissance, to the energy with which British intellects addressed the rise of science and the meaning of the Industrial Revolution for liberal education and its proper objects, the British tradition was a beacon to the world. And when America's Revolution created a nation that would become the next great home for liberal learning, it was in large part founded by classically-trained men of British descent. In recent years the ideal of a liberal education has fallen from view in Britain, but that failure of memory is uncharacteristic, as witnessed by the words of men such as Thomas Carlyle and John Stuart Mill, for whom the term was a conventional one.

Chapter IV

Against the Darkness

After the fall of Rome, only the dedication of a few men kept the tradition of liberal learning alive. In the eighth century, Britain was home to Alcuin, one of the last truly learned men in Europe: tending the flame of liberal thought in humble retreat, but ready, when called upon, to aid in a great restoration of civilisation, albeit in the service of Christian expansionism. For Alcuin, the liberal arts were less an aid to scripture in St. Augustine's manner as scripture was a call to liberal learning in the service of Christ. He quoted Proverbs [9.1] in his Grammatica *as proof that the seven liberal arts had divine approval: 'Wisdom hath builded her house, she hath hewn out her seven pillars'. Alcuin eventually left the School of York, invited to put the Emperor Charlemagne and his empire to instruction once again. But the Carolingian Renaissance was itself precarious and did not reach Alcuin's homeland. Behind him, the Danes began their brutal raids on the British coast. Their first bloody incursions, recorded in the* Anglo-Saxon Chronicle, *included the sack of the bastion of Christian civilisation at Lindisfarne. They recall to us the dangers of the period and the uncertain fate of the tradition. King Alfred the Great, still fighting the invaders in the ninth century, made it part of his fight to encourage literacy and translate not just Christian works but The Consolations of Philosophy into Old English — a book written by another civilised man fallen into the hands of barbarians. By the tenth century, as Ælfric's* Grammar *attests, liberal learning was well-established in the country, and though Ælfric was the first to refer to his language as 'Englisc', he did so in the service of classical learning. In his landmark textbook, he encourages the young to learn Latin by providing translations in English as a guide. This was the first grammar written in a European vernacular: like Alcuin's service as Europe's schoolmaster, it is a further reminder of Britain's vital role in the liberal education tradition. These sources still speak directly to us: we can sense the affection the men had for their students, their love of learning and their conviction that this justified their lives. Their Christian beliefs and their love of liberal learning are largely reconciled. As Alcuin's epitaph says, 'My name was Alchuine, who e'er wisdom loved./ For me, who read my stone, pour prayers of thought'.*

(a) *The Anglo-Saxon Chronicle*: The Coming of the Northmen

AD 787 This year King Bertric took Edburga the daughter of Offa to wife. And in his days came first three ships of the Northmen from the land of robbers. The reeve then rode thereto, and would drive them to the king's town; for he knew not what they were; and there was he slain. These were the first ships of the Danish men that sought the land of the English nation.

AD 793 This year came dreadful fore-warnings over the land of the Northumbrians, terrifying the people most woefully: these were immense sheets of light rushing through the air, and whirlwinds, and fiery dragons flying across the firmament. These tremendous tokens were soon followed by a great famine: and not long after, on the sixth day before the ides of January in the same year, the harrowing inroads of heathen men made lamentable havoc in the church of God in Holy-island, by rapine and slaughter.

(b) Alcuin of York (735-804): With Faith, Learning is Restored

Urbibus egregiis – A Poem of Exile

> For noble cities, whose new roof-tops rise,
> Even above the stars loud praises fly;
> In song whom books of poets ancient laud
> Were bathed in gold, their wealth innumerable.[1]
> But this small cell you see, its woodland roof
> Rustic, built in the desert, nobler is.
> This flowers with sacred studies, reads the laws
> Of God and treats the secrets of old men.
> There do they sell and twist a thousand lies
> Of old men, to embroil their friend in harm.
> Here holy truth is sought in many ways
> With peaceful speech through logic's mysteries.
> There oft deep drinking takes away the sense,
> The lord is barely led by servants' hands.

---

1   These two lines literally translate as, 'Those whom the books of the poet-bearing ancients celebrate, these were multiplex in gold and their wealth could not be counted'. The sense is that learned men (like Cicero) were once at home in great cities, rich and respected for their learning. Alcuin scarcely exaggerates. It is a sign of the turning fortunes of liberal education that from instructing the golden age of Athens, preparing the Roman public orator and aiding the theological inquiry of an Augustine, it had become the ward of a provincial monk. But, as the ivy-covered tomb of Archimedes reclaimed by Cicero had already shown, such a fall from favour could occur and need not be permanent. Alcuin, and men like St. Bede whose work he continued, preserved learning against better times, when it could return to the great cities it had once so profitably schooled.

Here evening sees the readers' fasts prolonged,
And feeds with sacred feasts their sober hearts.
To Thee may our prayers come, O Christ most mild.
To us, O Christ, may Thy Grace soon arrive.

On the Saints of the Church of York — describing the School of York's library

To th'other he bequeathed both wisdom's mark,
And zeal for it, and also its abode,
And all the books his famous master had
Collected from all parts, beneath one roof
Preserving this egregious treasure-store.
There shall you find our ancient fathers' trace,
Whate'er the Roman in the Latian world
Has for himself, and what bright Greece transferred
To Latins, what the Hebrew people drank
From showers supernal, and what Africa
Did sprinkle forth from its light-flooded eye.
What knowledge had Jerome and Hilary,
Archbishop Ambrose and St. Augustine,
St. Athanasius, old Orosius' works:
What lofty Gregory and Pope Leo taught;
The sparks from Basil and Fulgentius.
Cassiodorus too, John Chrysostom,
What Aldhelm and the master Bede did teach,
What Victorinus and Boethius wrote,
The old historians, Pompeius, Pliny,
The shrewd Aristotle, great Cicero,
The orator. Sedulius' poems,
Also Juvencus', Alcimus', Clemens',
Prosper's, Paulinus', those of Arator,
What Fortunatus and Lactantius wrote.
The writings of Vergilius Maro and
Of Statius, Lucan and the masters of
The art of grammar; Probus, Focas, and
Donatus, Priscian, Servius, and still
Euticius, Pompey and Comminian.
You shall find many more, o reader, there,
Masters renowned in studies, art and speech,
Who wrote full many volumes with clear sense;

To write their names down in the present song
Methought would stretch the limits of my quill.

A Letter to the Monks of Wearmouth and Jarrow (AD 793)

Remember what noble fathers you had. Do not be degenerate sons to such progenitors. Look at the treasure-stores of your books; consider the beauty of your churches, the loveliness of your buildings, the orderliness of the regular life. Recall again how blessed is the man who from these most lovely dwellings moves across to the joys of the heavenly kingdom.

Let your boys be accustomed to stand to sing praises of our king above, not to dig out the holes of foxes, nor to follow the fleeing paths of hares. How impious it is to neglect Christ's obsequies and follow the tracks of foxes! Let your boys learn the sacred scriptures, that when they grow up they may be able to teach others. He who does not learn in his childhood, does not learn in old age. Think again of the noblest priest of our times, master Bede. How much zeal did he have for learning in his youth, how much praise does he now receive among men, and how much greater the glory of recompense in God's presence! So, on his example, wake up your sleeping minds. Sit by your masters, open your books, look at the letters, and understand their meaning, that you may be able both to feed yourselves and to provide the fodder of the spiritual life to others. Avoid secret binges and furtive drunkenness like the pit of hell, for as Solomon says, "Stolen waters are sweet, and bread eaten in secret is pleasant. But he knoweth not that the dead are there; and that her guests are in the depths of hell", [Proverbs 9.17–18] wanting it to be understood that at such feasts devils are present.

As sons of God, what befits you are nobility of manners, holiness of life, and modesty of garments. A man's laughter, his clothing and his gait say what he is—according to Solomon [Ecclesiasticus 19.29]. What appears praiseworthy among the laity, that is fine clothing, is recognised to be a matter for rebuke among clerics and most of all among monks. But the leading apostle himself also forbade even women from wearing precious garments and having their hair in plaits [1 Peter 3.3]. If this had not been a sin, Pope Gregory tells us, the shepherd of the church would never have banned women from the delights of clothing. Let all things be done decently and in order [I Corinthians 14.40], that God may be praised in your good style of living and your honour grow among men and the reward for your merits multiply with God.

A Letter to Charlemagne (AD 796/7)

To King David,[2] my most pious Lord, most glorious and most worthy of every honour, Flaccus Albinus wishes the eternal salvation of true blessedness in Christ. At every hour and every moment the sweetness of your holy affection abundantly refreshes the eagerness of my heart; and the appearance of your beauty, which I used very often lovingly to ponder, desirously fills all the veins of my memory with great joy; and the name and sight of your goodness is stored like the beauty of many riches in my heart.

Therefore it is a great joy to me to hear of the happiness of your most sweet prosperity. As you know, I have directed this little boy, a small dependant of my smallness, to learn of it, so that happily I may join in praise of the mercy of Jesus Christ, our Lord God, in respect of his acts of grace in the health of your highness. And not only ought I, the least little servant of our Saviour, to join in rejoicing at the prosperity and exaltation of your most illustrious power. But the whole of the holy church of God shall be obliged with a unanimous shout of love to give thanks to our omnipotent Lord God, since He has given to the Christian people by a most merciful gift in these last and dangerous times of the world so pious, wise and just a leader and defender, one who will vie in his every intention to correct wrongs, to strengthen the right, and to raise up what is holy, and will rejoice in spreading the name of our Lord God on high through many areas of the world, and will try to light the light of the Catholic faith in its furthest parts.

This is, O sweetest David, your glory, praise and reward in the judgment of the great day and in the perpetual company of the saints, that you study most diligently to correct the people entrusted to your excellency by God, and you attempt to lead their souls long blinded by the darkness of ignorance to the light of true faith.

Remuneration from God will never fail the best wills and good strivings. But he who works more in the will of God shall receive more rewards in the kingdom of God. The time of this life runs quickly, flees and does not return; but the ineffable piety of God foresaw for the human race short labour, but eternal coronation. Therefore time ought to be precious

---

2   Alcuin and his circle addressed one another by nicknames that expressed their learning, their ambition and their fondness for one another. So Charlemagne is addressed as the biblical King David; Alcuin (who elsewhere modestly calls himself 'Albinus, the humble Levite', ie, a descendant of the ancient tribe of Temple guardians and teachers of the law), refers to himself as Flaccus, another name for Horace, the great lyric poet of Augustinian Rome. Other common nicknames were taken from animals, perhaps in imitation of the iconographical tradition of representing the Four Evangelists as beasts. Thus a Bishop may be an eagle (traditionally the figure of John), while a young pupil is addressed affectionately as a calf (the figure of Luke).

to us, lest we lose through negligence what we shall be able to have for ever through the exercise of a good life. Nor shall we be able to love anything so much on earth as blessed repose shall be loved in heaven. He who wishes to have this then let him strive now to earn it by good works. Therefore the door to heaven is open in common to all, but those alone are allowed to enter who make haste towards it by the multiple fruits of their goodness.

I, your Flaccus, following your exhortation and your excellent wishes aim to administer to some under the roofs of St Martin's the honey of the sacred scriptures; others I study to inebriate with the vintage wine of the ancient teachings; some I shall set out to nourish with the fruits of grammatical subtlety; some I strive to enlighten in the ordering of the stars, as though they were the painted ceiling of some great man's house; becoming many things to many men, that I may educate many to the furtherment of the holy church of God, and to the honour of your imperial kingdom, so that God's grace towards me may not be empty nor the bountifulness of your goodness without issue.

However, I your humble servant, am missing from my portion the more esoteric books of scholarly learning which I had in my homeland through the good and most devoted zeal of my master and even through some little sweat on my own part. Therefore do I say this to your excellency, if it should please your counsel ever most desirous of all wisdom that I should send back some of my boys to take from there some things I need and bring back to France the flowers of Britain, so that not only in York may there be an enclosed garden, but that in Tours also there may be emissions of paradise with its many fruits, that the south wind arising may blow upon the gardens of the Loire and its perfumes may flow, and that in our age may come to pass what follows in the *Song of Songs*, from where I took this analogy: "May my beloved come into his garden and eat the bounty of his fruits, and let him say to his young men: 'Eat my friends, drink and let us become drunk my dearest ones. I sleep, yet my heart keeps watch", or that saying of the prophet Isaiah which exhorts to the acquisition of learning: "All ye who thirst, come to the waters. And ye who have no money, hurry, buy and eat; come, buy without money and without any exchange both wine and milk."

These are things which your most noble mind is not ignorant of — as we are exhorted by every page of sacred scripture to the acquisition of wisdom — that there is nothing higher for the attainment of the blessed life, nothing more pleasant for its exercise, nothing stronger against vice, nothing more praiseworthy in every dignity. Even according to the sayings of the philosophers, there is nothing more essential for ruling a people, nothing better for setting one's life's course in the direction of the best behaviour, than the beauty of wisdom, the praise of learning and the achievement of erudition. Wherefore does most wise Solomon proclaim in its praise: "Wisdom is better than all the most precious jewels, and everything desirable cannot be compared to it." It is this which exalts the lowly, which honours the lofty. "Through this do kings rule and the lawmakers make just decrees; through this do the rulers have power and the potentates decree justice. Blessed are those who guard its ways and blessed those who keep watch each day at its gates."

My Lord King, please exhort each of the young men in your excellency's palace to learn [wisdom] with all zeal and to gain possession of it by daily exercise, so that they may excel in it while they are in the age of their bloom, that they may be held worthy to bring their white hairs to honour and through wisdom be able to come to perpetual happiness. I shall not for my part be idle in these parts in sowing the seeds of wisdom among your servants, insofar as my modest intellect may allow, mindful of this wise saying: "Sow your seed in the morning and in the evening let not your hand grow idle: for you do not know what may grow greater, this or that, and if each grows equally it is better." In the morning of my life, when my studies flowered in conjunction with my age, I sowed my seeds in Britain, but now, as my blood grows cold, as though at eventide I do not cease from sowing in France. For, God's grace allowing it, I wish that both may grow.

Now my body is broken, my solace is in the wise dictum of St Jerome, who says in the epistle to Nepotianus: "Almost all the bodily functions change in old men, and all decrease, while wisdom alone increases." A little later he continues: "The old age of those who instructed their youth in the honourable arts and meditated night and day upon the law of the Lord, becomes more learned the older they are, smoother through experience, wiser by the passage of time; and it shall reap the sweetest harvest from its old studies." In this epistle on the praise of wisdom and the study of the ancients he who pleases to read can find more and discover how much the ancients desired to flourish in the beauty of wisdom.

A Letter to a Pupil (AD 798)

Albinus sends greetings to Maurus, a boy under the benediction of St. Benedict.

I am asking for the book which you promised to have written on my request, so that your promise may be kept and my joy be brought to pass. Though many drink, the fount of living water does not run dry. Thus your wisdom is not diminished even though my neediness slakes its thirst therefrom. Do not reject my request nor deny your promise, but let your truthfulness become my satisfaction. Love him who loves you and give to him who makes the request, that you may be able to please the one who possesses all, who gives these commands.

Live in good fortune with your boys and in the chalice of charity. Greet your brothers who pray for me.

A Letter to Charlemagne (AD 799)

Flaccus Albinus sends greetings to his most beloved lord, King David.

As I was journeying through the dry plains of broad Belgium the letter, sweeter than any honey, sent by your venerable authority, caught up with me.

[...]

But in having whisked me away from the dusty clods of the countryside to the most noble and piercing consideration of the heavenly heights, you attempt to renew in the secret places of my heart, from which it has never departed, the knowledge of Pythagoras' teachings, since you have never found me a laggard, only rather unlearned, in reflections upon honourable arts of this kind. Nor ought the annoying laziness of readers justly be put down to the master's benevolence, since perhaps, with many following the famous enthusiasm of your mind, a new Athens might be created in France, or rather, a much better one. For what is ennobled by the teaching of Christ our Lord is superior to any knowledge gained through academic exercises. The latter, taught merely by the Platonic disciplines, was formed and grew famous because of the seven arts. The former, enriched in addition by the sevenfold richness of the Holy Spirit, excels all the dignity of worldly wisdom. From whose gift I shall proffer anything I can worthily use in reply to your question.

A Letter to Charlemagne (AD 801)

To his most longed for David, most worthy of every honour, Father of his Fatherland, Albinus his pensioner wishes the salvation of present and future happiness.

Fortunate the people which is ruled by a pious and wise prince, as we read in the famous axiom of Plato, who said that kingdoms would have good fortune if the philosophers (that is, the lovers of wisdom) were to rule, or if kings devoted themselves to philosophy.[3] For nothing in this world can be compared to wisdom. It is this in fact which exalts the lowly, makes the powerful glorious, and is praiseworthy in every person. In this

---

3   Alcuin's source appears to have been *The Consolations of Philosophy* by Boethius, I.4, a work and a sentiment that also appealed to King Alfred the Great.

is the honour and beauty of the present life, and also the glory of perpetual happiness. It is only true wisdom which will make our eternal days happy.

My Lord David, I knew that always to love and to preach wisdom was your greatest care. You have endeavoured to exhort everyone to learn it, nay even to urge them by means of rewards and honours, and to assemble its lovers from various regions of the world to assist your good will. Among whom you took care to recruit even me, the meanest little household servant of that holy wisdom, from the furthest reaches of Britain. Would that I might have been as useful a servant in the house of God, as I was prompt to obey your will. For lovingly did I love in your most sacred breast what I knew you wished to find in me.

A Letter to Arno, Bishop of Salzburg (AD 801/2)

Albinus the pensioner wishes for his most beloved Eagle everlasting happiness in Christ.

I have sent this animal to you, a calf who is in my protection, for you to help him and snatch him from the hands of his enemies. Help him as much as you can, because the venerable bishop, Theodulph that is, is very angry with me. I have also sent in this boy's mouth, though the calf is, contrary to nature, a rational beast, something for him to moo in the ears of your holiness. For I keep him in my house to educate him for God. He will be able to progess, if God allow him the gift, in the study of reading and the discipline of the grammatical arts in the house of St. Martin. O Eagle, "Some trust in chariots, and some in horses; but we will remember the name of the Lord our God." [Psalm 20.7] Farewell and be strong for ever.

A Letter to a Pupil (AD 804)

Albinus sends greeting to Calf.

I beg you, my dearest son, to keep in mind the words of your father with perpetual diligence and to save yourself for eternal happiness. Let not the cleverness of the devil seduce you, let not bodily pleasure turn you aside, let not worldly ambition deceive you, let not sadness render you weak-minded, nor joy make you immoderate. In that boy's body be an old man in your ways, constant in mind, sedulous in God's work, watchful in prayer, joyous in obedience, devout in humility, peaceful in speech, honourable in deed, chaste of body, fervent in penitence, in love sufficient in God, always rejoicing in hope of the Lord's goodness, gladdened by fraternal love, lovable in piety towards your parents. Learn, that you may have something to teach, knowing that God speaks to you when you have read His sacred scriptures, and by the same token that you speak with God, when you have prayed to God with contrite heart. What is sweeter than to enjoy this reciprocity with God? Consider that He is always with you, and let his most sacred presence keep you from every sin and dishonesty of word or deed, and even of thought, so that you may appear fully clean in soul and body in the sight of the highest judge. And may the angels of God delight in your excellent works and deem it right to intercede for you, because for those whom they find devout in the work of God they do not cease to pray to God. Likewise do the spirits of the saints always give heed to our tears, if they know that we are ardent in the love of Christ and are performing good works.

Make sure that this little note is opened often before the eyes of your affection and retained in the treasure-store of your heart, so that it may speak to you always for your father's tongue ... and that he may find you joyful when he returns. Be mindful always that your throat should always be God's trumpet and your tongue a herald of salvation to everyone. The nearer the day of reward approaches, the more you should study to pile up the good fortune of your reward.

Propositions of Alcuin: For Sharpening Young Men's Minds[4]

(i) Two men were driving some cattle along the road. One of them said to the other, "Give me two cows and then I'll have the same number as you have yourself." The second man, however, replied, "No, you give me two cows and then I'll have double the number you have." Let him who can can tell me how many cows each man had?

(ii) There were three monks who each had a sister and needed to get across a river. Now each of the monks lusted after the sister of the one next to him. When they got to the river, they could only find a small boat, which could carry no more than two of them over. Let him who can tell me how they managed to cross the river without even one of the sisters being molested?

(iii) A bishop ordered twelve loaves of bread to be shared out among his clergy. His instructions were that each priest should receive two loaves, each deacon a half-loaf and each lector a quarter-loaf. However, the number of clerics should be equal to the number of loaves. Who can tell me how many priests, deacons and lectors there ought to be?

---

4   The earliest surviving copies of this textbook date from the ninth century. Although the attribution to Alcuin is sometimes considered spurious (perhaps even then a false claim of 'celebrity endorsement' was worth making) it is not implausible, and the problems give a genuine insight into the classroom exercises of the period.

(c) Alfred the Great (849-899): Britain's Philosopher-King

Bishop Asser's *Annals of the Reign of Alfred the Great*

On a certain day we were both of us sitting in the king's chamber, talking on all kinds of subjects, as usual, and it happened that I read to him a quotation out of a certain book. He heard it attentively with both his ears, and addressed me with a thoughtful mind, showing me at the same moment a book which he carried in his bosom, wherein the daily courses and psalms, and prayers which he had read in his youth, were written, and he commanded me to write the same quotation in that book.

Hearing this, and perceiving his ingenuous benevolence, and devout desire of studying the words of divine wisdom, I gave, though in secret, boundless thanks to Almighty God, who had implanted such a love of wisdom in the king's heart. But I could not find any empty space in that book wherein to write the quotation, for it was already full of various matters; wherefore I made a little delay, principally that I might stir up the bright intellect of the king to a higher acquaintance with the divine testimonies. Upon his urging me to make haste and write it quickly, I said to him, "Are you willing that I should write that quotation on some leaf apart? For it is not certain whether we shall not find one or more other such extracts which will please you; and if that should so happen, we shall be glad that we have kept them apart."

"Your plan is good," said he, and I gladly made haste to get ready a sheet, in the beginning of which I wrote what he bade me; and on that same day, I wrote therein, as I had anticipated, no less than three other quotations which pleased him; and from that time we daily talked together, and found out other quotations which pleased him, so that the sheet became full, and deservedly so; according as it is written, "The just man builds upon a moderate foundation, and by degrees passes to greater things."

Thus, like a most productive bee, he flew here and there, asking questions, as he went, until he had eagerly and unceasingly collected many various flowers of divine Scriptures, with which he thickly stored the cells of his mind.

Now when that first quotation was copied, he was eager at once to read, and to interpret in Saxon, and then to teach others; even as we read of that happy robber, who recognized his Lord, aye, the Lord of all men, as he was hanging on the blessed cross, and, saluting him with his bodily eyes only, because elsewhere he was all pierced with nails, cried, "Lord, remember me when thou comest into thy kingdom!"
for it was only at the end of his life that he began to learn the rudiments of the Christian faith. But the king, inspired by God, began to study the rudi-

ments of divine Scripture on the sacred solemnity of St. Martin [Nov. 11], and he continued to learn the flowers collected by certain masters, and to reduce them into the form of one book, as he was then able, although mixed one with another, until it became almost
as large as a psalter. This book he called his *Enchiridion* or *Manual*, because he carefully kept it at hand day and night, and found, as he told me, no small consolation therein.

King Alfred's *Introduction* to Gregory the Great's *Pastoral Care*

King Alfred bids greet bishop Wærferth, lovingly and friendly in his words; and I bid thee to make it known that it hath very often come into my mind what wise men formerly were throughout the English race, both of the spiritual and of the secular condition, and how happy the times then were through the English race, and how the kings, who then had the government of this folk, obeyed God and his messengers, and how they held both their peace, their customs, and their government at home, and also increased their country abroad, and how they then sped both in war and in wisdom, and also the religious orders, how earnest they were, both about their doctrine and about their learning, and about all the services that they should do to God, and how men from abroad sought wisdom and instruction in this land, and how we must now get them from without, if we would have them.

So clean was it [learning] now fallen off among the English race that there were very few on this side of the Humber that were able to understand their service in English, or even to turn a letter from Latin into English; and I think that there were not many beyond the Humber. — So few there were of them that I cannot think of even one on the south of the Thames, when I first took to the kingdom. To God Almighty be thanks that we now have any teacher in the stall, and therefore I have commanded thee that thou do as I believe thou wilt — that thou, who from the things of this world art at leisure for this, as thou often mayest, that thou bestow the wisdom that God has given thee wherever thou mayest bestow it.

Think what punishment shall come upon us for this world, when we have not ourselves loved it in the least degree, and also have not left it to other men to do so. We have had the name alone that we were Christians, and very few the virtues. When I then called to mind all this, then I remembered how I saw, ere that all in them was laid waste and burnt up, how the churches throughout all the English race stood filled with treasures and books, and also a great multitude of God's servants, but they knew very little use of those books, for that they could not understand anything of them, for that they were not written in their own language, such as they, our elders, spoke, who erewhile held these places; they loved wisdom, and through that got wealth, and left it to us. Here men may yet see their path, but we know not how to tread in their footsteps, inasmuch as we have both lost that wealth and wisdom, for that we would not with our minds stoop to their tracks.

When I then called to mind all this, I then wondered greatly about those good and wise men that have been of old among the English race, and who had fully learned all the books, that they have not been willing to turn any part of them into their own language. But then I soon again answered myself and said, "They did not think that men would ever become so reckless, and that learning should fall off in such a way. Of set purpose, then, they let it alone, and wished that there should be more wisdom in this land the more languages we knew." Then I remembered how the Law was first found in the Hebrew tongue, and again, when the Greeks learnt it, then they turned the whole of it into their own language, and also all the other books. And again the Latins also in the same way, when they had learned it, turned it all through wise interpreters into their own language, and likewise all other Christian nations have translated some part into their own speech. Wherefore I think it better, if it also appears so to you, that we too should translate some books, which are the most necessary for all men to understand — that we should turn these into that tongue which we all can know, and so bring it about, as we very easily may, with God's help, if we have rest, that all the youth that now is among the English race, of free men, that have property, so that they can apply themselves to these things, may be committed to others for the sake of instruction, so long as they have no power for any other employments, until the time that they may know well how to read English writing. Let men afterwards further teach them Latin, those whom they are willing further to teach, and whom they wish to advance to a higher state.

When I then called to mind how the learning of the Latin tongue before this was fallen away throughout the English race, though many knew how to read writing in English — then began I, among other unlike and manifold businesses of this kingdom, to turn into English the book that is named in Latin *Pastoralis*, and in English the *Hind's Book*,[5] one-while word for word, another-while meaning for meaning, so far as I learned it with Phlegmund, my archbishop, and with Asser, my bishop, and with Grimbold, my mass-priest, and with John, my mass-priest.

After I had learned them, so that I understood them, and so that I might read them with the fullest comprehension, I turned them into English, and

---

5   That is, *Regula Pastoralis*, Gregory the Great's *Of Pastoral Care*, the book to which this passage forms the introduction.

to each bishop's see in my kingdom will send one […] it is unknown how long there may be so learned bishops as now, thank God, are everywhere.

Alfred's Translation and Adaptation of Boethius' *Consolations of Philosophy*[6]

Lay XXIII (Chapter XXXV)

> Lo! Now on earth is he
> In every thing
> A happy man,
> If he may see
> The clearest
> Heaven-shining stream,
> The noble fountain
> Of all good;
> And of himself
> The swarthy mist, —
> The darkness of the mind, —
> Can dispel!
> We will as yet,
> With God's help,
> With old and fabulous
> Stories instruct
> Thy mind;
> That thou the better mayest
> Discover to the skies
> The right path
> To the eternal region
> Of our souls.

~

Chapter XL

Well! O wise men, well! Proceed ye all in the way which the illustrious examples of the good men, and of the men anxious for glory, who were before you, point out to you. O, ye weak and idle! Why are ye so useless and so enervated? Why will ye not enquire about the wise men, and about the men anxious for glory, who were before you; what they were? And why will ye not then, after ye have learned their manners, imitate them as ye best may? For they endeavoured after honour in this world, and sought

---

6 Alfred prepared two adaptation/translations of Boethius: *The Lays*, a free adaptation in poetic metre; and a prose translation. An example is provided from each.

good fame by good works, and set a good example to those who should be after them. Therefore they now dwell above the stars, in everlasting happiness, for their good works.

(d) Ælfric of Eynsham (c.955-1010): Latin For An 'Englisc'-Speaking People

The Preface to Ælfric's *Grammar*[7]

HERE BEGINS THE PREFACE OF THIS BOOK

I Ælfric, little wisdom as I possess, have laboured to translate into your language these excerpts from Priscian (the smaller and the larger editions) for you young boys, so that once you have read over the eight parts of Donatus in that book you are able to copy each language (that is Latin and English) to help your youthfulness until such time as you reach a more perfect understanding through your studies. I am well aware that there are many who will rebuke me for having wanted to occupy my intellect with such studies, that is in turning the *Ars Grammatica* into English. But I consider that this reading will be suitable for ignorant little boys, not for old men. I know that words can be translated in many ways, but I always follow a simple translation to avoid causing annoyance. However, if it displeases anyone, let him speak of our translation as he will: we are content with the way we learned in the school of Æthelwold, the venerable prelate, who imbued many towards the good by educating them well. It is to be noted, however, that in many places the art of grammar does not easily translate into English, for example in the area of metrics, on which I say nothing here. Nonetheless, we reckon that this translation can be of help to the little ones, as we have already said. [...] Farewell in the Lord, little boys.

---

7 Translated from the Latin, rather than transliterated from the accompanying Anglo-Saxon. The 'Englisc' version begins: '*Ic Ælfric wolde þas lytlan boc awendan to engliscum gereorde of ðam stæfcræfte, þe is gehaten GRAMMATICA, syððan ic a þwa bec awende on hundeahtagigum spellum, forðan ðe stæfcræfte is seo cæg, ðe ðæra boca andgit unlicð; and ic þohte, þæt ðeos boc mihte fremjan jungum cildum to anginne þæs cræftes, oððæt hi to maran andgyte becumon.*' ['I Ælfric decided this little book to translate to the English language of the art of letters known as GRAMMATICA, after I then two books translated of eighty homilies, because this art of letters is the key, that books to understanding unlocks; and I thought, that this book might aid young children to begin these crafts, until they more wise become.']

Chapter V

Twelfth-Century Revival

The twelfth century brought a classical revival to European learning. John of Salisbury's education was based upon the work of Quintilian, showing how liberal education can reach across the centuries to reinspire the human mind. John's writing defends the study of great works as refreshment for the thinking mind. Long before Isaac Newtons use of the phrase, John of Salisbury spoke of standing on the shoulders of giants — and acknowledged that this too he had learned from Bernard of Chartres, a vivid account of whose teaching methods he also recorded for posterity. John died as Bishop of Chartres, and his life of learning flourished on the European mainland, for learning was by this time a truly European project, a fact also evident in the need to include St. Thomas Aquinas, an Italian by birth and dwelling, here. In the extract, Aquinas discusses the true role of the teacher, like St. Augustine before him, but bringing the characteristics of Aristotelian logic (Aristotle having been recently rediscovered through the translations prepared in Islamic Spain) to problems of Christian doctrine. Although not British, St. Thomas is an indispensable figure in the tradition: no man did more to combine Aristotelian thought with Christian theology, uniting reason and faith. For this he was named by the Catholic Church as Doctor Communis, *the universal and timeless instructor of Catholics and the model teacher for those preparing for the priesthood; but his intellectual impact has been even wider and deeper than that might imply. GK Chesterton wrote in his biography of Aquinas,* The Dumb Ox, *'It will not be possible to conceal much longer from anybody the fact that St. Thomas Aquinas was one of the great liberators of the human intellect.*

(a) John of Salisbury (c. 1115-1176):
Standing on the Shoulders of Giants

Metalogicon

Book I

Chapter 12

Although there are many kinds of arts, it is the liberal arts that are the very first to spring to the mind of the philosopher. All of these are contained in the Trivium or Quadrivium and are reported to have acquired such efficacy among our ancestors who studied them diligently, that they clarified every reading, raised the intellect to every challenge, and were sufficient for solving the difficulties posed by all the knotty problems which can be resolved. For in understanding books or in resolving problems those to whom either the force of all language was expounded by the Trivium course, or the secrets of the whole of nature by the law of the Quadrivium, did not need a teacher.

[...]

[T]hey are called liberal either because the ancients ensured that their children [*liberi*] were instructed in them, or because their goal is man's freedom, that he may be free [*liber*] to spend his time in learning, and they very often free him from those cares which wisdom does not allow us to share. They often exclude even the necessities of life, so that the way may be swifter for the impulsion of the mind towards philosophy.

Chapter 24

Bernard of Chartres, the most copious font of learning in Gaul of modern times, used to follow this method and would demonstrate in his reading of the authors what was simple and set down according to the rules. He used to set out clearly the grammatical figures, the rhetorical colours, the types of argument and how the passage for reading set before them related to other areas of study.

He did this not so as to teach everything in one go, but according to his pupils' abilities to dole out to them at the due time the correct measure of learning. Because the splendour of speech derives either from its properties, that is when an adjective or verb are elegantly conjoined with a noun, or from metaphor, that is when a word is for good reason transferred to another meaning, he would inculcate these lessons when the occasion arose in the minds of his audience.

And since memory is fortified by exercise, and the intellect is sharpened to imitate what people hear, he would urge on some by admonitions and others by the strap and punishments.

Everyone was compelled each day to repeat the next day some of what they had heard on the previous day, some more, some less. Among them the next day was the pupil of the previous one. Their evening exercise, called *declinatio*, was stuffed with such a huge amount of grammar that anyone who spent his time on it for an entire year would have to hand, provided he were not too stupid, the proper method of speaking and writing, and would not be able to be ignorant of the correct meaning of the words in common use.

However, because it is not right for any school or any day to be without religion, the sort of material set forth was such as to edify faith and character and from which those gathered together might be motivated to pursue the good, as though they were at a *collatio*.[1] The final passage of this *declinatio*, or rather philosophical *collatio*, set forth the imprints of piety and commended the souls of the dead to their Redeemer through the devout offering of the sixth psalm in the penitentials[2] and the Lord's Prayer.

Bernard would explain the poets or orators prescribed as introductory exercises for the boys in imitating prose or poetry, demonstrating the way their words were joined together and the elegant endings of their discourses. When anyone had taken a piece of cloth from someone else and used it to enhance the beauty of his own work, he would expose the theft he had detected, but very often did not impose a penalty. In this way he encouraged the exposed plagiarist, even if his inept disposition of the material had merited punishment, by modest indulgence to ascend towards properly expressing the authorities' form and he caused those who imitated their forebears to be models for imitation by their descendants.

Among the first lessons, he taught and fixed in his pupils' minds the virtue of economy, what is to be praised in the beauty of the facts and what in words, where slenderness of speech almost to the point of emaciation is appropriate, where orotundity is needed, where excess lies and where moderation in all things. He advised them to run through histories and poems, but with close attention, like riders urged to flight by no spurs. He demanded from everyone with diligent insistence as a daily due something memorised. He told them to avoid what was superfluous, and that

---

1   In Benedictine monasteries *collatio* meant the reading of sacred scripture, at set hours, usually after the main meal of the day. See *Rule of St. Benedict*, chapter 42.

2   Psalm 130, 'Out of the depths have I cried unto thee, O Lord.'

what was written by the famous authors was sufficient for their purposes...

[...]

And because in the whole preliminary training of those who are to be educated nothing is more useful than to grow accustomed to the final goal of the art, the pupils would constantly write prose and poetry every day, and exercise themselves in mutual comparisons.

Nothing is more useful for the attainment of eloquence than this exercise, nothing which provides a swifter route to knowledge. Moreover, it also has much to offer in terms of the way we live, so long as charity holds the reins of diligence and humility is retained while progress is being made in the study of letters.

Book III

Chapter 4

Moreover, we must show reverence towards the words of the authoritative writers, who are to be used with respect and assiduousness, both because they carry before them a certain majesty from the great names of antiquity, but also because lack of knowledge of them imposes a penalty, since they are extremely powerful aids to encouragement and discouragement. For they seize hold of the ignorant like a whirlwind and drive them along or lay them low struck with fear: the words of philosophers when previously unheard are thunderbolts.

Even though the meaning of modern writers may be the same as that of the older ones, age is more venerable. I recall that the Palatine Peripatetic, Peter Abelard, said (and I regard it as true) that it would be simple for someone in our times to compose a book about dialectic which was in no way inferior either in its conception of the truth or in its elegance of expression, but that it would be impossible or at least very difficult for it to attain the enjoyment of authoritativeness.

This he asserted was to be ascribed to our forebears, whose intellects flowered and who because they were gifted with amazing inventiveness left the fruits of their labours to their descendants. And so what many spent their time upon, sweating profusely upon their creative labours, can now be learned easily and quickly by one individual.

Our age however enjoys the benefit of the preceding one, and often knows more, not because it excels in its own intellectual qualities, but because it relies upon the strength of others, and the rich wisdom of our fathers. Bernard of Chartres used to say that we were like dwarfs sitting on the shoulders of giants, with the result that we are able to see more and further than they could, not because of the acuity of our own eyesight or the size of our bodies, but because we are raised and lifted up on high by the massiveness of the giants.

On this basis I would find it easy to agree that teachers of the arts even in their *Introductions* pass down the prerequisites of the art and many articles of truth equally as well, and sometimes better, than the ancients. Is anyone content with what even Aristotle teaches in *On Interpretation*? Who does not add to it matter derived from elsewhere?

Everyone gathers the sum of the whole art and passes it on in simple language. They dress the meanings of the authorities as it were in everyday clothing, which somehow or other becomes more glorious when it is more obviously marked by the gravity of antiquity. We must therefore learn by heart the words of the authors, but most particularly those which lay out their full views and can be communicated easily to many. These words preserve the integrity of knowledge and beside this contain within themselves as much hidden as explicit force.

(b) St. Thomas Aquinas (c. 1225-1274): The Need For Teachers

Quæstiones Disputatæ De Veritate

Question 11: The Teacher–Article 2

> *"Can one be called his own teacher?"*

It seems the answer is "yes", because

1. an action ought to be attributed more to the principal cause than to the instrumental; but the principal cause of knowledge caused in us is the agent intellect, although the man outside who teaches is as it were an instrumental cause, providing the intellectual agent with the instruments by which he may lead him to knowledge; therefore the agent intellect is more teacher than the man outside; if therefore because of his being labelled "outside" the person who speaks outside is said to be the teacher of him who listens, much more is he who hears to be called his own teacher because of the light from the agent intellect.

2. Besides, no one learns anything except according to what leads to the certainty of understanding; but the certainty of understanding is naturally present in us through principles known in the light of the agent intellect; therefore it is principally the place of the agent intellect to be the teacher, and this brings us to the same conclusion as before.

3. Furthermore, to teach is more God's than man's place. Hence (Matthew 23.8) the dictum "Your teacher is one". But God teaches us in so far as he gives us the light of reason by which we are able to make

judgments. Therefore it is to that light that the action of teaching ought principally to be attributed, and so we reach the same conclusion as before.

4.   Furthermore, to know something through discovery is better than to learn from another, as appears in the first book of the *Ethics*[3]. If therefore it is from that manner of acquisition by which someone learns knowledge from another that the name of teacher is taken, so that one is the teacher of the other, so much the more ought the name of teacher to be received from the manner of receiving knowledge through discovery, so that someone is called his own teacher.

5.   Furthermore, just as someone is brought to virtue by another and by himself, so someone is led to knowledge both by himself through discovery and by another through learning; but those who arrive at the works of the virtues without an external instructor or legislator are said to be a law unto themselves (*Romans* 2.14): "When the gentiles who do not have the law do naturally what the law requires, they are a law unto themselves". Therefore he who acquires knowledge through himself also ought to be called his own teacher.

6.   Furthermore, a teacher is the cause of knowledge in the same way that a physician is of health, as the saying goes; but a physician heals himself; therefore someone can teach himself.

Against this

1.   is what the Philosopher[4] says in *Physics* book 8, namely that it is impossible for a teacher to learn, because a teacher must have knowledge, but a learner must not possess it; therefore it cannot be that someone may teach himself or be able to be called his own teacher.

2.   Furthermore, the role of teacher brings with it a relationship of superiority, like that of master; but this sort of relationship cannot exist within a person with regard to himself; for no one can be his own father or master; therefore no one can be called his own teacher either.

Reply

We should say that without doubt someone can through the light of reason inborn in him and without the support of outside teaching arrive at knowledge of many things he did not know, as is apparent in everyone who acquires knowledge through discovery; and thus in some way a person is the cause of his own acquisition of knowledge. However, he should not because of this be called his own teacher or be said to teach himself.

---

3   By Aristotle.
4   Aristotle.

For we find in the world of nature two modes of agent principles, as can be seen from the Philosopher's[5] *Metaphysics* 7. One agent is that which contains in itself that which is in effect caused by it, either in the same way as in univocal agents or in a higher way as in equivocal agents; but there are some agents in which only a part of what is done exists beforehand, for example as a movement causes health or some warm medicine in which warmth is found either actually or virtually, but the warmth is not the whole of health but only part of it. In the first agents, therefore, there exists the complete cause of action, but not in the agents of the second kind, because this second type causes something because it is in action, whence since it is not in the act of inducing the effect except in part, it will not be fully an agent.

But learning brings the complete action of knowledge in the person teaching or the master; hence it is necessary that he who teaches or is the master have the knowledge which he causes explicitly and fully in the other, as it is acquired by learning in the learner. But when someone acquires knowledge through an internal principle, that which is the agent cause of the knowledge does not possess the knowledge to be acquired except partially, that is as much as pertains to the seminal reasons which are the common principles; and therefore from such causality the name of teacher or master cannot properly speaking be derived.

Answers To Objections

1. In answer to the first objection we should say that, although the agent intellect is in some respect a more principal cause than the man teaching externally, nonetheless the knowledge does not pre-exist in it completely as it does in the teacher, and so the argument does not follow.

2. To the second objection we should make the same answer as to the first.

3. To the third we should respond that God explicitly knows everything which a man is taught through Him. Hence the title of teacher can suitably be attributed to Him. But for the reason already stated, the same is not true of the agent intellect.

4. To the fourth we should reply that although the manner in the acquisition of knowledge through discovery is more complete on the part of the person receiving the knowledge, inasmuch as he is designated as more apt to learn, nonetheless on the part of the person who causes the knowledge the mode via teaching is more complete, because the person teaching, who explicitly knows the whole knowledge, is able more expeditiously to lead someone to knowledge than someone can

---

5   Aristotle's.

be led by himself through that which he knows beforehand of the principles of knowledge in their generality.

5. To the fifth our response should be that the law operates in much the same way in respect of action as a principle does in matters of speculation, but not in the same way as a teacher. Hence it does not follow that because someone may be a law unto himself he can be his own teacher.

6. To the sixth we should reply that a physician heals insofar as he possesses healing beforehand not in actuality but in the understanding of the art, but a teacher teaches inasmuch as he possesses knowledge in actuality. Hence, he who does not possess healing in actuality is able to heal himself because he has healing in his understanding of the art. It cannot be, however, that someone has knowledge in actuality and at the same time does not have it, so that he is able to be taught by himself.

New Learning:
The Renaissance Humanists

The revival of the twelfth century effloresced with the Renaissance, reaching England in the sixteenth century. As in ancient Rome, liberal learning again became the proper training of statesmen like St. Thomas More – the diplomat Richard Pace even wrote a book defending this claim. Petrarch, the forefather of Italian humanism, already a source for Chaucer in the fourteenth century, now became the most popular poet of the English Renaissance, translated by Elizabeth I and influencing poets such as Wyatt, Sidney, Shakespeare and Donne. Henry Parker's translation bears witness to Petrarch's classical debt. The battle to incorporate the rediscovered classical authors within the educational system still had to be won. While scholastics resisted the trend, it was the humanists who won the day, thanks to such voices as St. Thomas More, whose letter to the University of Oxford is a classic defence of liberal learning. More's spiritual adviser, John Colet, was, like More, a friend of Erasmus and a lover of the new learning. Colet was inspired to found St. Paul's School – concrete testament to his passion. His curriculum would give as much weight to Greek as to Latin. More also ensured that his daughters enjoyed an excellent education, while George Buchanan, whose work on the limits of kingship was one of the most radical of the sixteenth century, penned a poem to the infant James VI on the education for self-mastery that he saw as proper to a king. The two great predecessors of King James, Henry VIII and Elizabeth I, had been exceptionally well-educated in the liberal arts, and if Henry had ultimately disappointed the promise of his youth, Elizabeth had provided the standard for intelligent kingship. Her education at the hands of Roger Ascham, and that of Lady Jane Grey, is recalled in two extracts from Ascham's writing.

(a) John Colet: A True Education Requires both Greek and Latin

Statuta Paulinæ Scholæ [The Statutes of Saint Paul's School] (1512)

John Colett the sonne of Henrye Colett, Dean of Paules, desiring nothyng more thanne education and bringing uppe children in good maners and literature in the yere of our Lorde A M fyve hundreth and twelfe bylded a scole in the estende of Paulis churche for CLIII to be taught fre in the same. And ordeyned there a maister, and a surmaister, and a chappelyn, with sufficiente and perpetuale stipendes ever to endure, and sett patrones and defenders governours and rulers of that same schoole the most honest and faithful fellowshipe of the mercers of London. And for because nothing can continue longe and endure in good ordre withoute lawes and statutes, I the saide John have here expressed and shewed my minde what I wolde shoulde be truly and diligentlye observed and kept of the sayde maister and surmaister, and chapelyn, and of the mercers governours of the schole that in this boke may appere to what intent I founde this schole.

[...]

What shall be taught.

As touching in this scole what shall be taught of the maisters and learned of the scolers, it passeth my witte to devyse, and determyne in particular, but in general to speake and somewhat to saye my mynde, I would they were taught always in good literature bothe Laten and Greke, and good autors such as have the verrye Romayne eloquence joyned with wisdom, specially Cristen autors, that wrote theire wisdome with clean and chaste Laten, other in verse or in prose, for my intent is by this scole specially to encrease knowlege and worshippinge of God and our Lord Christ Jesu, and good Cristen life and maners in the children. And for that entent I will the children learne first above all the catechizon in Englishe and after the accidens, that I made, or some other, yf any be better to the purpose, to induce children more spedely to Laten speeche. And then *Institutum Christiani Hominis*, which that learned Erasmus made at my requeste, and the boke called *Copia* of the same Erasmus. And then other authors Christian, as Lactantius, Prudentius, and Proba and Sedulius, and Juvencus and Baptista Mantuanus, and suche other as shall be thought convenient and most to purpose unto the true Laten speeche, all barbary, all corruption, all Laten adulterate which ignorant blinde foles brought into this worlde and with the same hath dystained and poysonyd the olde Laten speche and the veraye Romayne tongue whiche in the tyme of Tully and Salust, and Virgill, and Terence, was usid, whiche also sainte Jerome and sainte

Ambrose and saint Austen and many holy doctors lernid in theyre tymes. I saye that fylthines and all suche abusion whiche the later blynde worlde brought in whiche more rather may be called blotterature then litterature, I utterly abannyshe and exclude out of this scole, and charge the maisters that they teache alwaye that is beste, and instruct the children in Greke and redynge Laten in redynge unto them suche autors that hathe with wisdome joyned the pure chaste eloquence.

(b) Richard Pace: The Statesman needs a Liberal Education

De Fructu Qui Ex Doctrina Percipitur [The Fruits of Liberal Education] (1517)[1]

Such is the force of learning that it raises the humble on high, but brings the lofty equal with the divine. It is as though it also has the capacity to render you even more famous if your fortune should be rather prosperous, but if you are oppressed by adversity, to console you, a thing I have often experienced myself.

Moreover, since utility is the most highly regarded thing in human affairs, young men ought to consider and ponder how many individuals in the past and present, and how many born in obscure positions, learning has rendered most noble and illustrious.

Finally, true nobility is the one created by virtue, rather than that bestowed by a famous and long family succession. This issue has long been a matter of discussion by the most erudite men. Those who have held the contrary view were the ones who brought upon the human race the corruption of all good habits. For it is no rash dictum that honour is added to nobility from virtue and not to virtues from nobility.

Therefore, since from this evidence I think it sufficiently clear how great the excellence of learning is and how necessarily it should be sought by every wish, I shall now turn my pen to other matters which relate to the argument.

Since we have advised above that the company of dishonest and evil men is to be avoided, it follows that we should give instructions as to whose company studious young men should cultivate. Actually, the old proverb "equal with equals" gives this information succinctly. Thus young men who are dedicated to the study of literature ought to make

---

1   Remarkably, the book was written without reference to a library, while Pace was working as a diplomat in Switzerland. Intended, in a gesture that Seneca would have approved, as a Stoic consolation while his professional life was beset with difficulties, Pace dedicated his treatise to John Colet and his pupils at St Paul's School, and to learners and teachers everywhere. While himself not the equal of More or Colet, Pace's appreciation and knowledge of the liberal learning is undeniable.

friends only with learned and honourable men, frequent their houses, and consult them. If they have any doubts, let them labour with all their strength to demonstrate that they wish to learn and seek with all their heart nothing so much as learning.

For if he sees in a young man this kind of nature and desire for learning, any really learned man will most gladly teach him and (as the saying goes) spur the running steed. This happened to me first at Padua, when as a young man I began to bend myself to the study of literature, through the agency of Cuthbert Tunstall and William Latymer, men of great renown and perfectly rounded learning. Moreover, so great is their wisdom, uprightness of life, and honesty of character, that it is scarcely possible to say whether it is their learning which gives lustre to their characters, or their characters to their learning. Then I had instruction from Leonico and Leoniceno, men of the same stripe, and also from our Erasmus in various places (an education which continues in the present, since either his books accompany me or I go in pursuit of them), and from Paolo Bombasio at Bologna, where in a great hall he commented to great acclaim on all the good books. For it is to these men alone that I owe any small bit of learning that I may possess, and it is because of this that in these trifles of mine I wanted to show that I do not perform the role of ungrateful pupil, but remember my teachers: after all, even Aristophanes' rustic considers they are worthy of being honoured at least with flour.[2]

It is from association with this sort of men, youths, that not only good literature, but also good character is learned, the two things of which the perfect human life consists. From a learned mouth you will hear nothing but learned words, and this conduces to the speedy learning of many lessons. For somehow it often happens that what we hear, provided it is erudite, sticks more firmly in the memory than what we read. So do not neglect this, as the firmest foundation upon which to build learning, in case an inauspicious beginning should lead to an inauspicious end.

(c) St. Thomas More: In Defence of the "New" Learning

A Letter to John Colet (1512)

I am not really surprised if they are bursting with envy of your most illustrious school. They can see that just as the Greeks emerged from the Trojan horse and destroyed the barbarous Troy, so from your school emerge those who prove and undermine their ignorance.

---

2   Probably a reference to Strepsiades in Aristophanes' *Clouds*: 'For this lesson alone, Jove, all in my power — / You must bring me your tub, and I'll fill him with flour'.

A Letter to his Daughters (1517)

Thomas More to his most beloved daughters Margaret, Elisabeth and Cecilia and to Margaret Giggs, as dear as though she had been his daughter.

I cannot properly explain, my most pleasant girls, what great delight your elegant letters give me, and none the less since I see that although you are continually changing locations as you travel, you have not left aside any of your usual pursuits, either in exercises of logic, in the composition of declamations, or in the writing of verses. Now I very clearly can persuade myself that I am, as is reasonable, dear to you, when you take such account of my absence that you vie with each other to do what you know would be a delight to me if I were present. As I see your disposition towards me gives me joy, so shall I ensure on my return that you shall experience its utility. For you must be fully persuaded, that there is nothing which brings me more relief among this tedious business than when I read what emanates from you. From which I perceive to be true what your teacher, who loves you so much, writes so amiably about you, namely that if your letter did not declare your outstanding zeal for letters, he could appear to have been indulging his affection rather than the truth. As it is, however, from what you write you gain credence for him, so that I believe true what he boasts almost unbelievably, how finely and acutely you discourse. And so my heart longs to rush home, so that I may match my pupil[3] with you and listen. He is rather lazy in this matter, because he is not able to abandon the hope that he may find you fall below the claims of your teacher. I conceive the hope, however, since I know you are tenacious of your purpose, that you will soon surpass your teacher if not in discoursing, at least in not deserting the contest. Farewell, my dearest girls.

A Letter to the University of Oxford (29 March 1518)

Thomas More sends many greetings to the reverend fathers, the commissary, proctors, and the rest of the senate of the scholars of Oxford.

[...]

Now learn what sort of matter this is. When I was in London, I heard that recently already on a good number of occasions certain scholars of your academy, whether through hatred of Greek literature or some perverse enthusiasm for another literature, though in my opinion more likely because of their misguided desire for sport and trifling, had deliberately conspired together to call themselves Trojans. One of their number,

---

3   The 'pupil' may refer to More's son, John.

advanced in age but not in wisdom, as they say, chose for himself the name of Priam, another that of Hector, another likewise that of Paris, or of some other of the ancient Trojans, with the rest following the same notion, with no other purpose than to poke fun, with jests and jokes, at those committed to the study of Greek literature, as though they were a faction opposed to the Greeks. And so they say that this was how it happened that no one who had had even a taste of that language could stand up whether at his house or in public without being pointed at, greeted with uproarious laughter, and made the butt of jokes by one of those ridiculous Trojans, who are actually mocking only all the good literature of which they are ignorant. So much so that one might most aptly fit to those appalling Trojans the old adage "Phrygians are late learners".

When I heard many people assiduously reporting many things about this matter, although it displeased everyone and was especially upsetting to me that there were some scholars among you who with such idiocies both abused their leisure and caused annoyance to the good studies of others, nonetheless because I could see that there could never be anywhere the prospect that out of such a large body of people everyone would be wise, temperate and modest I began to regard the matter in my own mind as unworthy of notice.

However, when I accompanied our most invincible king here to Abingdon, I learned that those idiocies had finally begun to move towards madness. Well it seems that one of the Trojans, in his own opinion a wise man, a jolly jester, as his supporters might say in mitigation, but a lunatic, in the judgment of others who consider what he has done, during this sacred season of Lent in a public meeting-place has made a babbling attack not just upon Greek literature and good Latinity, but pretty liberally against all the liberal arts.

[...]

And so as far as secular literature is concerned, although no one denies that someone can attain salvation without not only that literature but any whatsoever, nevertheless secular learning, as he calls it, does prepare the soul for virtue. However that may be, almost no one denies that the study of literature is almost the only reason why Oxford is so crowded. It is clear that any decent woman could teach her children pretty well at home that virtue which is rough and illiterate. Besides, students who come to us do not head straightaway towards the study of theology. Some of them must learn the laws also. Moreover, wisdom in human affairs is also something to be gained, a thing which is so useful for a theologian that he might be able to sing a sweet enough song among his peers, but would certainly sing a foolish one before the ordinary people. I do not know if there is anywhere from which this skill can be drunk in deeper measure than from the poets, orators and historians.

[...]

I am not such a fool, most literate men, as to take upon myself the protection of Greek literature in the presence of such wise persons as yourselves. I can easily recognise that its utility has been perceived and understood by you. To whom in fact is it not obvious that it was the Greeks who discovered all the most important things and who handed down most accurately what they had discovered, both in the other arts and in theology itself?

[...]

May God keep safe this most illustrious Academy of yours and render it daily more and more flourishing in all good literature and in virtue.

Abingdon, 4th days before the Kalends of April 1518

A Letter to William Gonell (22 May 1518)

I have received your letter, my Gonell, which is as always most elegant and full of affection. I perceive from your letter your affection for my children, your diligence from theirs. I was mightily pleased by all their epistles. But in particular I feel that Elisabeth has displayed such modesty of character in the absence of her mother as some normally do not in the presence of theirs. Make sure she learns that this is more pleasing to me than all the letters of all mortal men.

For just as I prefer the learning which is joined with virtue to all the treasure-stores of the kings, so if you separate probity of character, what else does literary fame confer than a celebrated and glorious infamy? This is especially so in women, since most people will gladly attack the idea of educating them as a revolutionary thing and as arguing the case against men for their sloth and they will accuse literature of what is actually a fault of nature, reckoning that their own ignorance will be counted as virtue as a result of the faults of the educated.

On the contrary, if a woman adds to outstanding mental virtues even a moderate skill in letters (a thing which I pray, nay I expect for certain with you as their teacher, all mine will achieve), I think that she has gained more true good than if she had acquired the riches of Croesus along with the beauty of Helen.

[...]

Nor do I think it matters to the harvest whether it is a man or a woman who has done the sowing. If each can lay claim to the name of human being, whose nature is distinguished from the beasts by reason, I claim that each

can equally lay claim to literary learning, through which reason is cultivated and like a field brings forth its crop once the seeds of good lessons
have been planted there. But if the feminine soil be of its very nature thin
and more wont to bring forth fern than crops (a saying which many use to
put women off from letters), my view is on the contrary that a woman's
intellect is so much the more diligently to be cultivated by literature and
the good disciplines, in order that a fault of nature may be redressed by
hard work. This was the view of very wise and at the same time very holy
men. To mention only two, Jerome and Augustine did not simply encourage excellent married women and very honourable maidens to engage in
literary study, but to help them make progress more readily they provided
diligent exegesis for them of hidden meanings in the Scriptures, and wrote
to tender little girls letters stuffed with such erudition that even now old
men who profess to be teachers of sacred literature can scarcely read them
properly, let alone understand them.

[...]

Besides, you will make my children, who are dear to me first by nature's
law, and secondly dearer through their studies and their virtue, most dear
to me through this increment in their learning and good character.

Farewell.

A Letter to Margaret More (1518)

I enjoyed your letter, my dearest Margaret, in which you informed me how
Shaw is. I will enjoy future ones the more if you have reported on your and
your brother's studies, what you read together every day, how pleasur-
ably you converse, what you compose, and how you spend your day
among the sweetest fruits of literature. For although nothing could not
cause me pleasure which you write, nonetheless those offerings are the
most honey-sweet which cannot be written to me except by you and your
brother.

[...]

Please make sure I know what is going on with your studies, Margaret. For
rather than allow my own to grow torpid with inertia, I would immediately bid farewell to my other cares and business, even with some loss to
my fortunes, and give my attention to my children and my family. Among
these there is nothing dearer to me than you, my dearest daughter.

Farewell.

A Letter to his School (1521)[4]

Thomas More sends greetings to his whole school.

Note the greeting shortcut I have discovered, to save myself wasting both time and paper, which otherwise would have had to be taken up in greeting you all individually by a roll-call of names! In fact my labour in this would have been superfluous, since although you are all dear to me under different names, none of which should be omitted in an ambitious greeting, nonetheless no one is dearer by almost any appellation than each of you is by virtue of the name "scholar". To such an extent does the enthusiasm for learning bind me to you more tightly almost than the actual bond of blood. I rejoice, therefore, that Master Drew has returned safely: as you know, I was concerned for his well-being. If I did not love you so very much, I would obviously be envious of your great good fortune in having so many great teachers. However, I think Master Nicholas is now surplus to your requirements, since you have learned so well whatever astronomy he has in his grasp. Indeed, I hear you are so far advanced in this study that not only can you spot the pole-star or the dog-star or any other member of the star herd, but you can even (a thing which demands a skilled and complete astronomer) among those outstanding and primary stellar entities distinguish the sun from the moon! Bravo! I applaud this new and admirable skill of yours, with which you thus mount the stars. While you are looking up so assiduously, perhaps you might think from time to time that this sacred period of Lent admonishes you and that excellent and most holy poem of Boethius[5] sings in your ears. By the latter we are taught to lift our minds up to heaven at the same time, in case though the body be raised on high the intellect may be laid low upon the earth, following the lifestyle of the beasts.

Farewell, all my most dear ones. From the Court, 23rd March.

---

4   More's school at his home was sometimes compared to a latter-day revival of Plato's Academy — and in his enthusiasm to educate his daughters he does echo Plato's conclusion in his *Republic* that women should be educated alongside men as Guardians of the state.

5   *Consolations of Philosophy*, V.5: 'only the race of men raises its head on high/and lightly stands with body erect and looks down upon the earth/ This figure gives advice, unless earthbound you are a fool./ You who seek the heavens with your gaze and lift up your forehead,/ make sure you lift on high also your mind, lest weighed down/ your mind may slip down while your body is raised on high.' More quotes the last three words 'corpore celsius levato' to end the letter just before his farewell greeting.

(d) Roger Ascham: Ladies of Great Learning

A Letter to Sturm **(1550)**

St. John's, April 4.

There are many honourable ladies now who surpass Thomes More's daughters in all kinds of learning; but among all of them the brightest star is my illustrious Lady Elizabeth, the king's sister; so that I have no difficulty in finding subject for writing in her praise, but only in setting bounds to what I write. I will write nothing however which I have not myself witnessed. She had me for her tutor in Greek and Latin two years; but now I am released from the Court and restored to my old literary leisure here, where by her beneficence I hold an honest place in this University.

It is difficult to say whether the gifts of nature or of fortune are most to be admired in that illustrious lady. The praise which Aristotle gives wholly centres in her — beauty, stature, prudence, and industry. She has just passed her sixteenth birthday, and shows such dignity and gentleness as are wonderful at her age and in her rank.

Her study of true religion and learning is most energetic. Her mind has no womanly weakness, her perseverance is equal to that of a man, and her memory long keeps what it quickly picks up. She talks French and Italian as well as English: she has often talked to me readily and well in Latin, and moderately so in Greek. When she writes Greek and Latin, nothing is more beautiful than her hand-writing. She is as much delighted with music as she is skilful in the art. In adornment she is elegant rather than showy, and by her contempt of gold and head-dresses, she reminds one of Hippolyte rather than of Phædra.

She read with me almost all Cicero, and great part of Titus Livius; for she drew all her knowledge of Latin from those two authors. She used to give the morning of the day to the Greek Testament, and afterwards read select orations of Isocrates and the tragedies of Sophocles. For I thought that from those sources she might gain purity of style, and her mind derive instruction that would be of value to her to meet every contingency of life.

To these I added Saint Cyprian and Melanchthon's Common Places, &c., as best suited, after the Holy Scriptures, to teach her the foundations of religion, together with elegant language and sound doctrine. Whatever she reads she at once perceives any word that has a doubtful or curious meaning. She cannot endure those foolish imitators of Erasmus, who have tied up the Latin tongue in those wretched fetters of proverbs. She likes a style that grows out of the subject; chaste because it is suitable, and beautiful because it is clear. She very much admires modest metaphors, and comparisons of contraries well put together and contrasting felicitously with one another. Her ears are so well practised in discriminating all these things, and her judgment is so good, that in all Greek, Latin, and English composition, there is nothing so loose on the one hand or so concise on the other, which she does not immediately attend to, and either reject with disgust or receive with pleasure, as the case may be.

I am not inventing anything, my dear Sturm; it is all true: but I only seek to give you an outline of her excellence, and whilst doing so, I have been pleased to recall to my mind the dear memory of my most illustrious lady.

The Scholemaster (1570)

Therfore, to love or to hate, to like or contemne, to plie this waie or that waie to good or to bad, ye shall have as ye use a child in his youth.

And one example, whether love or feare doth worke more in a child, for vertue and learning, I will gladlie report: which maie be had with some pleasure, and folowed with more profit. Before I went into Germanie, I came to Brodegate in Lecetershire, to take my leave of that noble Ladie Jane Grey, to whom I was exceding moch beholdinge.

Hir parentes, the Duke and Duches, with all the Grey houshould, Gentlemen and Gentlewomen, were huntinge in the Parke: I founde her, in her Chamber, readinge Plato's *Phædo* in Greeke, and that with as moch delite, as som gentleman wold read a merie tale in Boccacio[6]. After salutation, and dewtie done, with som other taulke, I asked hir, why she wold lease soch pastime in the Parke? Smiling she answered me: I know all their sporte in the Parke is but a shadoe to that pleasure, that I find in Plato: Alas good folke, they never felt, what trewe pleasure ment.

And howe came you Madame, quoth I, to this deepe knowledge of pleasure, and what did chieflie allure you unto it: seinge, not many women, but verie fewe men have atteined thereunto. I will tell you, quoth she, and tell you a troth, which perchance ye will mervell at. One of the greatest benefites, that ever God gave me, is, that he sent me so sharpe and severe Parentes, and so gentle a scholemaster.

For when I am in presence either of father or mother, whether I speake, kepe silence, sit, stand, or go, eate, drinke, be merie, or sad, be sowyng, plaiyng, dauncing, or doing anie thing els, I must do it, as it were, in soch weight, mesure, and number, even so perfitelie, as God made the world, or else I am so sharplie taunted, so cruellie threatened, yea presentlie some tymes, with pinches, nippes, and bobbes, and other waies, which I will not name, for the honor I beare them, so without measure misordered, that I thinke my selfe in hell, till tyme cum, that I must go to M. Elmer, who

---

6   Whose *Decameron* includes many witty and salacious tales.

teacheth me so gentlie, so pleasantlie, with soch faire allurementes to learning, that I thinke all the tyme nothing, whiles I am with him. And when I am called from him, I fall on weeping, because, what soever I do els, but learning, is ful of grief, trouble, feare, and whole misliking unto me: And thus my booke, hath bene so moch my pleasure, & bringeth dayly to me more pleasure & more, that in respect of it, all other pleasures, in very deede, be but trifles and troubles unto me. I remember this talke gladly, both bicause it is so worthy of memorie, & bicause also, it was the last talke that ever I had, and the last tyme, that ever I saw that noble and worthie Ladie.

[…]

Dion of Prussæus, that wise Philosopher, & excellent orator of all his tyme, did cum to the great learning & utterance that was in him, by reading and folowing onelie two bookes, Plato's *Phædo*, and Demosthenes' most notable oration 'Peri tes Parapresbeias'.[7] And a better, and nerer example herein, may be our most noble Queene Elizabeth, who never toke yet, Greeke nor Latin Grammer in her hand, after the first declining of a nowne and a verbe, but onely by this double translating of Demosthenes and Isocrates dailie without missing everie forenone, and likewise som part of Tully[8] every afternone, for the space of a yeare or two, hath atteyned to soch a perfite understanding in both the tonges, and to soch a readie utterance of the Latin, and that wyth soch a judgement, as they be fewe in nomber in both the universities, or els where in England, that be, in both tonges, comparable with her Majestie. And to conclude in a short room, the commodities of double translation, surelie the mynde by dailie marking, first, the cause and matter: than, the wordes and phrases: next, the order and composition: after the reason and argumentes: than the formes and figures of both the tonges: lastelie, the measure and compas of everie sentence, must nedes, by litle and litle drawe unto it the like shape of eloquence, as the author doth use, which is read.

7   'On the False Embassy'.
8   Cicero [from his forenames, Marcus Tullius].

(e) Henry Parker, Lord Morley:
The Heroes Of The Past Inspire Us Forward

A Translation of Petrarch's *Triumph of Fame* (1554)[9]

I coulde not in noo wyse away put my syght
From these greate honorable men of myght
When as me thoughte one to me dyd saye
Loke on the lefte hande there see thou may
The dyvyne Plato that goeth I say full nye
Unto the marke of fame even by and by
Next unto Plato Aristotle there he is
Pytagoras foloweth that mekely calde Iwys
Phylosophy he dyd geve it that name
Socrates and Xenophontes folowed the same
And that fyery old auncient man
To whome the musys were so fra[n]dely than
That descrybed Argo Micena and Troye
Howe that for Helene they lost all their joye
And he dyd wryte of Lærtes sonne also
And of Achilles that was the Troyanes woe
He was the fyrst paynter it is so tolde
Of the auncient and venerable actes olde
There went with hym in that place hand in hand
The Mantuan poete I do well understand
Stryving which of them should goo before
And there folowed after in hast more and more

[...]

I cannot saye in ordre nether wryte nor tell
Of one and other that dyd there exell
Nor howe I dyd them se nor when
Nor who went foremost nor hynmost then
For it were so to do to great a wondre
They went not fare these clarkes a sondre
But so thycke that both eye and mynd
In lokyng on them theyr names I could not find

[...]

9   The first English translation of the poem, especially significant given Petrarch's importance as
    the founder of Renaissance humanism. The extracts here are taken from Chapter III. The poem
    is a hymn to worldly greatness, but also to its ultimate emptiness—fame is a "second death"
    and only spiritual humility can save even the wisest.

There followed after [Th]ucides in that pres
That ordeyned [with] wisedome the howres doutles
And wrote of the battels & wher they were done
And Herodotus with his style holesome
And he beganne the crafty sciense of Geometre
The triangle and the rounde Arball in degree

[...]

There was also Dicearco the curyouse
Quintilian, Sceneke,[10] and Plutarke the famouse

[...]

There was also that Phylozopher [that] in very dede
Spune the subtle and wonderouse crafty threde
Hys wyt was so excellent and his learning so fine
That he semed to have a knowledge devyne
[Z]e[n]one of the Father of the Stoykes secte
Above the rest he was best electe
Well declared he as he dyd there stande
By the palme and closyng of hys hande
Howe the truth was in eche season and case
For he so declared it with his wyse face.

(e) George Buchanan: A King Must Be Bound By Wisdom[11]

Genethliacon[12] Jacobi Principis Scotorum (1566)

These precepts let him learn in tender age,
And practise in mature, and let him deem
He reigns more widely, than if he conjoin'd
The dusk Hindoos to the Hesperian shore,
If of himself, and of his passions King.
When firmer strength shall rule his limbs and mind,
His boyish murmurs, and his struggling words
The Graces sweet will fashion, and will give

---

10 Seneca.
11 Buchanan not only tutored James VI and was a pioneer in discussing the limits of kingship, he
    also instructed the young Michel de Montaigne at Bordeaux. His skill as a poet was remarked
    on for more than two centuries, ultimately dying out only as his work, all in Latin, proved
    inaccessible to Europe's elites. As late as 1783, Boswell records in his *Life of Johnson* that
    Buchanan made even Dr. Johnson praise a Scotsman, remarking, "I should not have said of
    Buchanan, had he been an Englishman, what I will now say of him as a Scotchman — that he
    was the only man of genius his country ever produced."
12 'Genethliacon' = A birthday ode.

His rude breast to the Muses to be train'd;
Thence will he learn the marks, by which what grieves
Or pleases, he, though absent, may express
To absent friends beloved; what certain marks
Discriminate the specious from the true;
What contradicts, or necessarily follows;
What kind of language soothes inflamèd wrath,
What kindles it when smouldering; what force rules
The orbs of heaven; or whether Nature rolls
Her maze eternal of her proper force.
Next he'll begin by the Socratic chart
To know himself, if by Socratic chart
Truth can indeed be known: now firmer age,
Fit to distinguish sacred from profane,
Adapts him for the heaven-begotten Muses:
Thence will he get the precepts that subdue
Rebellious passions; from the sacred fount
Learn the true art of ruling commonwealths
In peace and war. If careful to this rule
He all his acts conform, he will succeed
And happily to his forefathers' throne.

Chapter VII

Persistence Through Enlightenment, Romanticism & Industrialisation

The Age of Enlightenment preferred rationality to tradition and might have been expected to reject the old ways of liberal learning. There were modernising educational voices at the time who sought to introduce systems born of pure reason. However, even David Hume had to acknowledge the need for a test of time in constructing a canon of great works. Adam Smith, introducing the economic transformation of industrialisation that lies implicit in his theory of the division of labour, was aware of the Greco-Roman tradition, acknowledged that the specialisation he advocated worked against the creation of fully-rounded human beings, and proposed the state should work to correct this tendency through its national education system. In Samuel Johnson, himself at one time a schoolmaster, we find a practical man who worked for helpful changes but without rejecting the traditional system. In his 'Vision of Theodore' he offers an allegorical account of human life in which Education is a hard taskmistress and the goal is faith informed by reason. After the Enlightenment, the Romantic reaction against rationalism produced Rousseau's Emile, the classic 'alternative' to liberal education. Yet in Coleridge's Biographia he once more rejects the trend away from tradition and celebrates his own rigorous classical education.

(a) Samuel Johnson: Education Battles With Bad Habits

Scheme for the Classes of a Grammar School (c. 1736?)[1]

When the introduction, or formation of nouns and verbs, is perfectly mastered, let them learn

Corderius, by Mr. Clarke; beginning at the same time to translate out of the introduction, that by this means they may learn the syntax. Then let them proceed to

Erasmus, with an English translation, by the same author.

Class II. Learns Eutropius and Cornelius Nepos, or Justin, with the translation.

N.B. The first class gets for their part every morning the rules which they have learned before, and in the afternoon learns the Latin rules of the nouns and verbs.

They are examined in the rules which they have learned, every Thursday and Saturday.

The second class doth the same whilst they are in Eutropius; afterwards their part is in the irregular nouns and verbs, and in the rules for making and scanning verses. They are examined as in the first.

Class III. Ovid's *Metamorphoses* in the morning, and Cæsar's *Commentaries* in the afternoon.

Part is in the Latin rules till they are perfect in them, afterwards in Mr. Leeds's *Greek Grammar*. Examined as before.

Afterwards they proceed to Virgil, beginning at the same time to write themes and verses, and to learn Greek from thence passing on to Horace, &c. as shall seem most proper.

---

1   From *The Gentleman's Magazine*, 55, April 1785, 266. A Mr. Urban wrote from Ross in Herefordshire with this manuscript, 'communicated to me by a friend'. Aged 27, Johnson set up a private academy in Edial, near Lichfield, advertising in *The Gentleman's Magazine* of 1736 that here 'young gentlemen are boarded and taught the Latin and Greek languages, by SAMUEL JOHNSON.' The manuscript is believed to date from this period. Johnson was not a natural teacher, and few pupils were put forward. The academy closed within two years.

The Vision of Theodore, the hermit of Teneriffe, found in his cell (1748)[2]

I looked and beheld a mountain higher than Teneriffe, to the summit of which the human eye could never reach; when I had tired myself with gazing upon its height, I turned my eyes towards its foot, which I could easily discover, but was amazed to find it without foundation, and placed inconceivably in emptiness and darkness. Thus I stood terrified and confused; above were tracks inscrutable, and below was total vacuity. But my protector, with a voice of admonition, cried out, "Theodore, be not affrighted, but raise thy eyes again; the Mountain of Existence is before thee, survey it and be wise."

I then looked with more deliberate attention, and observed the bottom of the mountain to be of gentle rise, and overspread with flowers; the middle to be more steep, embarrassed with crags, and interrupted by precipices, over which hung branches loaded with fruits, and among which were scattered palaces and bowers. The tracts which my eye could reach nearest the top were generally barren; but there were among the clefts of the rocks a few hardy evergreens, which though they did not give much pleasure to the sight or smell, yet seemed to cheer the labour and facilitate the steps of those who were clambering among them.

Then, beginning to examine more minutely the different parts, I observed at a great distance a multitude of both sexes issuing into view from the bottom of the mountain. Their first actions I could not accurately discern; but, as they every moment approached nearer, I found that they amused themselves with gathering flowers under the superintendence of a modest virgin in a white robe, who seemed not over-solicitous to confine them to any settled pace or certain track; for she knew that the whole ground was smooth and solid, and that they could not easily be hurt or bewildered. When, as it often happened, they plucked a thistle for a flower, Innocence, so was she called, would smile at the mistake. Happy, said I, are they who are under so gentle a government, and yet are safe. But I had no opportunity to dwell long on the consideration of their felicity; for I found that Innocence continued her attendance but a little way, and seemed to consider only the flowery bottom of the mountain as her proper province. Those whom she abandoned scarcely knew that they were left, before they perceived themselves in the hands of Education, a nymph more severe in her aspect, and imperious in her commands, who confined them to certain paths, in their opinion too narrow and too rough. These

2   Published anonymously in volume II of *The Præceptor* by Robert Dodsley. Not always highly rated today, Thomas Percy records, in a letter to Boswell, that Johnson 'attributed the palm over all he ever wrote' to this allegory of life's journey toward wisdom.

they were continually solicited to leave by Appetite, whom Education could never fright away, though she sometimes awed her to such timidity that the effects of her presence were scarcely perceptible. Some went back to the first part of the mountain, and seemed desirous of continuing busied in plucking flowers, but were no longer guarded by Innocence; and such as Education could not force back proceeded up the mountain by some miry road, in which they were seldom seen, and scarcely ever regarded.

As Education led her troop up the mountain, nothing was more observable than that she was frequently giving them cautions to beware of Habits; and was calling out to one or another at every step, that a Habit was insnaring them; that they would be under the dominion of Habit before they perceived their danger; and that those whom Habit should once subdue, had little hope of regaining their liberty.

[...]

(b) David Hume:
A Canon is Formed by Uniform Consent of Nations and Ages

Of the Standard of Taste (1757)

The same Homer, who pleased at Athens and Rome two thousand years ago, is still admired at Paris and at London. All the changes of climate, government, religion, and language, have not been able to obscure his glory. Authority or prejudice may give a temporary vogue to a bad poet or orator, but his reputation will never be durable or general. When his compositions are examined by posterity or by foreigners, the enchantment is dissipated, and his faults appear in their true colours. On the contrary, a real genius, the longer his works endure, and the more wide they are spread, the more sincere is the admiration which he meets with. Envy and jealousy have too much place in a narrow circle; and even familiar acquaintance with his person may diminish the applause due to his performances. But when these obstructions are removed, the beauties, which are naturally fitted to excite agreeable sentiments, immediately display their energy; and while the world endures, they maintain their authority over the minds of men.

It appears then, that, amidst all the variety and caprice of taste, there are certain general principles of approbation or blame, whose influence a careful eye may trace in all operations of the mind. Some particular forms or qualities, from the original structure of the internal fabric, are calculated to please, and others to displease; and if they fail of their effect in any particular instance, it is from some apparent defect or imperfection in the organ. A man in a fever would not insist on his palate as able to decide concerning flavours; nor would one, affected with the jaundice, pretend to give a verdict with regard to colours. In each creature, there is a sound and a defective state; and the former alone can be supposed to afford us a true standard of taste and sentiment. If, in the sound state of the organ, there be an entire or a considerable uniformity of sentiment among men, we may thence derive an idea of the perfect beauty; in like manner as the appearance of objects in daylight, to the eye of a man in health, is denominated their true and real colour, even while colour is allowed to be merely a phantasm of the senses.

Many and frequent are the defects in the internal organs, which prevent or weaken the influence of those general principles, on which depends our sentiment of beauty or deformity. Though some objects, by the structure of the mind, be naturally calculated to give pleasure, it is not to be expected that in every individual the pleasure will be equally felt. Particular incidents and situations occur, which either throw a false light on the objects, or hinder the true from conveying to the imagination the proper sentiment and perception.

One obvious cause, why many feel not the proper sentiment of beauty, is the want of that *delicacy* of imagination, which is requisite to convey a sensibility of those finer emotions. This delicacy every one pretends to: every one talks of it; and would reduce every kind of taste or sentiment to its standard. But as our intention in this essay is to mingle some light of the understanding with the feelings of sentiment, it will be proper to give a more accurate definition of delicacy, than has hitherto been attempted. And not to draw our philosophy from too profound a source, we shall have recourse to a noted story in Don Quixote.[3]

It is with good reason, says Sancho to the squire with the great nose, that I pretend to have a judgment in wine: this is a quality hereditary in our family. Two of my kinsmen were once called to give their opinion of a hogshead, which was supposed to be excellent, being old and of a good vintage. One of them tastes it; considers it; and after mature reflection pronounces the wine to be good, were it not for a small taste of leather, which he perceived in it. The other, after using the same precautions, gives also his verdict in favour of the wine; but with the reserve of a taste of iron, which he could easily distinguish. You cannot imagine how much they were both ridiculed for their judgment. But who laughed in the end? On emptying the hogshead, there was found at the bottom an old key with a leathern thong tied to it.

The great resemblance between mental and bodily taste will easily teach us to apply this story. Though it be certain, that beauty and deformity,

3   Part II, Chapter 13.

more than sweet and bitter, are not qualities in objects, but belong entirely to the sentiment, internal or external, it must be allowed that there are certain qualities in objects which are fitted by nature to produce those particular feelings. Now as these qualities may be found in a smaller degree, or may be mixed and confounded with each other, it often happens that the taste is not affected with such minute qualities, or is not able to distinguish all the particular flavours, amidst the disorder in which they are presented. Where the organs are so fine as to allow nothing to escape them and at the same time so exact as to perceive every ingredient in the composition: this we call delicacy of taste, whether we employ these terms in the literal or metaphorical sense. Here then the general rules of beauty are of use, being drawn from established models, and from the observation of what pleases or displeases, when presented singly and in a high degree; and if the same qualities, in a continued composition and in a small degree, affect not the organs with a sensible delight or uneasiness, we exclude the person from all pretensions to this delicacy. To produce these general rules or avowed patterns of composition is like finding the key with the leathern thong, which justified the verdict of Sancho's kinsmen, and confounded those pretended judges who had condemned them. Though the hogshead had never been emptied, the taste of the one was still equally delicate, and that of the other equally dull and languid; but it would have been more difficult to have proved the superiority of the former, to the conviction of every by-stander. In like manner, though the beauties of writing had never been methodized, or reduced to general principles; though no excellent models had ever been acknowledged; the different degrees of taste would still have subsisted, and the judgment of one man had been preferable to that of another; but it would not have been so easy to silence the bad critic, who might always insist upon his particular sentiment, and refuse to submit to his antagonist. But when we show him an avowed principle of art; when we illustrate this principle by examples, whose operation, from his own particular taste, he acknowledges to be conformable to the principle; when we prove that the same principle may be applied to the present case, where he did not perceive or feel its influence: he must conclude, upon the whole, that the fault lies in himself, and that he wants the delicacy which is requisite to make him sensible of every beauty and every blemish in any composition or discourse.

It is acknowledged to be the perfection of every sense or faculty, to perceive with exactness its most minute objects, and allow nothing to escape its notice and observation. The smaller the objects are, which become sensible to the eye, the finer is that organ, and the more elaborate its make and composition. A good palate is not tried by strong flavours, but by a mix-

ture of small ingredients, where we are still sensible of each part, notwithstanding its minuteness and its confusion with the rest. In like manner, a
quick and acute perception of beauty and deformity must be the perfection
of our mental taste; nor can a man be satisfied with himself while he sus-
pects that any excellence or blemish in a discourse has passed him unob-
served. In this case, the perfection of the man and the perfection of the
sense of feeling are found to be united. A very delicate palate, on many
occasions, may be a great inconvenience both to a man himself and to his
friends; but a delicate taste of wit or beauty must always be a desirable
quality, because it is the source of all the finest and most innocent enjoy-
ments of which human nature is susceptible. In this decision the sentiments of all mankind are agreed. Wherever you can ascertain a delicacy of
taste, it is sure to meet with approbation; and the best way of ascertaining
it is to appeal to those models and principles, which have been established
by the uniform consent and experience of nations and ages.

But though there be naturally a wide difference in point of delicacy
between one person and another, nothing tends further to increase and
improve this talent, than *practice* in a particular art, and the frequent survey or contemplation of a particular species of beauty. When objects of any
kind are first presented to the eye or imagination, the sentiment, which
attends them, is obscure and confused; and the mind is, in a great measure,
incapable of pronouncing concerning their merits or defects. The taste cannot perceive the several excellences of the performance, much less distinguish the particular character of each excellency and ascertain its quality
and degree. If it pronounce the whole in general to be beautiful or
deformed, it is the utmost that can be expected; and even this judgment, a
person, so unpractised, will be apt to deliver with great hesitation and
reserve. But allow him to acquire experience in those objects, his feeling
becomes more exact and nice: he not only perceives the beauties and
defects of each part, but marks the distinguishing species of each quality,
and assigns it suitable praise or blame. A clear and distinct sentiment
attends him through the whole survey of the objects; and he discerns that
very degree and kind of approbation or displeasure, which each part is
naturally fitted to produce. The mist dissipates, which seemed formerly to
hang over the object: the organ acquires greater perfection in its operations; and can pronounce, without danger of mistake, concerning the merits of every performance. In a word, the same address and dexterity, which
practice gives to the execution of any work, is also acquired by the same
means in the judging of it.

So advantageous is practice to the discernment of beauty, that, before
we can give judgment of any work of importance, it will even be requisite,

that that very individual performance be more than once perused by us, and be surveyed in different lights with attention and deliberation. There is a flutter or hurry of thought which attends the first perusal of any piece, and which confounds the genuine sentiment of beauty. The relation of the parts is not discerned: The true characters of style are little distinguished: The several perfections and defects seem wrapped up in a species of confusion, and present themselves indistinctly to the imagination. Not to mention, that there is a species of beauty, which, as it is florid and superficial, pleases at first but being found incompatible with a just expression either of reason or passion, soon palls upon the taste, and is then rejected with disdain, at least rated at a much lower value.

It is impossible to continue in the practice of contemplating any order of beauty, without being frequently obliged to form *comparisons* between the several species and degrees of excellence, and estimating their proportion to each other. A man who has had no opportunity of comparing the different kinds of beauty, is indeed totally unqualified to pronounce an opinion with regard to any object presented to him. By comparison alone we fix the epithets of praise or blame, and learn how to assign the due degree of each. The coarsest daubing contains a certain lustre of colours and exactness of imitation, which are so far beauties, and would affect the mind of a peasant or Indian with the highest admiration. The most vulgar ballads are not entirely destitute of harmony or nature; and none but a person familiarized to superior beauties would pronounce their numbers harsh, or narration uninteresting. A great inferiority of beauty gives pain to a person conversant in the highest excellence of the kind, and is for that reason pronounced a deformity; as the most finished object with which we are acquainted is naturally supposed to have reached the pinnacle of perfection, and to be entitled to the highest applause. One accustomed to see, and examine, and weigh the several performances admired in different ages and nations can alone rate the merits of a work exhibited to his view, and assign its proper rank among the productions of genius.

But to enable a critic the more fully to execute this undertaking, he must preserve his mind free from all prejudice, and allow nothing to enter into his consideration but the very object which is submitted to his examination. We may observe that every work of art, in order to produce its due effect on the mind, must be surveyed in a certain point of view, and not be fully relished by persons whose situation, real or imaginary, is not conformable to that which is required by the performance. An orator addresses himself to a particular audience, and must have a regard to their particular genius, interests, opinions, passions, and prejudices; otherwise he hopes in vain to govern their resolutions, and inflame their affections.

Should they even have entertained some prepossessions against him, however unreasonable, he must not overlook this disadvantage; but, before he enters upon the subject, must endeavour to conciliate their affection, and acquire their good graces. A critic of a different age or notion, who should peruse this discourse, must have all these circumstances in his eye, and must place himself in the same situation as the audience, in order to form a true judgment of the oration. In like manner, when any work is addressed to the public, though I should have a friendship or enmity with the author, I must depart from this situation and, considering myself as a man in general, forget, if possible, my individual being and my peculiar circumstances. A person influenced by prejudice complies not with this condition, but obstinately maintains his natural position, without placing himself in that point of view which the performance supposes. If the work be addressed to persons of a different age or nation, he makes no allowance for their peculiar views and prejudices; but, full of the manners of his own age and country, rashly condemns what seemed admirable in the eyes of those for whom alone the discourse was calculated. If the work be executed for the public, he never sufficiently enlarges his comprehension, or forgets his interest as a friend or enemy, as a rival or commentator. By this means his sentiments are perverted; nor have the same beauties and blemishes the same influence upon him, as if he had imposed a proper violence on his imagination, and had forgotten himself for a moment. So far his taste evidently departs from the true standard, and of consequence loses all credit and authority.

It is well known, that in all questions submitted to the understanding prejudice is destructive of sound judgment, and perverts all operations of the intellectual faculties: it is no less contrary to good taste; nor has it less influence to corrupt our sentiment of beauty. It belongs to *good sense* to check its influence in both cases; and in this respect, as well as in many others, reason, if not an essential part of taste, is at least requisite to the operations of this latter faculty. In all the nobler productions of genius, there is a mutual relation and correspondence of parts; nor can either the beauties or blemishes be perceived by him whose thought is not capacious enough to comprehend all those parts, and compare them with each other, in order to perceive the consistence and uniformity of the whole. Every work of art has also a certain end or purpose for which it is calculated; and is to be deemed more or less perfect, as it is more or less fitted to attain this end. The object of eloquence is to persuade, of history to instruct, of poetry to please by means of the passions and the imagination. These ends we must carry constantly in our view when we peruse any performance; and we must be able to judge how far the means employed are adapted to their respective purposes. Besides, every kind of composition, even the most poetical, is nothing but a chain of propositions and reasonings; not always, indeed, the justest and most exact, but still plausible and specious, however disguised by the colouring of the imagination. The persons introduced in tragedy and epic poetry must be represented as reasoning, and thinking, and concluding, and acting, suitably to their character and circumstances; and without judgment, as well as taste and invention, a poet can never hope to succeed in so delicate an undertaking. Not to mention, that the same excellence of faculties which contributes to the improvement of reason, the same clearness of conception, the same exactness of distinction, the same vivacity of apprehension, are essential to the operations of true taste, and are its infallible concomitants. It seldom or never happens that a man of sense, who has experience in any art, cannot judge of its beauty; and it is no less rare to meet with a man who has a just taste without a sound understanding.

Thus, though the principles of taste be universal, and, nearly, if not entirely the same in all men; yet few are qualified to give judgment on any work of art, or establish their own sentiment as the standard of beauty. The organs of internal sensation are seldom so perfect as to allow the general principles their full play, and produce a feeling correspondent to those principles. They either labour under some defect, or are vitiated by some disorder; and by that means excite a sentiment which may be pronounced erroneous. When the critic has no delicacy, he judges without any distinction, and is only affected by the grosser and more palpable qualities of the object: the finer touches pass unnoticed and disregarded. Where he is not aided by practice, his verdict is attended with confusion and hesitation. Where no comparison has been employed, the most frivolous beauties, such as rather merit the name of defects, are the object of his admiration. Where he lies under the influence of prejudice, all his natural sentiments are perverted. Where good sense is wanting, he is not qualified to discern the beauties of design and reasoning, which are the highest and most excellent. Under some or other of these imperfections, the generality of men labour; and hence a true judge in the finer arts is observed, even during the most polished ages, to be so rare a character: strong sense, united to delicate sentiment, improved by practice, perfected by comparison, and cleared of all prejudice, can alone entitle critics to this valuable character; and the joint verdict of such, wherever they are to be found, is the true standard of taste and beauty.

(c) Adam Smith: Economic Pragmatism Does Not Exclude Liberal Education

An Inquiry Into the Nature and Causes of the Wealth of Nations (1776)

Of the Expense of the Institutions for the Education of Youth[4]

In the republics of ancient Greece, every free citizen was instructed, under the direction of the public magistrate, in gymnastic exercises and in music. By gymnastic exercises it was intended to harden his body, to sharpen his courage, and to prepare him for the fatigues and dangers of war; and as the Greek militia was, by all accounts, one of the best that ever was in the world, this part of their public education must have answered completely the purpose for which it was intended. By the other part, music, it was proposed, at least by the philosophers and historians who have given us an account of those institutions, to humanize the mind, to soften the temper, and to dispose it for performing all the social and moral duties both of public and private life.

[...]

In the progress of the division of labour, the employment of the far greater part of those who live by labour, that is, of the great body of the people, comes to be confined to a few very simple operations, frequently to one or two. But the understandings of the greater part of men are necessarily formed by their ordinary employments. The man whose whole life is spent in performing a few simple operations, of which the effects are perhaps always the same, or very nearly the same, has no occasion to exert his understanding or to exercise his invention in finding out expedients for removing difficulties which never occur. He naturally loses, therefore, the habit of such exertion, and generally becomes as stupid and ignorant as it is possible for a human creature to become.[5] The torpor of his mind renders him not only incapable of relishing or bearing a part in any rational conversation, but of conceiving any generous, noble, or tender sentiment, and consequently of forming any just judgment concerning many even of the ordinary duties of private life. Of the great and extensive interests of his country he is altogether incapable of judging, and unless very particular pains have been taken to render him otherwise, he is equally incapable of defending his country in war. The uniformity of his stationary life naturally corrupts the courage of his mind, and makes him regard with abhor-

---

4   Book V, Chapter 1, Part 3, Article II.
5   A concern that would be taken up by many others, including John Stuart Mill (see the following section).

rence the irregular, uncertain, and adventurous life of a soldier. It corrupts even the activity of his body, and renders him incapable of exerting his strength with vigour and perseverance in any other employment than that to which he has been bred. His dexterity at his own particular trade seems, in this manner, to be acquired at the expense of his intellectual, social, and martial virtues. But in every improved and civilised society this is the state into which the labouring poor, that is, the great body of the people, must necessarily fall, unless government takes some pains to prevent it.

[...]

Even though the martial spirit of the people were of no use towards the defence of the society, yet to prevent that sort of mental mutilation, deformity, and wretchedness, which cowardice necessarily involves in it, from spreading themselves through the great body of the people, would still deserve the most serious attention of government, in the same manner as it would deserve its most serious attention to prevent a leprosy or any other loathsome and offensive disease, though neither mortal nor dangerous, from spreading itself among them, though perhaps no other public good might result from such attention besides the prevention of so great a public evil.

The same thing may be said of the gross ignorance and stupidity which, in a civilised society, seem so frequently to benumb the understandings of all the inferior ranks of people. A man without the proper use of the intellectual faculties of a man, is, if possible, more contemptible than even a coward, and seems to be mutilated and deformed in a still more essential part of the character of human nature. Though the state was to derive no advantage from the instruction of the inferior ranks of people, it would still deserve its attention that they should not be altogether uninstructed.

(d) Samuel Taylor Coleridge: Romantic Classicist

Biographia Literaria (1817)

At school[6] I enjoyed the inestimable advantage of a very sensible though at the same time a very severe master.[7] He early moulded my taste to the preference of Demosthenes to Cicero, of Homer and Theocritus to Virgil, and again of Virgil to Ovid. He habituated me to compare Lucretius, (in such extracts as I then read) Terence, and above all the chaster poems of Catullus, not only with the Roman poets of the, so called, silver and brazen ages; but with even those of the Augustan era: and on grounds of plain

---

6   Christ's Hospital, in Horsham, West Sussex.
7   Rev. James Bowyer.

sense and universal logic to see and assert the superiority of the former in the truth and nativeness, both of their thoughts and diction. At the same time that we were studying the Greek Tragic Poets, he made us read Shakespeare and Milton as lessons: and they were the lessons too, which required most time and trouble to *bring up*, so as to escape his censure. I learnt from him, that Poetry, even that of the loftiest and, seemingly, that of the wildest odes, had a logic of its own, as severe as that of science; and more difficult, because more subtle, more complex, and dependent on more, and more fugitive causes. In the truly great poets, he would say, there is a reason assignable, not only for every word, but for the position of every word; and I well remember that, availing himself of the synonyms to the Homer of Didymus, he made us attempt to show, with regard to each, *why* it would not have answered the same purpose; and *wherein* consisted the peculiar fitness of the word in the original text.

In our own English compositions, (at least for the last three years of our school education,) he showed no mercy to phrase, metaphor, or image, unsupported by a sound sense, or where the same sense might have been conveyed with equal force and dignity in plainer words. Lute, harp, and lyre, muse, muses, and inspirations, Pegasus, Parnassus, and Hippocrene were all an abomination to him. In fancy I can almost hear him now, exclaiming *"Harp? Harp? Lyre? Pen and ink, boy, you mean! Muse, boy, Muse? Your Nurse's daughter, you mean! Pierian spring? Oh aye! The cloister-pump, I suppose!"* Nay, certain introductions, similes, and examples, were placed by name on a list of interdiction. Among the similes, there was, I remember, that of the Manchineel fruit,[8] as suiting equally well with too many subjects; in which however it yielded the palm at once to the example of Alexander and Clytus,[9] which was equally good and apt, whatever might be the theme. Was it ambition? Alexander and Clytus! — Flattery? Alexander and Clytus! — Anger? Drunkenness? Pride? Friendship? Ingratitude? Late repentance? Still, still Alexander and Clytus! At length, the praises of agriculture having been exemplified in the sagacious observation that, had Alexander been holding the plough, he would not have run his friend Clytus through with a spear, this tried, and serviceable old friend was ban-

---

8   A highly poisonous tropical tree with fruit resembling apples and a sap that blisters the skin. Growing in the Caribbean, it became a source of fascination for Europeans: some fifty years after Coleridge wrote his *Biographia*, the 1865 opera by Meyerbeer, *L'Africaine*, featured a heroine who kills herself by inhaling the scent of Manchineel blossom.

9   Alexander the Great murdered his childhood friend Clytus (today more commonly transliterated as Cleitus, sometimes known as 'Cleitus the black') in a fit of drunken rage and paranoia after Clytus compared him to a Persian tyrant rather than a king of Greece; realising his error, Alexander took to his bed for days without food.

ished by public edict *in secula seculorum*.[10] I have sometimes ventured to think, that a list of this kind, or an index expurgatorius of certain well known and ever returning phrases, both introductory, and transitional, including a large assortment of modest egoisms, and flattering illeisms,[11] &c., &c., might be hung up in our law-courts, and both houses of parliament, with great advantage to the public, as an important saving of national time, an incalculable relief to his Majesty's ministers, but above all, as insuring the thanks of country attornies, and their clients, who have private bills to carry through the house.

Be this as it may, there was one custom of our master's, which I cannot pass over in silence, because I think it imitable and worthy of imitation. He would often permit our exercises, under some pretext of want of time, to accumulate, till each lad had four or five to be looked over. Then placing the whole number *abreast* on his desk, he would ask the writer, why this or that sentence might not have found as appropriate a place under this or that other thesis: and if no satisfying answer could be returned, and two faults of the same kind were found in one exercise, the irrevocable verdict followed, the exercise was torn up, and another on the same subject to be produced, in addition to the tasks of the day. The reader will, I trust, excuse this tribute of recollection to a man, whose severities, even now, not seldom furnish the dreams, by which the blind fancy would fain interpret to the mind the painful sensations of distempered sleep; but neither lessen nor dim the deep sense of my moral and intellectual obligations. He sent us to the University excellent Latin and Greek scholars, and tolerable Hebraists. Yet our classical knowledge was the least of the good gifts, which we derived from his zealous and conscientious tutorage. He is now gone to his final reward, full of years, and full of honors, even of those honors, which were dearest to his heart, as gratefully bestowed by that school, and still binding him to the interests of that school, in which he had been himself educated, and to which during his whole life he was a dedicated thing.

[...]

There are indeed modes of teaching which have produced, and are producing, youths of a very different stamp; modes of teaching, in comparison with which we have been called on to despise our great public schools, and universities, in whose halls are hung Armoury of the invincible knights of old — modes, by which children are to be metamorphosed into

10   Literally, 'for ages of ages': For ever and ever.
11   Apparently an invention of Coleridge, the word refers to the tic of referring to oneself in the third person. See Shakespeare's *Julius Cæsar*, I.2: 'I rather tell thee what is to be fear'd/ Than what I fear; for always I am Cæsar.'

prodigies. And prodigies with a vengeance have I known thus produced! Prodigies of self-conceit, shallowness, arrogance, and infidelity! Instead of storing the memory, during the period when the memory is the predominant faculty, with facts for the after exercise of the judgment; and instead of awakening by the noblest models the fond and unmixed love and admiration, which is the natural and graceful temper of early youth; *these* nurslings of improved pedagogy are taught to dispute and decide; to suspect all, but their own and their lecturer's wisdom; and to hold nothing sacred from their contempt, but their own contemptible arrogance: boy-graduates in all the technicals, and in all the dirty passions and impudence of anonymous criticism. To such dispositions alone can the admonition of Pliny be requisite, "*Neque enim debet operibus ejus obesse, quod vivit. An si inter eos, quos nunquam vidimus, floruisset, non solum libros ejus, verum etiam imagines conquireremus, ejusdem nunc honor præsentis, et gratia quasi satietate languescit? At hoc pravum, malignumque est, non admirari hominem admiratione dignissimum, quia videre, complecti, nec laudare tantum, verum etiam amare contingit.*"[12]

---

12   *Epistles*, Book I, Letter 16. 'Let it be no objection to such an author, that he is still living. If he flourished in a distant part of the world, we should not only procure his books, but we should have his picture in our houses: and shall his fame be tarnished, because we have the man before our eyes? Shall malignity make us cease to admire him, because we see him, hear him, esteem and love him?'

Chapter VIII

Restating the Ideal: Diligence and Devotion

In the Victorian era, religious revival went hand-in-hand with a renewed empha-
sis on self-help, hard work and a regard for tradition. It was fertile ground for the
ideals of liberal education and Cardinal Newman provides one of the great state-
ments of Christian humanism and of liberal education's didascalic nature in his
Idea of a University. *The contemporary obsession with assessment and valida-*
tion is memorably challenged in his suggestion that a university without courses,
simply bringing students into shared residence, would be preferable to an exam
factory. John Stuart Mill's address to the University of St. Andrews shows how
much ground the great liberal and Newman shared on education, if not on matters
of faith. Carlyle and Ruskin, two very different men who developed a deep friend-
ship out of their shared intellectual interests, shine a wider light on the period's
attitudes to education. Ruskin's concern to bring the voice of learning to a mass
audience, harking back to the optimism of Quintilian, was a great influence on the
movement for workers' education, the fruits of which are explored in section VII.
But in Carlyle's address, we find his conventional praise of liberal education mov-
ing beyond the concern that an education in verbal fluency might encourage mere
sophistry (a fear as old as Isocrates and Plato), and the acknowledgement that def-
erence of students to authority is necessary in order to lead them toward freedom,
to a desire to replace this central pillar of liberal education with something more
practical and wholly subservient to authority: a return to the plain man of action
Stesimbrotos of Thasos saw in Cimon the Athenian. Here, Carlyle betrays his fas-
cination with the Great Men of history and also, perhaps surprisingly, positions
himself as someone tempted by new ideas about a pragmatic education founded on
certainty, not debate, ideas that would be championed by Thomas Huxley and
those who sought to make natural science the keystone of modern education, as
section VI makes clear.

(a) Cardinal Newman: Knowledge Forms One Whole

The Idea of a University (1852–58; 1873)[1]

Discourse V

I have said that all branches of knowledge are connected together, because the subject-matter of knowledge is intimately united in itself, as being the acts and the work of the Creator. Hence it is that the Sciences, into which our knowledge may be said to be cast, have multiplied bearings one on another, and an internal sympathy, and admit, or rather demand, comparison and adjustment. They complete, correct, balance each other. This consideration, if well-founded, must be taken into account, not only as regards the attainment of truth, which is their common end, but as regards the influence which they exercise upon those whose education consists in the study of them. I have said already, that to give undue prominence to one is to be unjust to another; to neglect or supersede these is to divert those from their proper object. It is to unsettle the boundary lines between science and science, to disturb their action, to destroy the harmony which binds them together. Such a proceeding will have a corresponding effect when introduced into a place of education. There is no science but tells a different tale, when viewed as a portion of a whole, from what it is likely to suggest when taken by itself, without the safeguard, as I may call it, of others.

[...]

It is a great point then to enlarge the range of studies which a University professes, even for the sake of the students; and, though they cannot pursue every subject which is open to them, they will be the gainers by living among those and under those who represent the whole circle. This I conceive to be the advantage of a seat of universal learning, considered as a place of education. An assemblage of learned men, zealous for their own sciences, and rivals of each other, are brought, by familiar intercourse and for the sake of intellectual peace, to adjust together the claims and relations of their respective subjects of investigation. They learn to respect, to consult, to aid each other. Thus is created a pure and clear atmosphere of thought, which the student also breathes, though in his own case he only pursues a few sciences out of the multitude. He profits by an intellectual tradition, which is independent of particular teachers, which guides him in his choice of subjects, and duly interprets for him those which he

1   Originally largely delivered as lectures by Newman in 1852 for the Catholic University of Ireland in Dublin, where he became the first rector on its establishment in 1854. The discourses were published as *The Idea of a University* in 1873.

chooses. He apprehends the great outlines of knowledge, the principles on which it rests, the scale of its parts, its lights and its shades, its great points and its little, as he otherwise cannot apprehend them. Hence it is that his education is called "Liberal." A habit of mind is formed which lasts through life, of which the attributes are, freedom, equitableness, calmness, moderation, and wisdom; or what in a former Discourse I have ventured to call a philosophical habit. This then I would assign as the special fruit of the education furnished at a University, as contrasted with other places of teaching or modes of teaching. This is the main purpose of a University in its treatment of its students.

Discourse VI

A Hospital heals a broken limb or cures a fever: what does an Institution effect, which professes the health, not of the body, not of the soul, but of the intellect? What is this good, which in former times, as well as our own, has been found worth the notice, the appropriation, of the Catholic Church?

[...]

[A] truly great intellect, and recognized to be such by the common opinion of mankind, such as the intellect of Aristotle, or of St. Thomas, or of Newton, or of Goethe, (I purposely take instances within and without the Catholic pale, when I would speak of the intellect as such,) is one which takes a connected view of old and new, past and present, far and near, and which has an insight into the influence of all these one on another; without which there is no whole, and no centre. It possesses the knowledge, not only of things, but also of their mutual and true relations; knowledge, not merely considered as acquirement, but as philosophy.

Accordingly, when this analytical, distributive, harmonizing process is away, the mind experiences no enlargement, and is not reckoned as enlightened or comprehensive, whatever it may add to its knowledge. For instance, a great memory, as I have already said, does not make a philosopher, any more than a dictionary can be called a grammar. There are men who embrace in their minds a vast multitude of ideas, but with little sensibility about their real relations towards each other. These may be antiquarians, annalists, naturalists; they may be learned in the law; they may be versed in statistics; they are most useful in their own place; I should shrink from speaking disrespectfully of them; still, there is nothing in such attainments to guarantee the absence of narrowness of mind. If they are nothing more than well-read men, or men of information, they have not what specially deserves the name of culture of mind, or fulfils the type of Liberal Education.

[...]

That only is true enlargement of mind which is the power of viewing many things at once as one whole, of referring them severally to their true place in the universal system, of understanding their respective values, and determining their mutual dependence. Thus is that form of Universal Knowledge, of which I have on a former occasion spoken, set up in the individual intellect, and constitutes its perfection. Possessed of this real illumination, the mind never views any part of the extended subject-matter of Knowledge without recollecting that it is but a part, or without the associations which spring from this recollection. It makes every thing in some sort lead to every thing else; it would communicate the image of the whole to every separate portion, till that whole becomes in imagination like a spirit, everywhere pervading and penetrating its component parts, and giving them one definite meaning. Just as our bodily organs, when mentioned, recall their function in the body, as the word "creation" suggests the Creator, and "subjects" a sovereign, so, in the mind of the Philosopher, as we are abstractedly conceiving of him, the elements of the physical and moral world, sciences, arts, pursuits, ranks, offices, events, opinions, individualities, are all viewed as one, with correlative functions, and as gradually by successive combinations converging, one and all, to the true centre.

To have even a portion of this illuminative reason and true philosophy is the highest state to which nature can aspire, in the way of intellect; it puts the mind above the influences of chance and necessity, above anxiety, suspense, unsettlement, and superstition, which is the lot of the many. Men, whose minds are possessed with some one object, take exaggerated views of its importance, are feverish in the pursuit of it, make it the measure of things which are utterly foreign to it, and are startled and despond if it happens to fail them. They are ever in alarm or in transport. Those on the other hand who have no object or principle whatever to hold by, lose their way, every step they take. They are thrown out, and do not know what to think or say, at every fresh juncture; they have no view of persons, or occurrences, or facts, which come suddenly upon them, and they hang upon the opinion of others, for want of internal resources. But the intellect, which has been disciplined to the perfection of its powers, which knows, and thinks while it knows, which has learned to leaven the dense mass of facts and events with the elastic force of reason, such an intellect cannot be partial, cannot be exclusive, cannot be impetuous, cannot be at a loss, cannot but be patient, collected, and majestically calm, because it discerns the end in every beginning, the origin in every end, the law in every interruption, the limit in each delay; because it ever knows where it stands, and how its path lies from one point to another. It is the τετραγονοσ of the Peripatetic,[2] and has the '*nil admirari*'[3] of the Stoic, —

> *Felix qui potuit rerum cognoscere causas,*
> *Atque metus omnes, et inexorabile fatum*
> *Subjecit pedibus, strepitumque Acherontis avari.*[4]

There are men who, when in difficulties, originate at the moment vast ideas or dazzling projects; who, under the influence of excitement, are able to cast a light, almost as if from inspiration, on a subject or course of action which comes before them; who have a sudden presence of mind equal to any emergency, rising with the occasion, and an undaunted magnanimous bearing, and an energy and keenness which is but made intense by opposition. This is genius, this is heroism; it is the exhibition of a natural gift, which no culture can teach, at which no Institution can aim; here, on the contrary, we are concerned, not with mere nature, but with training and teaching. That perfection of the Intellect, which is the result of Education, and its *beau ideal*, to be imparted to individuals in their respective measures, is the clear, calm, accurate vision and comprehension of all things, as far as the finite mind can embrace them, each in its place, and with its own characteristics upon it. It is almost prophetic from its knowledge of history; it is almost heart-searching from its knowledge of human nature; it has almost supernatural charity from its freedom from littleness and prejudice; it has almost the repose of faith, because nothing can startle it; it has almost the beauty and harmony of heavenly contemplation, so intimate is it with the eternal order of things and the music of the spheres.

[...]

I protest to you, Gentlemen, that if I had to choose between a so-called University, which dispensed with residence and tutorial superintendence, and gave its degrees to any person who passed an examination in a wide range of subjects, and a University which had no professors or examinations at all, but merely brought a number of young men together for three or four years, and then sent them away as the University of Oxford is said to have done some sixty years since, if I were asked which of these two methods was the better discipline of the intellect, — mind, I do not say which is morally the better, for it is plain that compulsory study must be a good and idleness an intolerable mischief, — but if I must determine which

---

2   The school of ancient Greek philosophy derived from Aristotle, for whom the ideal man was 'tetragonos', or 'foursquare'.

3   'Let nothing astonish you.'

4   Virgil, *Georgics*, II. 'How blest the sage whose soul can pierce each cause/ Of changeful Nature, and her wondrous laws:/Who tramples fear beneath his foot, and braves/ Fate, and stern death, and hell's resounding waves.'

of the two courses was the more successful in training, moulding, enlarging the mind, which sent out men the more fitted for their secular duties, which produced better public men, men of the world, men whose names would descend to posterity, I have no hesitation in giving the preference to that University which did nothing, over that which exacted of its members an acquaintance with every science under the sun. And, paradox as this may seem, still if results be the test of systems, the influence of the public schools and colleges of England, in the course of the last century, at least will bear out one side of the contrast as I have drawn it. What would come, on the other hand, of the ideal systems of education which have fascinated the imagination of this age, could they ever take effect, and whether they would not produce a generation frivolous, narrow-minded, and resourceless, intellectually considered, is a fair subject for debate; but so far is certain, that the Universities and scholastic establishments, to which I refer, and which did little more than bring together first boys and then youths in large numbers, these institutions, with miserable deformities on the side of morals, with a hollow profession of Christianity, and a heathen code of ethics, — I say, at least they can boast of a succession of heroes and statesmen, of literary men and philosophers, of men conspicuous for great natural virtues, for habits of business, for knowledge of life, for practical judgment, for cultivated tastes, for accomplishments, who have made England what it is, — able to subdue the earth, able to domineer over Catholics.

(b) Thomas Carlyle:
Education Requires Deference To Authority

Inaugural Address delivered to the University of Edinburgh (1866)[5]

There are now fifty-six years gone last November since I first entered your city, a boy of not quite fourteen — fifty-six years ago — to attend classes here and gain knowledge of all kinds, I know not what, with feelings of wonder and awe-struck expectation; and now, after a long, long course, this is what we have come to. (Cheers.) There is something touching and tragic, and yet at the same time beautiful, to see the third generation, as it were, of my dear old native land, rising up and saying, "Well, you are not alto-

---

5   Delivered after the publication of his last major work, *History of Friedrich II of Prussia, Called Frederick the Great*, and just days before the death of his wife Jane, Carlyle's oration was well-received. In London, *The Times* devoted a leader to the address, observing, 'A man may differ as much as he pleases from the doctrines of Mr. Carlyle, he may reject his historical teachings, and may distrust his politics, but he must be of a very unkindly disposition not to be touched by his reception at Edinburgh.' It was published as *On the Choice of Books* in the same year.

gether an unworthy labourer in the vineyard: you have toiled through a great variety of fortunes, and have had many judges." As the old proverb says, "He that builds by the wayside has many masters." We must expect a variety of judges; but the voice of young Scotland, through you, is really of some value to me, and I return you many thanks for it, though I cannot describe my emotions to you, and perhaps they will be much more conceivable if expressed in silence. (Cheers.)

[...]

I daresay you know, very many of you, that it is now seven hundred years since Universities were first set up in this Europe of ours. Abelard and other people had risen up with doctrines in them the people wished to hear of, and students flocked towards them from all parts of the world. There was no getting the thing recorded in books as you may now. You had to hear him speaking to you vocally, or else you could not learn at all what it was that he wanted to say. And so they gathered together the various people who had anything to teach, and formed themselves gradually, under the patronage of kings and other potentates who were anxious about the culture of their populations, nobly anxious for their benefit, and became a University.

I daresay, perhaps, you have heard it said that all that is greatly altered by the invention of printing, which took place about midway between us and the origin of Universities. A man has not now to go away to where a professor is actually speaking, because in most cases he can get his doctrine out of him through a book, and can read it, and read it again and again, and study it. I don't know that I know of any way in which the whole facts of a subject may be more completely taken in, if our studies are moulded in conformity with it. Nevertheless, Universities have, and will continue to have, an indispensable value in society—a very high value. I consider the very highest interests of man vitally intrusted to them.

[...]

I do not know whether it has been sufficiently brought home to you that there are two kinds of books. When a man is reading on any kind of subject, in most departments of books—in all books, if you take it in a wide sense—you will find that there is a division of good books and bad books—there is a good kind of a book and a bad kind of a book. I am not to assume that you are all very ill acquainted with this; but I may remind you that it is a very important consideration at present. It casts aside altogether the idea that people have that if they are reading any book—that if an ignorant man is reading any book, he is doing rather better than nothing at all. I entirely call that in question. I even venture to deny it. (Laughter and cheers.) It would be much safer and better would he have no concern with books at all than with some of them. You know these are my views. There are a number, an increasing number, of books that are decidedly to him not useful. (Hear.) But he will learn also that a certain number of books were written by a supreme, noble kind of people — not a very great number — but a great number adhere more or less to that side of things. In short, as I have written it down somewhere else, I conceive that books are like men's souls — divided into sheep and goats. (Laughter and applause.) Some of them are calculated to be of very great advantage in teaching — in forwarding the teaching of all generations. Others are going down, down, doing more and more, wilder and wilder mischief.

And for the rest, in regard to all your studies here, and whatever you may learn, you are to remember that the object is not particular knowledge — that you are going to get higher in technical perfections, and all that sort of thing. There is a higher aim lies at the rear of all that, especially among those who are intended for literary, for speaking pursuits — the sacred profession. You are ever to bear in mind that there lies behind that the acquisition of what may be called wisdom — namely, sound appreciation and just decision as to all the objects that come round about you, and the habit of behaving with justice and wisdom. In short, great is wisdom — great is the value of wisdom. It cannot be exaggerated. The highest achievement of man — "Blessed is he that getteth understanding."

[...]

Upon the whole, there is one reason why endowments are not given now as they were in old days, when they founded abbeys, colleges, and all kinds of things of that description, with such success as we know. All that has changed now. Why that has decayed away may in part be that people have become doubtful that colleges are now the real sources of that which I call wisdom, whether they are anything more — anything much more — than a cultivating of man in the specific arts. In fact, there has been a suspicion of that kind in the world for a long time. (A laugh.) That is an old saying, an old proverb, "An ounce of mother wit is worth a pound of clergy." (Laughter.) There is a suspicion that a man is perhaps not nearly so wise as he looks, or because he has poured out speech so copiously. (Laughter.)

When the seven free Arts on which the old Universities were based came to be modified a little, in order to be convenient for or to promote the wants of modern society — though, perhaps, some of them are obsolete enough even yet for some of us — there arose a feeling that mere vocality, mere culture of speech, if that is what comes out of a man, though he may be a great speaker, an eloquent orator, yet there is no real substance there — if that is what was required and aimed at by the man himself, and by the community that set him upon becoming a learned man.

[...]

What has been done by rushing after fine speech? I have written down some very fierce things about that, perhaps considerably more emphatic than I would wish them to be now; but they are deeply my conviction. (Hear, hear.) There is very great necessity indeed of getting a little more silent than we are. It seems to me the finest nations of the world — the English and the American — are going all away into wind and tongue. (Applause and laughter.) But it will appear sufficiently tragical by-and-by, long after I am away out of it. Silence is the eternal duty of a man. He won't get to any real understanding of what is complex, and, what is more than any other, pertinent to his interests, without maintaining silence. "Watch the tongue," is a very old precept, and a most true one. I do not want to discourage any of you from your Demosthenes, and your studies of the niceties of language, and all that. Believe me, I value that as much as any of you. I consider it a very graceful thing, and a proper thing, for every human creature to know what the implement which he uses in communicating his thoughts is, and how to make the very utmost of it. I want you to study Demosthenes, and know all his excellencies. At the same time, I must say that speech does not seem to me, on the whole, to have turned to any good account.

Why tell me that a man is a fine speaker if it is not the truth that he is speaking? Phocion, who did not speak at all, was a great deal nearer hitting the mark than Demosthenes. (Laughter.) He used to tell the Athenians — "You can't fight Philip. You have not the slightest chance with him. He is a man who holds his tongue; he has great disciplined armies; he can brag anybody you like in your cities here; and he is going on steadily with an unvarying aim towards his object: and he will infallibly beat any kind of men such as you, going on raging from shore to shore with all that rampant nonsense." Demosthenes said to him one day — "The Athenians will get mad some day and kill you." "Yes," Phocion says, "when they are mad; and you as soon as they get sane again." (Laughter.)

It is also told about him going to Messina on some deputation that the Athenians wanted on some kind of matter of an intricate and contentious nature, that Phocion went with some story in his mouth to speak about. He was a man of few words — no unveracity; and after he had gone on telling the story a certain time there was one burst of interruption. One man interrupted with something he tried to answer, and then another; and, finally, the people began bragging and bawling, and no end of debate, till it ended in the want of power in the people to say any more. Phocion drew back altogether, struck dumb, and would not speak another word to any man; and he left it to them to decide in any way they liked.

It appears to me there is a kind of eloquence in that which is equal to anything Demosthenes ever said — "Take your own way, and let me out altogether." (Applause.)

All these considerations, and manifold more connected with them — innumerable considerations, resulting from observation of the world at this moment — have led many people to doubt of the salutary effect of vocal education altogether. I do not mean to say it should be entirely excluded; but I look to something that will take hold of the matter much more closely, and not allow it slip out of our fingers, and remain worse than it was. For if a good speaker — an eloquent speaker — is not speaking the truth, is there a more horrid kind of object in creation? (Loud cheers.

[...]

Well, all that being the too well-known product of our method of vocal education — the mouth merely operating on the tongue of the pupil, and teaching him to wag it in a particular way (laughter) — it had made a great many thinking men entertain a very great distrust of this not very salutary way of procedure, and they have longed for some kind of practical way of working out the business. There would be room for a great deal of description about it if I went into it; but I must content myself with saying that the most remarkable piece of reading that you may be recommended to take and try if you can study is a book by Goethe — one of his last books, which he wrote when he was an old man, about seventy years of age — I think one of the most beautiful he ever wrote, full of mild wisdom, and which is found to be very touching by those who have eyes to discern and hearts to feel it. It is one of the pieces in *Wilhelm Meisters Travels*.

[...]

[He] introduces, in an aërial, flighty kind of way, here and there a touch which grows into a beautiful picture — a scheme of entirely mute education, at least with no more speech than is absolutely necessary for what they have to do.

[...]

Very wise and beautiful it is. It gives one an idea that something greatly better is possible for man in the world. I confess it seems to me it is a shadow of what will come, unless the world is to come to a conclusion that is perfectly frightful; some kind of scheme of education like that, presided over by the wisest and most sacred men that can be got in the world, and watching from a distance—a training in practicality at every turn; no speech in it except that speech that is to be followed by action, for that ought to be the rule as nearly as possible among them. For rarely should men speak at all unless it is to say that thing that is to be done; and let him go and do his part in it, and to say no more about it.

(c) John Stuart Mill:
Liberals Must Renew And Preserve The Great Tradition

Inaugural Address delivered to the University of St. Andrews (1867)

The proper function of an University in national education is tolerably well understood. At least there is a tolerably general agreement about what an University is not. It is not a place of professional education. Universities are not intended to teach the knowledge required to fit men for some special mode of gaining their livelihood. Their object is not to make skilful lawyers, or physicians, or engineers, but capable and cultivated human beings.

[...]

What professional men should carry away with them from an University, is not professional knowledge, but that which should direct the use of their professional knowledge, and bring the light of general culture to illuminate the technicalities of a special pursuit.

[...]

In every generation, and now more rapidly than ever, the things which it is necessary that somebody should know are more and more multiplied. Every department of knowledge becomes so loaded with details, that one who endeavours to know it with minute accuracy, must confine himself to a smaller and smaller portion of the whole extent: every science and art must be cut up into subdivisions, until each man's portion, the district which he thoroughly knows, bears about the same ratio to the whole range of useful knowledge that the art of putting on a pin's head does to the field of human industry.[6] Now, if in order to know that little completely, it is

---

6   A reference to the work of Adam Smith. Smith famously explains the economic benefits of the division of labour by considering a pin factory where 'One man draws out the wire, another straights it, a third cuts it, a fourth points it, a fifth grinds it at the top for receiving the head [...] the important business of making a pin is, in this manner, divided into about eighteen distinct operations, which, in some manufactories, are all performed by distinct hands', *Wealth of Nations*, Book I, Chapter 1. As the previous section shows, Smith shared Mill's concerns on the possible effects. John Ruskin, too, wrote in *The Stones of Venice* (1853) against the practice, complaining that it was the division not of labour, but men: 'Divided into mere segments of men—broken into small

necessary to remain wholly ignorant of all the rest, what will soon be the worth of a man, for any human purpose except his own infinitesimal fraction of human wants and requirements? His state will be even worse than that of simple ignorance. Experience proves that there is no one study or pursuit, which, practised to the exclusion of all others, does not narrow and pervert the mind; breeding in it a class of prejudices special to that pursuit, besides a general prejudice, common to all narrow specialities, against large views, from an incapacity to take in and appreciate the grounds of them. We should have to expect that human nature would be more and more dwarfed, and unfitted for great things, by its very proficiency in small ones. But matters are not so bad with us: there is no ground for so dreary an anticipation. It is not the utmost limit of human acquirement to know only one thing, but to combine a minute knowledge of one or a few things with a general knowledge of many things. [...] It is this combination which gives an enlightened public: a body of cultivated intellects, each taught by its attainments in its own province what real knowledge is, and knowing enough of other subjects to be able to discern who are those that know them better.

[...]

The only languages [...] and the only literature, to which I would allow a place in the ordinary curriculum, are those of the Greeks and Romans; and to these I would preserve the position in it which they at present occupy. That position is justified, by the great value, in education, of knowing well some other cultivated language and literature than one's own, and by the peculiar value of those particular languages and literatures.

[...]

---

fragments and crumbs of life; so that all the little piece of intelligence that is left in a man is not enough to make a pin, or a nail, but exhausts itself in making the point of a pin or the head of a nail.' Jean-Baptiste Say had also referred to the danger of mental narrowing in *Traité d'économie politique* (1803), I.VIII.24: 'A man, whose whole life is devoted to the execution of a single operation, will most assuredly acquire the faculty of executing it better and quicker than others; but he will, at the same time, be rendered less fit for every other occupation, corporeal or intellectual; his other faculties will be gradually blunted or extinguished; and the man, as an individual, will degenerate in consequence.' Pierre-Joseph Proudhon, in *Système des contradictions économiques* (1847), Chapter 3.1, quotes Say and further observes, 'All the economists, since Adam Smith, have pointed out the advantages and the inconveniences of the law of division, but at the same time insisting much more strenuously upon the first than the second, because such a course was more in harmony with their optimistic views'. However, Adam Smith, like Mill, did not simply rest upon optimism, but proposed education as the remedy for over-specialisation, still a more robust answer than Proudhon's vague call for 'a recomposition of labour which shall obviate the inconveniences of division while preserving its useful effects'.

[I]n studying the great writers of antiquity, we are not only learning to understand the ancient mind, but laying in a stock of wise thought and observation, still valuable to ourselves; and at the same time making ourselves familiar with a number of the most perfect and finished literary compositions which the human mind has produced — compositions which, from the altered conditions of human life, are likely to be seldom paralleled, in their sustained excellence, by the times to come.

[...]

The discoveries of the ancients in science have been greatly surpassed, and as much of them as is still valuable loses nothing by being incorporated in modern treatises: but what does not so well admit of being transferred bodily, and has been very imperfectly carried off even piecemeal, is the treasure which they accumulated of what may be called the wisdom of life: the rich store of experience of human nature and conduct, which the acute and observing minds of those ages, aided in their observations by the greater simplicity of manners and life, consigned to their writings, and most of which retains all its value. The speeches in Thucydides; the *Rhetoric, Ethics,* and *Politics* of Aristotle, the Dialogues of Plato; the Orations of Demosthenes; the *Satires,* and especially the *Epistles* of Horace; all the writings of Tacitus; the great work of Quintilian, a repertory of the best thoughts of the ancient world on all subjects connected with education; and, in a less formal manner, all that is left to us of the ancient historians, orators, philosophers, and even dramatists, are replete with remarks and maxims of singular good sense and penetration, applicable both to political and to private life, and the actual truths we find in them are even surpassed in value by the encouragement and help they give us in the pursuit of truth. Human invention has never produced anything so valuable, in the way both of stimulation and of discipline to the inquiring intellect, as the dialectics of the ancients, of which many of the works of Aristotle illustrate the theory, and those of Plato exhibit the practice. No modern writings come near to these, in teaching, both by precept and example, the way to investigate truth, on those subjects, so vastly important to us, which remain matters of controversy, from the difficulty or impossibility of bringing them to a directly experimental test. To question all things; never to turn away from any difficulty; to accept no doctrine either from ourselves or from other people without a rigid scrutiny by negative criticism, letting no fallacy, or incoherence, or confusion of thought, slip by unperceived; above all, to insist upon having the meaning of a word clearly understood before using it, and the meaning of a proposition before assenting to it; these are the lessons we learn from the ancient dialecticians. With all this vigorous management of the negative element, they inspire no scepticism about the reality of truth, or indifference to its pursuit. The noblest enthusiasm, both for the search after truth and for applying it to its highest uses, pervades these writers, Aristotle no less than Plato, though Plato has incomparably the greater power of imparting those feelings to others. In cultivating, therefore, the ancient languages as our best literary education, we are all the while laying an admirable foundation for ethical and philosophical culture. In purely literary excellence—in perfection of form—the pre-eminence of the ancients is not disputed. In every department which they attempted, and they attempted almost all, their composition, like their sculpture, has been to the greatest modern artists an example, to be looked up to with hopeless admiration, but of inappreciable value as a light on high, guiding their own endeavours. In prose and in poetry, in epic, lyric, or dramatic, as in historical, philosophical, and oratorical art, the pinnacle on which they stand is equally eminent. I am now speaking of the form, the artistic perfection of treatment: for, as regards substance, I consider modern poetry to be superior to ancient, in the same manner, though in a less degree, as modern science: it enters deeper into nature. The feelings of the modern mind are more various, more complex and manifold, than those of the ancients ever were. The modern mind is, what the ancient mind was not, brooding and self-conscious; and its meditative self-consciousness has discovered depths in the human soul which the Greeks and Romans did not dream of, and would not have understood. But what they had got to express, they expressed in a manner which few even of the greatest moderns have seriously attempted to rival. It must be remembered that they had more time, and that they wrote chiefly for a select class, possessed of leisure. To us who write in a hurry for people who read in a hurry, the attempt to give an equal degree of finish would be loss of time. But to be familiar with perfect models is not the less important to us because the element in which we work precludes even the effort to equal them. They shew us at least what excellence is, and make us desire it, and strive to get as near to it as is within our reach. And this is the value to us of the ancient writers, all the more emphatically, because their excellence does not admit of being copied, or directly imitated. It does not consist in a trick which can be learnt, but in the perfect adaptation of means to ends. The secret of the style of the great Greek and Roman authors, is that it is the perfection of good sense. In the first place, they never use a word without a meaning, or a word which adds nothing to the meaning. They always (to begin with) had a meaning; they knew what they wanted to say; and their whole purpose was to say it with the highest degree of exactness and completeness, and bring it home to the mind with the greatest possible clearness and vividness. It never entered into their thoughts to conceive of a piece of writing as beautiful in itself, abstractedly from what it had to express: its beauty must all be subservient to the most perfect expression of the sense. The *curiosa felicitas* which their critics ascribed in a pre-eminent degree to Horace, expresses the standard at which they all aimed.[7] Their style is exactly described by Swift's definition, "the right words in the right places."[8] Look at an oration of Demosthenes: there is nothing in it which calls attention to itself as style at all: it is only after a close examination we perceive that every word is what it should be, and where it should be, to lead the hearer smoothly and imperceptibly into the state of mind which the orator wishes to produce.

[...]

For all these reasons I think it important to retain these two languages and literatures in the place they occupy, as a part of liberal education, that is, of the education of all who are not obliged by their circumstances to discontinue their scholastic studies at a very early age. But the same reasons which vindicate the place of classical studies in general education, shew also the proper limitation of them. They should be carried as far as is sufficient to enable the pupil, in after life, to read the great works of ancient literature with ease. Those who have leisure and inclination to make scholarship, or ancient history, or general philology, their pursuit, of course require much more, but there is no room for more in general education. The laborious idleness in which the school-time is wasted away in the English classical schools deserves the severest reprehension. To what purpose should the most precious years of early life be irreparably squandered in learning to write bad Latin and Greek verses? I do not see that we are much the better even for those who end by writing good ones.

[...]

Much more might be said respecting classical instruction, and literary cultivation in general, as a part of liberal education. But it is time to speak of the uses of scientific instruction: or rather its indispensable necessity, for it is recommended by every consideration which pleads for any high order of intellectual education at all.

The most obvious part of the value of scientific instruction, the mere information that it gives, speaks for itself. We are born into a world which we have not made; a world whose phenomena take place according to fixed laws, of which we do not bring any knowledge into the world with us. In such a world we are appointed to live, and in it all our work is to be

7 'A studied ease', used by Petronius of Horace in *Satyricon*, CXVIII.
8 *A Letter to a Young Clergyman, Lately Entered into Holy Orders* (1719–20). Actually 'Proper words in proper places make the true definition of a style'.

done. Our whole working power depends on knowing the laws of the world — in other words, the properties of the things which we have to work with, and to work among, and to work upon. [...] This, however, is but the simplest and most obvious part of the utility of science, and the part which, if neglected in youth, may be the most easily made up for afterwards. It is more important to understand the value of scientific instruction as a training and disciplining process, to fit the intellect for the proper work of a human being. Facts are the materials of our knowledge, but the mind itself is the instrument: and it is easier to acquire facts, than to judge what they prove, and how, through the facts which we know, to get to those which we want to know.

The most incessant occupation of the human intellect throughout life is the ascertainment of truth. We are always needing to know what is actually true about something or other. It is not given to us all to discover great general truths that are a light to all men and to future generations; though with a better general education the number of those who could do so would be far greater than it is. But we all require the ability to judge between the conflicting opinions which are offered to us as vital truths; to choose what doctrines we will receive in the matter of religion, for example; to judge whether we ought to be Tories, Whigs, or Radicals, or to what length it is our duty to go with each; to form a rational conviction on great questions of legislation and internal policy, and on the manner in which our country should behave to dependencies and to foreign nations. And the need we have of knowing how to discriminate truth, is not confined to the larger truths. All through life it is our most pressing interest to find out the truth about all the matters we are concerned with. If we are farmers we want to find what will truly improve our soil; if merchants, what will truly influence the markets of our commodities; if judges, or jurymen, or advocates, who it was that truly did an unlawful act, or to whom a disputed right truly belongs. Every time we have to make a new resolution or alter an old one, in any situation in life, we shall go wrong unless we know the truth about the facts on which our resolution depends. Now, however different these searches for truth may look, and however unlike they really are in their subject-matter, the methods of getting at truth, and the tests of truth, are in all cases much the same. There are but two roads by which truth can be discovered; observation, and reasoning: observation, of course, including experiment. We all observe, and we all reason, and therefore, more or less successfully, we all ascertain truths: but most of us do it very ill, and could not get on at all were we not able to fall back on others who do it better. If we could not do it in any degree, we should be mere instruments in the hands of those who could: they would be able to reduce us to slavery. Then how shall we best learn to do this? By being shewn the way in which it has already been successfully done. The processes by which truth is attained, reasoning and observation, have been carried to their greatest known perfection in the physical sciences. As classical literature furnishes the most perfect types of the art of expression, so do the physical sciences those of the art of thinking. Mathematics, and its application to astronomy and natural philosophy, are the most complete example of the discovery of truths by reasoning; experimental science, of their discovery by direct observation. In all these cases we know that we can trust the operation, because the conclusions to which it has led have been found true by subsequent trial. It is by the study of these, then, that we may hope to qualify ourselves for distinguishing truth, in cases where there do not exist the same ready means of verification.

[...]

The moral or religious influence which an university can exercise, consists less in any express teaching, than in the pervading tone of the place. Whatever it teaches, it should teach as penetrated by a sense of duty; it should present all knowledge as chiefly a means to worthiness of life, given for the double purpose of making each of us practically useful to his fellow-creatures, and of elevating the character of the species itself; exalting and dignifying our nature. There is nothing which spreads more contagiously from teacher to pupil than elevation of sentiment: often and often have students caught from the living influence of a professor, a contempt for mean and selfish objects, and a noble ambition to leave the world better than they found it, which they have carried with them throughout life. In these respects, teachers of every kind have natural and peculiar means of doing with effect, what every one who mixes with his fellow-beings, or addresses himself to them in any character, should feel bound to do to the extent of his capacity and opportunities. What is special to an university on these subjects belongs chiefly, like the rest of its work, to the intellectual department. An university exists for the purpose of laying open to each succeeding generation, as far as the conditions of the case admit, the accumulated treasure of the thoughts of mankind. As an indispensable part of this, it has to make known to them what mankind at large, their own country, and the best and wisest individual men, have thought on the great subjects of morals and religion.

[...]

All the arts of expression tend to keep alive and in activity the feelings they express. Do you think that the great Italian painters would have filled the place they did in the European mind, would have been universally ranked

among the greatest men of their time, if their productions had done nothing for it but to serve as the decoration of a public hall or a private *salon*?
Their Nativities and Crucifixions, their glorious Madonnas and Saints,
were to their susceptible Southern countrymen the great school not only of
devotional, but of all the elevated and all the imaginative feelings. We
colder Northerns may approach to a conception of this function of art
when we listen to an oratorio of Handel, or give ourselves up to the emotions excited by a Gothic cathedral. Even apart from any specific emotional
expression, the mere contemplation of beauty of a high order produces in
no small degree this elevating effect on the character.

[...]

Art, when really cultivated, and not merely practised empirically, maintains, what it first gave the conception of, an ideal Beauty, to be eternally
aimed at, though surpassing what can be actually attained; and by this
idea it trains us never to be completely satisfied with imperfection in what
we ourselves do and are: to idealize, as much as possible, every work we
do, and most of all, our own characters and lives.

And now, having travelled with you over the whole range of the materials and training which an University supplies as a preparation for the
higher uses of life, it is almost needless to add any exhortation to you to
profit by the gift. Now is your opportunity for gaining a degree of insight
into subjects larger and far more ennobling than the minutiæ of a business
or a profession, and for acquiring a facility of using your minds on all that
concerns the higher interests of man, which you will carry with you into
the occupations of active life, and which will prevent even the short inter-
vals of time which that may leave you, from being altogether lost for noble
purposes.

(d) John Ruskin: Everyone Should Read The Great Books

Of Kings' Treasuries (1865)[9]

I want to speak to you about books; and about the way we read them, and
could, or should read them. A grave subject, you will say; and a wide one!
Yes; so wide that I shall make no effort to touch the compass of it. I will try
only to bring before you a few simple thoughts about reading, which press
themselves upon me every day more deeply, as I watch the course of the
public mind with respect to our daily enlarging means of education; and
the answeringly wider spreading, on the levels, of the irrigation of
literature.

9   Lecture 1 in *Sesames and Lilies.*

[...]

Nearly all our associations are determined by chance or necessity; and restricted within a narrow circle. We cannot know whom we would; and those whom we know, we cannot have at our side when we most need them. All the higher circles of human intelligence are, to those beneath, only momentarily and partially open. We may, by good fortune, obtain a glimpse of a great poet, and hear the sound of his voice; or put a question to a man of science, and be answered good-humouredly. We may intrude ten minutes' talk on a cabinet minister, answered probably with words worse than silence, being deceptive; or snatch, once or twice in our lives, the privilege of throwing a bouquet in the path of a Princess, or arresting the kind glance of a Queen. And yet these momentary chances we covet; and spend our years, and passions, and powers in pursuit of little more than these; while, meantime, there is a society continually open to us, of people who will talk to us as long as we like, whatever our rank or occupation; — talk to us in the best words they can choose, and with thanks if we listen to them. And this society, because it is so numerous and so gentle, — and can be kept waiting round us all day long, not to grant audience, but to gain it; — kings and statesmen lingering patiently in those plainly furnished and narrow ante-rooms, our bookcase shelves, — we make no account of that company, — perhaps never listen to a word they would say, all day long!

You may tell me, perhaps, or think within yourselves, that the apathy with which we regard this company of the noble, who are praying us to listen to them; and the passion with which we pursue the company, probably of the ignoble, who despise us, or who have nothing to teach us, are grounded in this, — that we can see the faces of the living men, and it is themselves, and not their sayings, with which we desire to become familiar. But it is not so. Suppose you never were to see their faces; — suppose you could be put behind a screen in the statesman's cabinet, or the prince's chamber, would you not be glad to listen to their words, though you were forbidden to advance beyond the screen? And when the screen is only a little less, folded in two, instead of four, and you can be hidden behind the cover of the two boards that bind a book, and listen, all day long, not to the casual talk, but to the studied, determined, chosen addresses of the wisest of men; — this station of audience, and honourable privy council, you despise!

But perhaps you will say that it is because the living people talk of things that are passing, and are of immediate interest to you, that you desire to hear them. Nay; that cannot be so, for the living people will themselves tell you about passing matters much better in their writings than in their care-

less talk. But I admit that this motive does influence you, so far as you prefer those rapid and ephemeral writings to slow and enduring writings—books, properly so called. For all books are divisible into two
classes, the books of the hour, and the books of all time. Mark this distinction—it is not one of quality only. It is not merely the bad book that does
not last, and the good one that does. It is a distinction of species. There are
good books for the hour, and good ones for all time; bad books for the
hour, and bad ones for all time. I must define the two kinds before I go
farther.

The good book of the hour, then,—I do not speak of the bad ones,—is
simply the useful or pleasant talk of some person whom you cannot otherwise converse with, printed for you. [...] The book of talk is printed only
because its author cannot speak to thousands of people at once; if he could,
he would—the volume is mere *multiplication* of his voice. You cannot talk
to your friend in India; if you could, you would; you write instead: that is
mere *conveyance* of voice. But a book is written, not to multiply the voice
merely, not to carry it merely, but to preserve it. The author has something
to say which he perceives to be true and useful, or helpfully beautiful. So
far as he knows, no one has yet said it; so far as he knows, no one else can
say it. He is bound to say it, clearly and melodiously if he may; clearly at all
events. In the sum of his life he finds this to be the thing, or group of things,
manifest to him;—this, the piece of true knowledge, or sight, which his
share of sunshine and earth has permitted him to seize. He would fain set
it down for ever; engrave it on rock, if he could; saying, "This is the best of
me; for the rest, I ate, and drank, and slept, loved, and hated, like another;
my life was as the vapour, and is not; but this I saw and knew: this, if anything of mine, is worth your memory." That is his "writing;" it is, in his
small human way, and with whatever degree of true inspiration is in him,
his inscription, or scripture. That is a "Book."

[...]

Strange! to think how the Moth-kings lay up treasures for the moth; and
the Rust-kings, who are to their peoples' strength as rust to armour, lay up
treasures for the rust; and the Robber-kings, treasures for the robber; but
how few kings have ever laid up treasures that needed no guarding—treasures of which, the more thieves there were, the better! Broidered robe,
only to be rent; helm and sword, only to be dimmed; jewel and gold, only
to be scattered;—there have been three kinds of kings who have gathered
these. Suppose there ever should arise a Fourth order of kings, who had
read, in some obscure writing of long ago, that there was a Fourth kind of
treasure, which the jewel and gold could not equal, neither should it be
valued with pure gold. A web more fair in the weaving, by Athena's shut-

tle; an armour, forged in diviner fire by Vulcanian force; a gold only to be mined in the sun's red heart, where he sets over the Delphian cliffs;—deep-pictured tissue, impenetrable armour, potable gold!—the three great Angels of Conduct, Toil, and Thought, still calling to us, and waiting at the posts of our doors, to lead us, with their winged power, and guide us, with their inescapable eyes, by the path which no fowl knoweth, and which the vulture's eye has not seen! Suppose kings should ever arise, who heard and believed this word, and at last gathered and brought forth treasures of—Wisdom—for their people?

Think what an amazing business *that* would be! How inconceivable, in the state of our present national wisdom! That we should bring up our peasants to a book exercise instead of a bayonet exercise!—organise, drill, maintain with pay, and good generalship, armies of thinkers, instead of armies of stabbers!—find national amusement in reading-rooms as well as rifle-grounds; give prizes for a fair shot at a fact, as well as for a leaden splash on a target. What an absurd idea it seems, put fairly in words, that the wealth of the capitalists of civilised nations should ever come to support literature instead of war!

[...]

It will be long, yet, before that comes to pass. Nevertheless, I hope it will not be long before royal or national libraries will be founded in every considerable city, with a royal series of books in them; the same series in every one of them, chosen books, the best in every kind, prepared for that national series in the most perfect way possible; their text printed all on leaves of equal size, broad of margin, and divided into pleasant volumes, light in the hand, beautiful, and strong, and thorough as examples of binders' work; and that these great libraries will be accessible to all clean and orderly persons at all times of the day and evening; strict law being enforced for this cleanliness and quietness.

I could shape for you other plans, for art-galleries, and for natural history galleries, and for many precious—many, it seems to me, needful—things; but this book plan is the easiest and needfullest, and would prove a considerable tonic to what we call our British constitution, which has fallen dropsical of late, and has an evil thirst, and evil hunger, and wants healthier feeding. You have got its corn laws repealed for it; try if you cannot get corn laws established for it, dealing in a better bread;—bread made of that old enchanted Arabian grain, the Sesame, which opens doors;—doors not of robbers', but of Kings' Treasuries.

Traffic (1866)[10]

Taste is not only a part and an index of morality — it is the ONLY morality. The first, and last, and closest trial question to any living creature is, "What do you like?" Tell me what you like, and I'll tell you what you are. Go out into the street, and ask the first man or woman you meet, what their "taste" is, and if they answer candidly, you know them, body and soul. "You, my friend in the rags, with the unsteady gait, what do *you* like?" "A pipe and a quartern of gin." I know you. "You, good woman, with the quick step and tidy bonnet, what do you like?" "A swept hearth and a clean tea-table, and my husband opposite me, and a baby at my breast." Good, I know you also. "You, little girl with the golden hair and the soft eyes, what do you like?" "My canary, and a run among the wood hyacinths." "You, little boy with the dirty hands and the low forehead, what do you like?" "A shy at the sparrows, and a game at pitch-farthing." Good; we know them all now. What more need we ask?

"Nay," perhaps you answer: "we need rather to ask what these people and children do, than what they like. If they *do* right, it is no matter that they like what is wrong; and if they *do* wrong, it is no matter that they like what is right. Doing is the great thing; and it does not matter that the man likes drinking, so that he does not drink; nor that the little girl likes to be kind to her canary, if she will not learn her lessons; nor that the little boy likes throwing stones at the sparrows, if he goes to the Sunday school." Indeed, for a short time, and in a provisional sense, this is true. For if, resolutely, people do what is right, in time they come to like doing it. But they only are in a right moral state when they *have* come to like doing it; and as long as they don't like it, they are still in a vicious state. The man is not in health of body who is always thirsting for the bottle in the cupboard, though he bravely bears his thirst; but the man who heartily enjoys water in the morning and wine in the evening, each in its proper quantity and time. And the entire object of true education is to make people not merely *do* the right things, but *enjoy* the right things — not merely industrious, but to love industry — not merely learned, but to love knowledge — not merely pure, but to love purity — not merely just, but to hunger and thirst after justice.

Of Wisdom and Folly in Art (1872)[11]

Remember always that you come to this University, — or, at least, your fathers came, — not to learn how to say things, but how to think them.

10 Lecture 2 in *The Crown of Wild Olive*.
11 Lecture I in *The Eagle's Nest*. The full title is 'The Function in Art of the Faculty Called by the Greeks σοφια'.

[...]

I say you come to the University for this; and perhaps some of you are much surprised to hear it! You did not know that you came to the University for any such purpose. Nay, perhaps you did not know that you had come to a University at all? You do not at this instant, some of you, I am well assured, know what a University means. Does it mean, for instance — can you answer me in a moment, whether it means — a place where everybody comes to learn something; or a place where somebody comes to learn everything? It means — or you are trying to make it mean — practically and at present, the first; but it means theoretically, and always, the last; a place where only certain persons come, to learn everything; that is to say, where those who wish to be able to think, come to learn to think: not to think of mathematics only, nor of morals, nor of surgery, nor chemistry, but of everything, rightly.

[...]

One of the simplest pieces of perfect art, which you are yourselves in the habit of practising, is the stroke of an oar given in true time. We have defined art to be the wise modification of matter by the body. With a good oar-stroke you displace a certain quantity of water in a wise way. Supposing you missed your stroke, and caught a crab, you would displace a certain quantity of water in a foolish way, not only ineffectually, but in a way the reverse of what you intended. The perfectness of the stroke implies not only absolutely accurate knowledge or science of the mode in which water resists the blade of an oar, but the having in past time met that resistance repeatedly with greater and greater rightness of adaptation to the end proposed. That end being perfectly simple, — the advance of the boat as far as possible with a given expenditure of strength, you at once recognize the degree in which the art falls short of, or the artlessness negatives, your purpose. But your being 'σοφοσ,[12] as an oarsman, implies much more than this mere art founded on pure science. The fact of your being able to row in a beautiful manner depends on other things than the knowledge of the force of water, or the repeated practice of certain actions in resistance to it. It implies the practice of those actions under a resolved discipline of the body, involving regulation of the passions. It signifies submission to the authority, and amicable concurrence with the humours of other persons; and so far as it is beautifully done at last, absolutely signifies therefore a moral and intellectual rightness, to the necessary extent influencing the character honourably and graciously. This is the *sophia*, or wit, of what is

12 'Sophos': 'wise'.

most honourable, which is concerned in rowing, without which it must become no rowing, or the reverse of rowing.

Let us next take example in an art which perhaps you will think (though I hope not) much inferior to rowing, but which is in reality a much higher art — dancing. I have just told you how to test the rank of arts — namely, by their corruptibility, as you judge of the fineness of organic substance. The μωρια (*moria*), or folly, of rowing, is only ridiculous, but the *moria*, or folly, of dancing, is much worse than ridiculous; and, therefore, you may know that its σοφια (*sophia*), or wisdom, will be much more beautiful than the wisdom of rowing. Suppose, for instance, a minuet danced by two lovers, both highly bred, both of noble character, and very much in love with each other. You would see, in that, an art of the most highly finished kind, under the government of a *sophia* which dealt with the strongest passions, and most exquisite perceptions of beauty, possible to humanity.

[...]

In the present course I have to show you the action of the final, or higher *sophia* which directs the skill of art to the best purposes; and of the final, or lower *moria* which misdirects them to the worst. And the two points I shall endeavour to bring before you throughout will be these: — First, that the object of University teaching is to form your conceptions; — not to acquaint you with arts, nor sciences. It is to give you a notion of what is meant by smith's work; for instance — but not to make you blacksmiths. It is to give you a notion of what is meant by medicine, but not to make you physicians. The proper academy for blacksmiths is a blacksmith's forge; the proper academy for physicians is an hospital. Here you are to be taken away from the forge, out of the hospital, out of all special and limited labour and thought, into the 'Universitas' of labour and thought, that you may in peace, in leisure, in calm of disinterested contemplation be enabled to conceive rightly the laws of nature, and the destinies of man.

Then the second thing I have to show you is that over these three kingdoms of imagination, art, and science, there reigns a virtue or faculty[13], which from all time, and by all great people, has been recognized as the appointed ruler and guide of every method of labour, or passion of soul; and the most glorious recompense of the toil, and crown of the ambition of man. "She is more precious than rubies, and all the things thou canst desire are not to be compared unto her. Lay fast hold upon her; let her not go; keep her, for she is thy life."

---

13   I.e., σοφια, or Wisdom.

Chapter IX

A Challenge from Science

Matthew Arnold's passion for education as 'the best that has been thought and said in the world' is famous. Here, instead of a quotation from Culture and Anarchy, *is a duel in lecture form, preceding the more notorious "Two Cultures?" CP Snow — FR Leavis debate by some eighty years, as the power of science first led it to stake a claim as the central subject for education. Thomas Huxley, the great defender of Darwin, was also active in educational reform, and saw scientific knowledge as essential for the improvement of the conditions of life among the workers of Britain. Arnold replies that his humanism includes scientific methods of study as well as literature, but that science ought not to be the main part of education.*

(a) Thomas Henry Huxley:
Scientific Training Is The Best Modern Education

Science and Culture (1881)[1]

[T]he establishment of a college under the conditions of Sir Josiah Mason's Trust has a significance apart from any which it could have possessed a hundred years ago. It appears to be an indication that we are reaching the crisis of the battle, or rather of the long series of battles, which have been fought over education in a campaign which began long before Priestley's time, and will probably not be finished just yet.

In the last century, the combatants were the champions of ancient literature, on the one side, and those of modern literature on the other; but, some thirty years ago, the contest became complicated by the appearance of a third army, ranged round the banner of Physical Science.

I am not aware that any one has authority to speak in the name of this new host. For it must be admitted to be somewhat of a guerilla force, composed largely of irregulars, each of whom fights pretty much for his own

---

1   An address delivered at the opening of Sir Josiah Mason's Science College, at Birmingham, on the 1st of October 1880; published in 1881 in *Science and Culture and other Essays.*

hand. But the impressions of a full private, who has seen a good deal of service in the ranks, respecting the present position of affairs and the conditions of a permanent peace, may not be devoid of interest; and I do not know that I could make a better use of the present opportunity than by laying them before you.

From the time that the first suggestion to introduce physical science into ordinary education was timidly whispered, until now, the advocates of scientific education have met with opposition of two kinds. On the one hand, they have been pooh-poohed by the men of business who pride themselves on being the representatives of practicality; while, on the other hand, they have been excommunicated by the classical scholars, in their capacity of Levites in charge of the ark of culture and monopolists of liberal education.

The practical men believed that the idol whom they worship—rule of thumb—has been the source of the past prosperity, and will suffice for the future welfare of the arts and manufactures. They were of opinion that science is speculative rubbish; that theory and practice have nothing to do with one another; and that the scientific habit of mind is an impediment, rather than an aid, in the conduct of ordinary affairs.

I have used the past tense in speaking of the practical men—for although they were very formidable thirty years ago, I am not sure that the pure species has not been extirpated. In fact, so far as mere argument goes, they have been subjected to such a *feu d'enfer* that it is a miracle if any have escaped. But I have remarked that your typical practical man has an unexpected resemblance to one of Milton's angels. His spiritual wounds, such as are inflicted by logical weapons, may be as deep as a well and as wide as a church door, but beyond shedding a few drops of ichor, celestial or otherwise, he is no whit the worse. So, if any of these opponents be left, I will not waste time in vain repetition of the demonstrative evidence of the practical value of science; but knowing that a parable will sometimes penetrate where syllogisms fail to effect an entrance, I will offer a story for their consideration.

Once upon a time, a boy, with nothing to depend upon but his own vigorous nature, was thrown into the thick of the struggle for existence in the midst of a great manufacturing population. He seems to have had a hard fight, inasmuch as, by the time he was thirty years of age, his total disposable funds amounted to twenty pounds. Nevertheless, middle life found him giving proof of his comprehension of the practical problems he had been roughly called upon to solve, by a career of remarkable prosperity.

Finally, having reached old age with its well-earned surroundings of 'honour, troops of friends', the hero of my story bethought himself of those who were making a like start in life, and how he could stretch out a helping hand to them.

After long and anxious reflection this successful practical man of business could devise nothing better than to provide them with the means of obtaining 'sound, extensive, and practical scientific knowledge'. And he devoted a large part of his wealth and five years of incessant work to this end.

I need not point the moral of a tale which, as the solid and spacious fabric of the Scientific College assures us, is no fable, nor can anything which I could say intensify the force of this practical answer to practical objections.

We may take it for granted then, that, in the opinion of those best qualified to judge, the diffusion of thorough scientific education is an absolutely essential condition of industrial progress; and that the College which has been opened to-day will confer an inestimable boon upon those whose livelihood is to be gained by the practice of the arts and manufactures of the district.

The only question worth discussion is, whether the conditions, under which the work of the College is to be carried out, are such as to give it the best possible chance of achieving permanent success.

Sir Josiah Mason, without doubt most wisely, has left very large freedom of action to the trustees, to whom he proposes ultimately to commit the administration of the College, so that they may be able to adjust its arrangements in accordance with the changing conditions of the future. But, with respect to three points, he has laid most explicit injunctions upon both administrators and teachers.

Party politics are forbidden to enter into the minds of either, so far as the work of the College is concerned; theology is as sternly banished from its precincts; and finally, it is especially declared that the College shall make no provision for 'mere literary instruction and education'.

It does not concern me at present to dwell upon the first two injunctions any longer than may be needful to express my full conviction of their wisdom. But the third prohibition brings us face to face with those other opponents of scientific education, who are by no means in the moribund condition of the practical man, but alive, alert, and formidable.

It is not impossible that we shall hear this express exclusion of 'literary instruction and education' from a College which, nevertheless, professes to give a high and efficient education, sharply criticised. Certainly the time was that the Levites of culture would have sounded their trumpets against its walls as against an educational Jericho.

How often have we not been told that the study of physical science is incompetent to confer culture; that it touches none of the higher problems of life; and, what is worse, that the continual devotion to scientific studies tends to generate a narrow and bigoted belief in the applicability of scientific methods to the search after truth of all kinds. How frequently one has reason to observe that no reply to a troublesome argument tells so well as calling its author a 'mere scientific specialist'. And, as I am afraid it is not permissible to speak of this form of opposition to scientific education in the past tense; may we not expect to be told that this, not only omission, but prohibition, of 'mere literary instruction and education' is a patent example of scientific narrow-mindedness?

I am not acquainted with Sir Josiah Mason's reasons for the action which he has taken; but if, as I apprehend is the case, he refers to the ordinary classical course of our schools and universities by the name of 'mere literary instruction and education', I venture to offer sundry reasons of my own in support of that action.

For I hold very strongly by two convictions — The first is, that neither the discipline nor the subject-matter of classical education is of such direct value to the student of physical science as to justify the expenditure of valuable time upon either; and the second is, that for the purpose of attaining real culture, an exclusively scientific education is at least as effectual as an exclusively literary education.

I need hardly point out to you that these opinions, especially the latter, are diametrically opposed to those of the great majority of educated Englishmen, influenced as they are by school and university traditions. In their belief, culture is obtainable only by a liberal education; and a liberal education is synonymous, not merely with education and instruction in literature, but in one particular form of literature, namely, that of Greek and Roman antiquity. They hold that the man who has learned Latin and Greek, however little, is educated; while he who is versed in other branches of knowledge, however deeply, is a more or less respectable specialist, not admissible into the cultured caste. The stamp of the educated man, the University degree, is not for him.

I am too well acquainted with the generous catholicity of spirit, the true sympathy with scientific thought, which pervades the writings of our chief apostle of culture[2] to identify him with these opinions; and yet one may cull from one and another of those epistles to the Philistines, which so much delight all who do not answer to that name, sentences which lend them some support.

2   Matthew Arnold, whose rejoinder to Huxley's talk is also included in this section. Matthew
    Arnold's notorious essays on the value of culture were collected as a book, *Culture and Anarchy*,
    in 1869, where the famous phrase 'the best that has been thought and said in the world'
    appeared.

Mr. Arnold tells us that the meaning of culture is, 'to know the best that has been thought and said in the world'. It is the criticism of life contained in literature. That criticism regards 'Europe as being, for intellectual and spiritual purposes, one great confederation, bound to a joint action and working to a common result; and whose members have, for their common outfit, a knowledge of Greek, Roman, and Eastern antiquity, and of one another. Special, local, and temporary advantages being put out of account, that modern nation will in the intellectual and spiritual sphere make most progress, which most thoroughly carries out this programme. And what is that but saying that we too, all of us, as individuals, the more thoroughly we carry it out, shall make the more progress?'[3]

We have here to deal with two distinct propositions. The first, that a criticism of life is the essence of culture; the second, that literature contains the materials which suffice for the construction of such a criticism.

I think that we must all assent to the first proposition. For culture certainly means something quite different from learning or technical skill. It implies the possession of an ideal, and the habit of critically estimating the value of things by comparison with a theoretic standard. Perfect culture should supply a complete theory of life, based upon a clear knowledge alike of its possibilities and of its limitations.

But we may agree to all this, and yet strongly dissent from the assumption that literature alone is competent to supply this knowledge. After having learnt all that Greek, Roman, and Eastern antiquity have thought and said, and all that modern literatures have to tell us, it is not self-evident that we have laid a sufficiently broad and deep foundation for that criticism of life which constitutes culture.

Indeed, to any one acquainted with the scope of physical science, it is not at all evident. Considering progress only in the 'intellectual and spiritual sphere', I find myself wholly unable to admit that either nations or individuals will really advance, if their common outfit draws nothing from the stores of physical science. I should say that an army, without weapons of precision and with no particular base of operations, might more hopefully enter upon a campaign on the Rhine, than a man, devoid of a knowledge of what physical science has done in the last century, upon a criticism of life.

---

3   A quote from Arnold's essay 'The Function of Criticism at the Present Time' (1864). Huxley reads 'common outfit' where Arnold wrote 'proper outfit'.

(b) Matthew Arnold:
Culture Requires More Than Factual Knowledge[4]

Literature and Science (1882)[5]

I am boldly going to ask whether the present movement for ousting letters from their old predominance in education, and for transferring the predominance in education to the natural sciences, whether this brisk and flourishing movement ought to prevail, and whether it is likely that in the end it really will prevail.

[…]

Some of you may have met with a phrase of mine which has been the object of a good deal of comment; an observation to the effect that in our culture, the aim being to know ourselves and the world, we have, as the means to this end, to know the best which has been thought and said in the world.

[…]

Now on my phrase […], Professor Huxley remarks that I assert literature to contain the materials which suffice for making us know ourselves and the world. But it is not by any means clear, says he, that after having learnt all which ancient and modern literatures have to tell us, we have laid a sufficiently broad and deep foundation for that criticism of life which constitutes culture. On the contrary, Professor Huxley declares that he finds himself 'wholly unable to admit that either nations or individuals will really advance, if their common outfit draws nothing from the stores of physical science. An army without weapons of precision and with no particular base of operations, might more hopefully enter upon a campaign on the Rhine, than a man devoid of a knowledge of what physical science has done in the last century, upon a criticism of life.'

This shows how needful it is, for those who are to discuss a matter together, to have a common understanding as to the sense of the terms they employ,—how needful, and how difficult. What Professor Huxley says, implies just the reproach which is so often brought against the study

4   And see Thomas Gradgrind in *Hard Times* by Charles Dickens (1854) as an early and powerful fictional rebuke to the belief that "In this life, we want nothing but Facts, sir; nothing but Facts!"

5   Delivered in response to TH Huxley's speech, as the Rede Lecture in Cambridge. Some eighty years later, in 1959, CP Snow would use the Rede Lecture's podium to deliver 'The Two Cultures and the Scientific Revolution', essentially reprising Huxley's arguments and inciting FR Leavis to take on the mantle of Arnold in his blistering response, 'Two Cultures? The Significance of CP Snow'. Arnold's lecture was published in *The Nineteenth Century*, a monthly review (LXVI, August 1882) and, slightly recast, was delivered by Arnold on an American lecture tour and published in *Discourses in America* (1885), the book by which Arnold hoped to be remembered.

of belles lettres, as they are called: that the study is an elegant one, but slight and ineffectual; a smattering of Greek and Latin and other ornamental things, of little use for any one whose object is to get at truth.

[...]

Let us, I say, be agreed about the meaning of the terms we are using. I talk of knowing the best which has been thought and uttered in the world; Professor Huxley says this means knowing *literature.Elements Principia belles lettres*, and taking no account of Rome's military and political and legal and administrative work in the world; and as, by knowing ancient Greece, I understand knowing her as the giver of Greek art, and the guide to a free and right use of reason and to scientific method, and the founder of our mathematics and physics and astronomy and biology—I understand knowing her as all this, and not merely knowing certain Greek poems, histories, and speeches—so as to the knowledge of modern nations also. By knowing modern nations, I mean not merely knowing their belles lettres, but knowing also what has been done by such men as Copernicus, Galileo, Newton, Darwin.[6]

[...]

There is, therefore, really no question between Professor Huxley and me as to whether knowing the results of the scientific study of nature is not required as a part of our culture, as well as knowing the products of literature and art. But to follow the processes by which those results are reached ought, say the friends of physical science, to be made the staple of education for the bulk of mankind. And here there does arise a question between those whom Professor Huxley calls with playful sarcasm 'the Levites of culture', and those whom the poor humanist is sometimes apt to regard as its Nebuchadnezzars.[7]

[...]

Professor Huxley is moved to lay it down that 'for the purpose of attaining real culture, an exclusively scientific education is at least as effectual as an exclusively literary education.' And a certain President of the Section for Mechanical Science in the British Association is, in Scripture phrase, 'very bold', and declares that if a man, in his education, 'has substituted litera-

---

6   TH Huxley had given himself the nickname 'Darwin's Bulldog' and was known for his strong public defence of the theory of evolution by natural selection.

7   Levites are one of the tribes of Israel, the hereditary caste of teachers and Temple guards. ('Humble Levite' was a nickname taken up by Alcuin of York). In the book of Jeremiah, Nebuchadnezzar conquers Jerusalem and the Temple is looted and destroyed. See Jeremiah 39.2 and also Ezra 1.7.

ture and history for natural science, he has chosen the less useful alternative.'

[...]

[H]ere, I confess, I part company with the friends of physical science, with
whom up to this point I have been agreeing. [...] At present it seems to me,
that those who are for giving to natural knowledge, as they call it, the chief
place in the education of the majority of mankind, leave one important
thing out of their account — the constitution of human nature.

[...]

Deny the facts altogether, I think, [the man of science] hardly can. He can
hardly deny, that when we set ourselves to enumerate the powers which
go to the building up of human life, and say that they are the power of conduct, the power of intellect and knowledge, the power of beauty, and the
power of social life and manners — he can hardly deny that this scheme,
though drawn in rough and plain lines and not pretending to scientific
exactness, does yet give a fairly true account of the matter. Human nature
is built up by these powers; we have the need for them all. This is evident
enough, and the friends of physical science will admit it. But perhaps they
may not have sufficiently observed another thing: namely, that these powers just mentioned are not isolated, but there is in the generality of mankind a perpetual tendency to relate them one to another in divers ways.
With one such way of relating them I am particularly concerned here. Following our instinct for intellect and knowledge, we acquire pieces of
knowledge; and presently, in the generality of men, there arises the desire
to relate these pieces of knowledge to our sense for conduct, to our sense
for beauty, and there is weariness and dissatisfaction if the desire is
balked. Now in this desire lies, I think, the strength of that hold which letters have upon us.

[...]

If we are studying physiology, it is interesting to know that the pulmonary
artery carries dark blood and the pulmonary vein carries bright blood,
departing in this respect from the common rule for the division of labour
between the veins and the arteries. But every one knows how we seek naturally to combine the pieces of our knowledge together, to bring them
under general rules, to relate them to principles; and how unsatisfactory
and tiresome it would be to go on for ever learning lists of exceptions, or
accumulating items of fact which must stand isolated.

    Well, that same need of relating our knowledge which operates here
within the sphere of our knowledge itself, we shall find operating, also,

outside that sphere. We feel, as we go on learning and knowing, the vast majority of mankind feel the need of relating what we have learnt and known to the sense which we have in us for conduct, to the sense which we have in us for beauty.

[...]

Knowledges which cannot be directly related to the sense for beauty, to the sense for conduct, are instrument-knowledges; they lead on to other knowledge, which can. A man who passes his life in instrument-knowledges is a specialist. They may be invaluable as instruments to something beyond, for those who have the gift thus to employ them; and they may be disciplines in themselves wherein it is useful to every one to have some schooling. But it is inconceivable that the generality of men should pass all their mental life with Greek accents or with formal logic. My friend Professor Sylvester, who holds transcendental doctrines as to the virtue of mathematics, is far away in America; and therefore, if in the Cambridge Senate House one may say such a thing without profaneness, I will hazard the opinion that for the majority of mankind a little of mathematics, also, goes a long way. Of course this is quite consistent with their being of immense importance as an instrument to something else; but it is the few who have the aptitude for thus using them, not the bulk of mankind.

The natural sciences do not stand on the same footing with these instrument-knowledges. Experience shows us that the generality of men will find more interest in learning that when a taper burns the wax is converted into carbonic acid and water, or in learning the explanation of the phenomenon of dew, or in learning how the circulation of the blood is carried on, than they find in learning that the genitive plural of pais and pas does not take the circumflex on the termination. And one piece of natural knowledge is added to another, and others to that, and at last we come to propositions so interesting as the proposition that 'our ancestor was a hairy quadruped furnished with a tail and pointed ears, probably arboreal in his habits.'[8] Or we come to propositions of such reach and importance as those which Professor Huxley brings us, when he says that the notions of our forefathers about the beginning and the end of the world were all wrong, and that nature is the expression of a definite order with which nothing interferes.

8   Charles Darwin, *The Descent of Man* (1871), vol. II, chapter 21, p. 389: 'We thus learn that man is descended from a hairy quadruped, furnished with a tail and pointed ears, probably arboreal in its habits, and an inhabitant of the Old World.'

Interesting, indeed, these results of science are, important they are, and
we should all be acquainted with them. But what I now wish you to mark
is, that we are still, when they are propounded to us and we receive them,
we are still in the sphere of intellect and knowledge. And for the generality
of men there will be found, I say, to arise, when they have duly taken in the
proposition that their ancestor was 'a hairy quadruped furnished with a
tail and pointed ears, probably arboreal in his habits', there will be found
to arise an invincible desire to relate this proposition to the sense within
them for conduct and to the sense for beauty. But this the men of science
will not do for us, and will hardly, even, profess to do. They will give us
other pieces of knowledge, other facts, about other animals and their
ancestors, or about plants, or about stones, or about stars; and they may
finally bring us to those 'general conceptions of the universe which have
been forced upon us,' says Professor Huxley, 'by physical science.' But still
it will be knowledge only which they give us; knowledge not put for us
into relation with our sense for conduct, our sense for beauty, and touched
with emotion by being so put; not thus put for us, and therefore, to the
majority of mankind, after a certain while unsatisfying, wearying.

Not to the born naturalist, I admit. But what do we mean by a born naturalist? We mean a man in whom the zeal for observing nature is so strong
and eminent that it marks him off from the bulk of mankind. Such a man
will pass his life happily in collecting natural knowledge and reasoning
upon it, and will ask for nothing, or hardly anything, more. I have heard it
said that the sagacious and admirable naturalist whom we have lately lost,
Mr. Darwin, once owned to a friend that for his part he did not experience
the necessity for two things which most men find so necessary to
them—poetry and religion; science and the domestic affections, he
thought, were enough.[9] To a born naturalist, I can well understand that

9   In fact Darwin's much-quoted comment from page 100 of his autobiography (published 1887;
     this passage composed 1 May 1881) shows that he had lost his taste for the humanities in the
     pursuit of science, and regretted the change:
       'I have said that in one respect my mind has changed during the last twenty or thirty years.
     Up to the age of thirty, or beyond it, poetry of many kinds, such as the works of Milton, Gray,
     Byron, Wordsworth, Coleridge, and Shelley, gave me great pleasure, and even as a schoolboy I
     took intense delight in Shakespeare, especially in the historical plays. I have also said that
     formerly pictures gave me considerable, and music very great delight. But now for many years
     I cannot endure to read a line of poetry: I have tried lately to read Shakespeare, and found it so
     intolerably dull that it nauseated me. I have also almost lost my taste for pictures or music.
     Music generally sets me thinking too energetically on what I have been at work on, instead of
     giving me pleasure. I retain some taste for fine scenery, but it does not cause me the exquisite
     delight which it formerly did. On the other hand, novels which are works of the imagination,
     though not of a very high order, have been for years a wonderful relief and pleasure to me, and
     I often bless all novelists. A surprising number have been read aloud to me, and I like all if
     moderately good, and if they do not end unhappily—against which a law ought to be passed.
     A novel, according to my taste, does not come into the first class unless it contains some person

this should seem so. So absorbing is his occupation with nature, so strong his love for his occupation, that he goes on acquiring natural knowledge and reasoning upon it, and has little time or inclination for thinking about getting it related to the desire in man for conduct, the desire in man for beauty. He relates it to them for himself as he goes along, so far as he feels the need; and he draws from the domestic affections all the additional solace necessary. But then Darwins are very rare.

[...]

Professor Huxley holds up to scorn mediæval education, with its neglect of the knowledge of nature, its poverty of literary studies, its formal logic devoted to 'showing how and why that which the Church said was true must be true.' But the great mediæval Universities were not brought into being, we may be sure, by the zeal for giving a jejune and contemptible education. Kings have been our nursing fathers, and queens have been our nursing mothers but not for this. Our Universities came into being because the supposed knowledge delivered by Scripture and the Church so deeply engaged men's hearts, and so simply, easily, and powerfully related itself to the desire for conduct, the desire for beauty [...].

[...]

But now, says Professor Huxley, conceptions of the universe fatal to the notions held by our forefathers have been forced upon us by physical science. Grant to him that they are thus fatal, that they must and will become current everywhere, and that every one will finally perceive them to be fatal to the beliefs of our forefathers. The need of humane letters, as they are truly called, because they serve the paramount desire in men that good should be for ever present to them, — the need of humane letters to establish a relation between the new conceptions and our instinct for beauty, our instinct for conduct, is only the more visible.

[...]

whom one can thoroughly love, and if a pretty woman all the better.
  'This curious and lamentable loss of the higher æsthetic tastes is all the odder, as books on history, biographies, and travels (independently of any scientific facts which they may contain), and essays on all sorts of subjects interest me as much as ever they did. My mind seems to have become a kind of machine for grinding general laws out of large collections of facts, but why this should have caused the atrophy of that part of the brain alone, on which the higher tastes depend, I cannot conceive. A man with a mind more highly organised or better constituted than mine, would not, I suppose, have thus suffered; and if I had to live my life again, I would have made a rule to read some poetry and listen to some music at least once every week; for perhaps the parts of my brain now atrophied would thus have been kept active through use. The loss of these tastes is a loss of happiness, and may possibly be injurious to the intellect, and more probably to the moral character, by enfeebling the emotional part of our nature.'

I mean that we shall find, as a matter of experience, if we know the best that has been thought and uttered in the world, we shall find that the art and poetry and eloquence of men who lived, perhaps, long ago, who had the most limited natural knowledge, who had the most erroneous conceptions about many important matters, we shall find that they have in fact not only the power of refreshing and delighting us, they have also the power, — such is the strength and worth, in essentials, of their authors' criticism of life, — they have a fortifying and elevating and quickening and suggestive power capable of wonderfully helping us to relate the results of modern science to our need for conduct, our need for beauty. Homer's conceptions of the physical universe were, I imagine, grotesque; but really, under the shock of hearing from modern science that 'the world is not subordinated to man's use, and that man is not the cynosure of things terrestrial', I could desire no better comfort than Homer's line [...],

τλητον γαρ Μοιραι θυμον θεσαν ανθρωποισιν[10]

for an enduring heart have the destinies appointed to the children of men.

And the more that men's minds are cleared, the more that the results of science are frankly accepted, the more that poetry and eloquence come to be studied as what they really are — the criticism of life by gifted men, alive and active with extraordinary power at an unusual number of points; so much the more will the value of humane letters, and of art also, which is an utterance having a like kind of power with theirs, be felt and acknowledged, and their place in education be secured.

Let us, all of us, avoid as much as possible any invidious comparison between the merits of humane letters, as means of education, and the merits of the natural sciences. But when some President of a Section for Mechanical Science insists on making the comparison, and tells us that 'he who in his training has substituted literature and history for natural science has chosen the less useful alternative', let us say to him that the student of humane letters only, will at least know also the great general conceptions brought in by modern physical science; for science, as Professor Huxley says, forces them upon us all. But the student of the natural sciences only, will, by our very hypothesis, know nothing of humane letters; not to mention that in setting himself to be perpetually accumulating natural knowledge, he sets himself to do what only specialists have the gift for doing genially. And so he will be unsatisfied, or at any rate incomplete, and even more incomplete than the student of humane letters.

10   *Iliad*, Book XXIV, 49. 'Fate gives the wound, and man is born to bear', in Alexander Pope's 1791 translation.

I once mentioned in a school-report how a young man in a training college, having to paraphrase the passage in Macbeth beginning,

Can'st thou not minister to a mind diseased?

turned this line into, 'Can you not wait upon the lunatic?' And I remarked what a curious state of things it would be, if every pupil of our primary schools knew that when a taper burns the wax is converted into carbonic acid and water, and thought at the same time that a good paraphrase for

Can'st thou not minister to a mind diseased?

was, 'Can you not wait upon the lunatic?' If one is driven to choose, I think I would rather have a young person ignorant about the converted wax, but aware that 'Can you not wait upon the lunatic?' is bad, than a young person whose education had left things the other way.

[...]

And indeed, to say the truth, I cannot really think that humane letters are in danger of being thrust out from their leading place in education, in spite of the array of authorities against them at this moment. So long as human nature is what it is, their attractions will remain irresistible. They will be studied more rationally, but they will not lose their place. What will happen will rather be that there will be crowded into education other matters besides, far too many; there will be, perhaps, a period of unsettlement and confusion and false tendency; but letters will not in the end lose their leading place. If they lose it for a time, they will get it back again. We shall be brought back to them by our wants and aspirations.

[...]

And so we have turned in favour of the humanities the *No wisdom, nor understanding, nor counsel, against the Eternal!*[11] which seemed against them when we started. The 'hairy quadruped furnished with a tail and pointed ears, probably arboreal in his habits' carried hidden in his nature, apparently, something destined to develop into a necessity for humane letters. The time warns me to stop; but most probably, if we went on, we might arrive at the further conclusion that our ancestor carried in his nature, also, a necessity for Greek. The attackers of the established course of study think that against Greek, at any rate, they have irresistible arguments. Literature may perhaps be needed in education, they say; but why on earth should it be Greek literature? Why not French or German? Nay, 'has not an

---

11   Proverbs, 21.30.

Englishman models in his own literature of every kind of excellence?'[12] [...] As I said of humane letters in general, Greek will come to be studied more rationally than at present; but it will be increasingly studied as men increasingly feel the need in them for beauty, and how powerfully Greek art and Greek literature can serve this need. Women will again study Greek, as Lady Jane Grey did; perhaps in that chain of forts with which the fair host of the Amazons is engirdling this University they are studying it already.

---

12   A loose paraphrase of Huxley's comment: 'every Englishman has, in his native tongue, an almost perfect instrument of literary expression; and, in his own literature, models of every kind of literary excellence. If an Englishman cannot get literary culture out of his Bible, his Shakespeare, his Milton, neither, in my belief, will the profoundest study of Homer and Sophocles, Virgil and Horace, give it to him.'

Chapter X

The Twentieth Century:
Liberal Education for All

"How can these men study?" Yet they go on — not only studying but making it possible for others to study, loyal and true to all that the educational movement means, casual labourers often on the brink of unemployment, oppressed at other times by overwork, living in one or two room tenements, tired after the day's labour, forming a band of men and women of which any country may well be proud.[1]

I was fascinated. My mind was being broken out of its shell. Here were wonderful things to know. Things that went beyond the small utilities of our lives, which was all that school had seemed to concern itself with until then. Knowledge of this sort could make all times, and places, your own. You could be anybody, and everybody, and still be yourself all the time.[2]

[H]ere at last the organising and the prophetic spirit meet and create a movement able to put the highest educational ideals into practice without lowering their standard; here at last is a hope for democracy to spread justice without destroying culture.[3]

In the late nineteenth and early twentieth century, the passion for bringing liberal education to a wider public without lowering the bar produced extraordinary results. Accounts of working men walking miles after a day of physical labour to spend their leisure time learning about the classical authors were not uncommon. Classic works, being out-of-copyright, were often the cheapest books available and read with enthusiasm by those at the bottom of the social scale. On BBC Radio, classical concerts were as popular as cricket matches. Jonathan Rose records in his

---

1   *University Tutorial Classes*, by Albert Mansbridge (1913), p. 83.
2   Richard Hillyer, born at the start of the twentieth century, and quoted by Jonathan Rose in *The Intellectual Life of the British Working Classes* (2001), p. 127. Rose comments, '[F]or those at the bottom of the social scale, the most old-fashioned literary canons could be terrifically liberating. What was dismally familiar to professional intellectuals was amazingly new to them.'
3   Werner Picht, a German observer of the Workers' Educational Association (WEA), writing in *The Highway*, June 1912. Reprinted in *Knowledge is Power: a short history of the Workers' Educational Association, 1903-1978* by Bernard Jennings (1979), p. 23.

book The Intellectual Life of the British Working Classes *(2001) and in his article for* City Journal *(Autumn 2004) 'The Classics in the Slums', instances of workers inspired into political careers by Shakespeare, such as Joseph Clynes (1869–1949), who went from the mill to the House of Commons and read* A Midsummer Night's Dream *as he waited for the votes to be counted. Once elected, Clynes rose to Deputy Leader of the House. Others simply found uplift and dignity in what they read, transcending the drudgery of their lives. Elizabeth Blackburn, a mill-worker born at the turn of the century, memorised Milton's 'Lycidas' to the rhythmic movement of the shuttles over the looms.*

An early contributor to this cultural blossoming was the University Extension Movement, which attempted to bring university-level material to working men and women, beginning around the 1870s. The enthusiasm for these challenging, stimulating courses could be remarkable.

> Two pitmen, brothers, who lived at a village five miles from one of the lecture centres, attended the course. They were able to get in by train, but the return service was inconvenient, and they were compelled to walk home. They did this for three months on dark nights, over wretchedly bad roads, and in all kinds of weather. On one occasion they returned in a severe storm, when the roads were so flooded that they lost their way and got up to their waists in water.[4]

In the 1880s, the University Settlement Movement went further, bringing a monastic spirit and a devotion to the life of the mind into deprived areas of industrial cities, with students living among the poor in a spirit of charitable service, providing instruction and assistance. Perhaps most famous today is Toynbee Hall, where the WEA was launched, while Mary Humphry Ward, author of the novel of religious controversy Robert Elsmere *(1888), the bestseller of its day, established several settlements, one of which, the Passmore Edwards Settlement, has now been renamed as the Mary Ward Centre and still offers adult education classes in Tavistock Place, London.*

In 1903, the Workers' Educational Association was established by Albert Mansbridge, allowing workers to take forward their education on their own terms. Mansbridge, a carpenter's son, began the WEA in response to the university extension movement's drift toward the middle class. He was a tremendous spokesman for the cause, and extant speeches, such as 'The Waters of Learning', a commencement address that he gave at the University of Pittsburgh in 1927, in which he looked back over the two and a half millennia of liberal educational tradition, capture some of his ability to lead and inspire this great movement for workers' education.

> If, perplexed by the multifarious contradictory activities of men, you are tempted to be pessimistic about your own importance, or to feel

---

4 A report from Northumberland in *The University Extension Movement* by Richard G. Moulton (1885), p. 18.

that you are a mere if sophisticated animal of no moment, with no purpose except to seek pleasure in life, then look down the roll of the past, or imagine the rivers of learning and purity in the world and bathe yourself in their living waters.

Look down, I say, or back through the years of our modern western civilisation, perhaps only a fragment of time in the long story of the world, but still full of noble teaching, wondrous achievements, and adventurous endeavour. Everywhere and always, far flung over the world, you will find men seeking to create reservoirs of thought and learning, which for us, at least, have their culmination in this our university.[5]

At the same time, DH Lawrence, writing from bitter experience as a teacher, published The Rainbow in 1915, recording the challenge a teacher could face in a classroom of ill-disciplined children, and delivering a warning about the practical and emotional difficulties involved in any actual form of of mass education.

Children will never naturally acquiesce to sitting in a class and submitting to knowledge. They must be compelled by a stronger, wiser will. Against which will they must always strive to revolt. So that the first great effort of every teacher of a large class must be to bring the will of the children into accordance with his own will. And this he can only do by an abnegation of his personal self, and an application of a system of laws, for the purpose of achieving a certain calculable result, the imparting of certain knowledge. Whereas Ursula thought she was going to become the first wise teacher by making the whole business personal, and using no compulsion. She believed entirely in her own personality.

So that she was in a very deep mess. In the first place she was offering to a class a relationship which only one or two of the children were sensitive enough to appreciate, so that the mass were left outsiders, therefore against her. Secondly, she was placing herself in passive antagonism to the one fixed authority of Mr. Harby, so that the scholars could more safely harry her.[6]

All three traditions — university extension classes; university settlements; and the WEA — still continue today in some form, but often without the focus on liberal education that marked their heyday. The Open University provides perhaps the strongest remaining bastion of this movement: still open, in the sense of having no entry requirements; still providing access to the humanities; and still producing work that is at least comparable with that produced in conventional university departments. RH Tawney's essay, 'An Experiment in Democratic Education', gives a flavour of the movement's early idealism and accomplishments.

5   'The Waters of Learning', first published in the *University of Pittsburgh Record*, II (1), October 1927 and published separately in the same year.
6   *The Rainbow*, Chapter 13.

The workers' education movement was the last great flowering of liberal educa-
tion in Britain and, in its desire to induct ordinary working men and women into
the great tradition, the most generous. For those involved, the liberal arts were
recognised as a genuinely liberating force, for people of any background, permit-
ting them to attend the millennia-long great conversation of Europe's best minds,
and to be inspired toward their own contributions. Its association with labour
unions and the cooperative movement were a firm reminder that liberal education
is not a force for conservatism, but rises above political partisanship. In America,
this ideal would be taken up in recent times by Earl Shorris in the Clemente
Course for the Humanities, outlined in his book Riches for the Poor *(2000).*
Operating initially in one of the toughest areas of New York City and later spread-
ing to other centres across the country, Shorris demonstrated that what had
occurred in early twentieth-century Britain could be more than a historical foot-
note. In Britain, while the passion for self-improvement persisted well into the
1950s, it ultimately dwindled before a combination of government neglect, ideologi-
cal suspicion and the broad cultural rebellion against established tradition of the
1960s. Richard Hoggart's memoirs of his work as a teacher in this great tradition
through the middle of the twentieth century are an excellent primary source to the
glories, and the ultimate diminution, of the movement, not quite to extinction, as
the Open University shows, but certainly to a much-reduced status. As Hoggart
notes, it is easy for those who were not involved to doubt it really happened.

> Her Majesty's Inspector, talking casually after listening to a univer-
> sity's annual lecture on Adult Education in 1984, was having no nos-
> talgic nonsense about the Great Days. "All that heroic stuff about
> marvellous three-year tutorial classes, wonderful worker-students
> with their superb written work, takes a lot of believing."[7]

Even at the time, in a discussion on University Extension classes, Mansbridge
acknowledged that it was unsurprising if outsiders were initially sceptical.

> In England alone, over eight thousand men and women have passed
> through these courses, which are organised in connection with every
> University and University College. If it were not for the clear demon-
> stration of experience, it would seem fatuous to expect that men and
> women who have undergone no educational training other than that
> provided in the few years of attendance at the elementary school
> would be willing to attend classes for three years, and, in some cases,
> for as many as seven or eight years. It must be remembered that the
> discipline of the class, though self-imposed, is severe. [...] "The
> instruction must aim at reaching, within the limits of the subject cov-
> ered, the standard of university work in honours."[8]

Yet happen it assuredly did.

---

7   *The Way We Live Now* (1995), p. 50.
8   Albert Mansbridge, *Education and the Working Classes* (1918), p. 8. Reprinted from *The*
     Contemporary Review, June 1918.

We have only to add, in conclusion, that no one could attend these classes without being struck by the zeal and earnestness of the students, their happy relations with the lecturer, the general atmosphere of comradeship and good feeling in the classes, and the strong appreciation by the students of the benefit which they are deriving from the work.[9]

That zeal and earnestness remains a magnificent testament to the universal value of a liberal education, and, as Hoggart reminds us (and as Earl Shorris's work in America, the Open University and indeed the still-extant WEA demonstrate), we should not assume the desire is now dead.

It is easy to assume that the great and widely-spread demand for further education by adults today is predominantly for vocational uses, retraining, refreshment or changes of direction; and such a demand does exist. But the full picture is more interesting. Just before its short life came to an end, the Advisory Council for Adult and Continuing Education ran the most thorough survey yet made of the demand for further education by adults. Of course it revealed that many want more education for practical purposes. But the most remarkable discovery was that a very substantial number of people seek further education for the traditional reasons. They express that need in lovely old-fashioned ways. They speak of wanting to be better educated so as to live a fuller life, so as to be more whole, so as to be able to understand their experience better, and the way their society is going. They want to understand and to criticise, but from a larger and less febrile perspective than they are generally offered; they are Arnoldians before they are anything else. Jude and his sister are not dead nor necessarily at university; they probably have Filofaxes; but they are still looking for larger meanings.[10]

(a) RH Tawney: Workers Need Education For Its Own Sake

An Experiment in Democratic Education (1914)[11]

I. The Idea

The truth is that educational problems cannot be considered in isolation from the aspirations of the great bodies of men and women for whose sake alone it is that educational problems are worth considering at all.

[...]

9   Extract from the 1910 Board of Education Report on Tutorial Classes by HMI JW Headlam and Professor LT Hobhouse, reprinted in *University Tutorial Classes* by Albert Mansbridge (1913), p. 162. Headlam and Hobhouse also reported that one student, in order to find a quiet time to study, 'went to bed at seven, got up at midnight, worked for two hours and then went to bed again.'

10   *A Sort of Clowning* (1990), p. 137. cf. pp. 93-5.

11   Reprinted from *The Political Quarterly*, 2, May 1914. Reprinted as a WEA pamphlet in the same year, it was published most recently in a collection of Tawney's essays, *The Radical Tradition*, edited by Rita Hinden (1964).

Society can be divided, it is thought, into those who work with their brains and those who work with their hands, and this division offers a decisive guide to educational policy. It is worth while to provide University education for the former. It is not worth while to provide it for the latter. 'A University', said a distinguished professor in the presence of the writer, 'is simply the professional school of the brain-working classes.'

Now it would, of course, be folly to deny that there are large fields of education in which this statement has considerable truth. The majority of men — one may hope an increasing majority — must live by working. Their work must be of different kinds, and to do different kinds of work they need specialized kinds of professional preparation. Doctors, lawyers, engineers, plumbers, and masons must, in fact, have trade schools of different kinds. The point at which this theory of the functions of the Universities is challenged by the educational movement of labour is its doctrine that [...] a 'humane education' is suitable for persons entering a certain restricted group of professions, to which attempts are now being made to add the direction of business, but that it is a matter with which the manual working classes have nothing to do.

Such a misinterpretation of the meaning of educational specialization is felt to be intellectually an imposture. If persons whose work is different require, as they do, different kinds of professional instruction, that is no reason why one should be excluded from the common heritage of civilization of which the other is made free by a University education, and from which, *ceteris paribus*[12], both, irrespective of their occupations, are equally capable, as human beings, of deriving spiritual sustenance.

Those who have seen the inside both of lawyers' chambers and of coal mines will not suppose that of the inhabitants of these places of gloom the former are more constantly inspired by the humanities than are the latter, or that conveyancing (*pace* the kindly shades of Maitland[13]) is in itself a more liberal art than hewing. And the differentiation of humane education according to class is felt to be worse than a mere intellectual error on the part of those by whom such education has hitherto been managed. It is felt to be one of those blunders which reveal coarseness of spirit even more than confusion of mind. It is felt to be morally insulting. On the lips of many of its advocates it *is* morally insulting. Stripped of its decent draperies of convention, what it means is that there is a class of masters whose right it is to enter at manhood on the knowledge which is the inheritance of the race, and a class of servants whose hands should be taught to labour

---

12   All other things being equal.
13   Frederick William Maitland, jurist and historian (1850-1906), who specialised in conveyancing cases, but was also a distinguished historian, notably of English law.

but whose eyes should be on the furrow which is watered with their sweat, whose virtue is contentment, and whose ignorance is the safety of the gay powers by whom their iron world is ruled.

"What," said an educated man to the writer, "you teach history and economics to miners and engineers? Take care. You will make them discontented and disloyal to us." That division of mankind into those who are ends and those who are means, whether made by slaveholders or by capitalists, is the ultimate and unforgivable wrong, with which there can be truce neither in education not in any other department of social life. To such wickedness only one answer is possible, *Ecrasez l'infame.*

But, it will be urged, secondary education is being improved. Rungs to connect it with the elementary schools at one end and with the Universities at the other are being constructed. In time every clever child will have a chance of winning a scholarship and passing from the elementary school to the University. What more do you desire?

[…]

It is certainly not the case, however, that the only avenue to humane education of the highest kind ought to be that which consists in a career of continuous school attendance from five to eighteen. In this matter we are still far too much at the mercy of the dogma of selection through competitive examinations which dominated the last half of the nineteenth century. Such selection has its use, and its use is to determine who are most suitable for a limited number of posts. But no one dreams of determining who shall enter elementary schools by a process of selection. On the contrary, we provide elementary education for all on the ground that it is indispensable to good citizenship.

In the same way, side by side with the selective system created by means of scholarships, there ought to be a system of higher education which aims at, even though it cannot attain, universal provision, which is accessible to all who care to use it, and which is maintained not in order to enable intellect to climb from one position to another, but to enable all to develop the faculties which, because they are the attributes of man, are not the attributes of any particular class or profession of men. To suppose that the goal of educational effort is merely to convert into doctors, barristers, and professors a certain number of persons who would otherwise have been manual workers is scarcely less unintelligent than to take the Smilesian advice, 'Remember, my boy, that your aim should be to be master of that business'[14] as an all-satisfying formula of economic progress, or to regard the existence of freed-men as making tolerable the institution of slavery.

Selection is wanted to save us from incompetence in high places: if only one could add to the scholarship system by which capacity travels up, a system of negative scholarships which would help incapacity to travel down! Universal provision is wanted because society is one, because we cannot put our minds in commission, because no class is good enough to do its thinking for another.

II. The Organization

Almost for the first time in English educational history the sedate rows of statistics which appear in Government Reports have suddenly begun to walk, to assert intellectual appetites, to demand that they shall be satisfied, to organize themselves in order to insist that they shall be satisfied — in short, to behave like men and women. The result, partially revealed in different ways by Ruskin College, by the Central Labour College, by the growth of innumerable classes and reading circles whose existence is almost unknown except to their members, perhaps, finds its completest expression in the Workers' Educational Association.

[...]

Founded in 1903 by a group of trade unionists and co-operators, the Workers' Educational Association is a federation which at the present time includes a very large number*[15] of working-class and educational organizations. Owing mainly to the inspiration of its founder and general secretary, Mr. Albert Mansbridge, its organization has grown in the last few years with remarkable and rather disconcerting rapidity. Its affiliated societies, which in 1906 numbered 283, were, at the date of its last Report, 2164; its local branches have risen from 13 at the earlier date to 158 at the later.

[...]

[T]he work of the Association is in a constant state of transformation, and there are already signs of a widening in its horizon which is likely to cause

14 Samuel Smiles, famous for his doctrine of 'Self-Help', the title of his 1859 book that preached the power of hard work, ambition and self-discipline to raise any individual to a higher position in life, but became a byword for rose-tinted sententiousness. The remark cited seems intended as a mocking distillation of Smiles rather than a direct quotation, but is perhaps a reference to *The Life of Thomas Telford* (1862), where Smiles quotes Telford's dictum that "I take care to be so far master of the business committed to me that none shall be able to eclipse me in that respect."

15 [Author's original note] E.g. 790 trade unions, trade union branches and trades councils, 326 co-operative education committees, 254 adult schools and classes, 163 working men's clubs and institutes, 61 teachers' associations, 20 University bodies, 15 local education authorities, and a number of miscellaneous working-class organizations.

it in the future to give increased attention to questions connected with the education of children and young persons. During the first ten years of its existence, however, its main task has been to create, with the assistance of the proper authorities, the nucleus of that system of humane education for adult workers, both men and women, which has attained some celebrity under the name of the University Tutorial Class movement.

[...]

A University Tutorial Class is really the nucleus of a University established in a place where no University exists. Its organization is simple. It consists of a group of not more than thirty students who agree to meet regularly once a week for twenty-four weeks during each of three successive winters for the purpose of study under a tutor appointed by a University, to follow the course of reading outlined by the tutor and to write fortnightly essays. [...] The classes meet every week for two hours at a time, of which the first normally consists of a lecture and the second of questions and discussion by the students. Books are obtained from the Universities and from local libraries.

[...]

Judged by the increase in their numbers, the University Tutorial Classes have met with a success unanticipated by the pioneers of the movement. In 1908 the University of Oxford provided a teacher for two classes, composed of some sixty students. At the present time thirteen Universities and University colleges in England and Wales conduct 142 classes, including about 3500 to 4000 students. The expectation that only in certain selected areas would a body of workers be found sufficiently enthusiastic and alert to give their evenings to study after a hard day's labour in the factory or in the mine has been quite falsified by the event. [...] In six years the students in the Tutorial Classes have increased from 60 to nearly 4000. In another ten years they could be increased from 4000 to 12000 if the men and the money needed to conduct the classes were available. If there was ever any truth in the saying that English people do not care for higher education — how should they when it was almost unattainable? — it has been disposed of by the simple process of offering them higher education for which they care.

[...]

It is as to the quality of the work done in the classes that the academic critic will naturally feel the greatest curiosity, and by which the movement will necessarily be judged by educationalists. The classes are fortunate in having from the first been closely watched by high academic authorities and by the inspectors of the Board of Education. The disposition, which was occasionally shown in their earlier years, to regard them as an amiable but quixotic attempt to provide cheap culture 'for the masses', by populariz- ing subjects which lose their meaning when they lose their austerity, has, therefore, been brought from the beginning to the test of facts, and is no longer held by persons whose experience or attainments entitle them to consideration.

The verdict given in their Report to the Board of Education by Professor LT Hobhouse and Mr. Headlam,[16] after an exhaustive examination of a large number of classes, that their work was 'in some respects better, and in others not so good, as that of an Oxford or Cambridge undergraduate', that the classes 'tend to accustom the student to the ideal of work familiar at a University', and that 'as regards the standard reached, there are stu- dents whose essays compare favourably with the best academic work', is substantially that of most observers who have had experience of teaching in a University and who have seen the work of the Tutorial Classes at first hand.

[...]

University Tutorial Classes are not, in short, an alternative to a University education, a pis aller[17] for those who cannot 'go to a University'. Nor are they merely a preparation for study in a University, though that is not, of course, incompatible with thinking it right for some students to go from them to residence in a University, just as in Germany men go regularly from one University to another. They are themselves a University educa- tion, carried on, it is true, under difficulties, but still carried on in such a way as to make their promotion one among the most important functions of a University. If this is not yet fully recognized it is because one of the besetting sins of those in high places in England — it is not that of the work- ing classes — is the bad utilitarianism which thinks that the object of educa- tion is not education, but some external result, such as professional success or industrial leadership. It is not in this spirit that a nation can be led to believe in the value of the things of the mind. In the matters of the intellect, as in matters of religion, 'high Heaven rejects the lore/ of nicely calculated less or more.'[18] And it is, perhaps, not fanciful to say that the disinterested desire of knowledge for its own sake, the belief in the free exercise of rea- son without regard to material results and because reason is divine, a faith not yet characteristic of English life, but which it is the highest spiritual

---

16   Reprinted in *University Tutorial Classes* by Albert Mansbridge (1913).
17   Last resort.
18   William Wordsworth, 'Inside of King's College Chapel, Cambridge' (c. 1821–1822).

end of Universities to develop, finds in the Tutorial Classes of the Workers' Educational Association as complete an expression as it does within the walls of some University cities. To these miners and weavers and engineers who pursue knowledge with the passion born of difficulties, knowledge can never be a means, but only an end; for what have they to gain from it save knowledge itself?

[...]

Historians tell us that decadent societies have been revivified through the irruption of new races. In England a new race of nearly 900,000 souls bursts upon us every year. They stand on the threshold with the world at their feet, like barbarians gazing upon the time-worn plains of an ancient civilization, and if, instead of rejuvenating the world they grind corn for the Philistines and doff bobbins for mill owners, the responsibility is ours into whose hands the prodigality of Nature pours life itself, and who let it slip aimlessly through the fingers that close so greedily on material riches.

Chapter XI

Worth Fighting For: Restatement in and after World War II

The civilisational struggle against Nazism, as with earlier moments of crisis, pro-duced a number of attempts to restate the Western educational ideal, several of which have become classic in their own right.

(a) Sir Richard Livingstone: Learning should be Collegial

Perhaps the most influential is also the least known. Sir Richard Winn Livingstone, a stalwart defender of classical education, published his first book on the subject, *A Defence of Classical Education*, in 1916, in the midst of the century's first Great War. In 1941, he published *The Future in Education*, Chapter IV of which, 'Cultural Studies in Adult Education', contains an able defence of liberal education.

> [T]hough slavery has gone, the ideal of a free man's education is not antiquated. Here, as so often the Greeks saw to the heart of the matter. [...] They saw clearly that men were breadwinners but also that they were, or ought to be, something more: that a man might be a doctor or a lawyer or a shopkeeper or an artisan or a clerk, but that he was also a man, and that education should recognise this and help each individ-ual to become, so far as his capacities allowed, what a man ought to be. That was the aim of a liberal education, and that is its aim — and clearly it is different from a technical education which simply enables us to earn our bread, but does not make us complete human beings.

Confident of his cause, and also influenced by Danish schools, Living-stone proposed to strengthen adult education. He feared the weakness of Western civilisation not from the external threat so much as the internal diminution of Christian faith and saw liberal education as a counterweight to the spiritual chaos of mass entertainment. He proposed, rather than the evening classes that had been the staple of the WEA and others, creating residential retreats where students could immerse themselves in their studies for several days at a time.

> No doubt the lamp of wisdom can burn in solitary shrines and even in dismal lecture halls. But for the many it will not burn brightly, if at all, unless fanned by that social, corporate life which exists in a residential university and which both educates and makes education attractive.[1]

After the devastation of the war, there would be no trouble in finding empty buildings to acquire.

> There will be no need to build colleges. All over the country great houses will be vacant, calling for occupation, purchasable for a song. Why should not each Local Education Authority start its own House of Education?[2]

Out of Livingstone's convictions, with the help of government backing, came a great national project. Some twenty education authorities had one of Livingstone's short-stay, residential colleges by 1951. Thirty still survive, such as Pendrell Hall in Staffordshire, although, as with the other movements to widen access to liberal learning, the courses available today are some distance from the curriculum Sir Richard Livingstone envisaged.

(b) CS Lewis:
Modern Education is an Attack on the Human Heritage

The Abolition of Man by CS Lewis, published in 1943, remains a powerful indictment of an education that sought only to debunk[3] and never to inspire or to guide, and that had forgotten the central goal of a liberal education was inner freedom, rather than political utility. As with the lecture by Dorothy Sayers discussed in this section, Lewis's book has had a considerable afterlife in America, especially among Christians, though rather less influence in Britain. Yet Lewis's gift for metaphor, his wide-ranging knowledge, citing both ancient authors and flawed modern schoolbooks with authority, and his evident indignation at what was being perpetrated in the name of education, make this extended essay an indispensable guide to the failings of much modern education and the virtues of the liberal education tradition. Lewis expressed it as the difference between a parent bird teaching a chick to fly and a poulterer deliberately clipping its wings for his own convenience.

---

1   *The Future in Education*, Chapter III.
2   Ibid.
3   cf. George Orwell, 'Inside the Whale' (1940): 'Patriotism, religion, the Empire, the family, the sanctity of marriage, the Old School Tie, birth, breeding, honour, discipline—anyone of ordinary education could turn the whole lot of them inside out in three minutes. But what do you achieve, after all, by getting rid of such primal things as patriotism and religion? You have not necessarily got rid of the need for *something to believe in*.'

[T]he difference between the old and the new will be an important one. Where the old initiated, the new merely 'conditions'. The old dealt with its pupils as grown birds deal with young birds when they teach them to fly; the new deals with them more as the poultry-keeper deals with young birds—making them thus or thus for purposes of which the birds know nothing. In a word, the old was a kind of propagation—men transmitting manhood to men; the new is merely propaganda.

(c) TS Eliot: Virgil Reminds Us of Our Duty to the Classics

On December 18, 1943, TS Eliot and six others, including Vita Sackville-West, published a letter in the *Times Literary Supplement*, announcing the formation of the Virgil Society, 'to bring together those men and women everywhere who are united in cherishing the central educational tradition of Western Europe. Among such persons the love of the poetry of Virgil is most likely to be found; and for such persons he is the fitting symbol of that tradition […] he is the witness to the continuity of our civilisation.' In 1944, Eliot gave the inaugural Virgil Society lecture, asking his audience 'What is a Classic?' The text itself has become a lasting memorial to Eliot's belief that only acknowledging the shared inheritance of the classics could heal Europe's wounds. As he said, '[T]he maintenance of the standard [of the classic] is the price of our freedom, the defence of freedom against chaos.'[4]

(d) Dorothy L Sayers: Unless Revived, the Tradition will Die

A lecture given by Dorothy L Sayers at an Oxford summer school in 1947, *The Lost Tools of Learning*, supplemented Eliot's focus on the great books of Greece and Rome by urging a curriculum re-centred on the mediæval trivium of grammar, logic and rhetoric. Sayers saw an education in these three skills as an education in the fundamentals of good thought and expression, with which students could progress rapidly, and without which limited expression, sloppy phrasing and flawed logic would drown out other achievements.

Almost forgotten in Britain, her talk forms the basis of the Christian Classical School movement in the United States. Douglas Wilson's 1991 book, *Recovering the Lost Tools of Learning: An Approach to Distinctively Christian Education*, describes his decision to start a school based on the principles she champions, and details a revived liberal curriculum centred on rhetoric and Christian humanism.

---

4   The Virgil Society continues to meet in London, at Senate House in Malet Street. Membership is £10 a year. [www.virgilsociety.org.uk]

Dorothy Sayers would have been startled by this posthumous legacy. Near the start of her address, she observes, 'However, it is in the highest degree improbable that the reforms I propose will ever be carried into effect.' Yet as she closes, she also fears a world without such reforms, in which the great tradition was already beginning to die out.

> Right down to the nineteenth century, our public affairs were mostly managed, and our books and journals were for the most part written, by people brought up in homes, and trained in places, where that tradition was still alive in the memory and almost in the blood
>
> [...]
>
> But one cannot live on capital forever. However firmly a tradition is rooted, if it is never watered, though it dies hard, yet in the end it dies.

SECTION THREE
After Tradition

From 1950-1970, the liberal education tradition entered upon a period that began hopefully but ended in defeat. From 1944, the grammar school system guaranteed access, if only for those few students who could pass the 11-plus exams, to an excellent course of liberal studies. Grammar was one branch of the mediæval trivium, and customarily associated with institutions that provided instruction in Latin grammar, marking out these schools as inheritors of the long educational tradition. At the same time, the workers' education movement continued, and Sir Richard Livingstone's residential courses opened up new forums for liberal studies among the working population. Keele University began a lonely experiment into a more rounded higher education in 1949. Ultimately, however, these projects, after many decades, were losing momentum. The latest great achievement of the period was the Open University, designed to exploit new communication technologies and founded in the closing years of the 1960s to help expand university access to all social levels. Yet this was not enough to halt the decline of the classical tradition. In 1960, the universities of Oxford and Cambridge both dropped Latin as a matriculation requirement. With formal entry into the nation's two greatest universities no longer requiring knowledge of the classical languages, these were soon sidelined in the classroom as well. The cultural current was running hard against liberal education, which lacked the theoretical definition that appealed to intellectuals and the novelty that struck the progessive and the scientific mind as a badge of honour. Having renewed and revived itself through countless struggles, preserved by Enlightenment thinkers and Romantics, defended through industrialisation and against the rising claims of science, the rise of the counter-culture proved its nemesis. Liberal education was just one among many traditions dismissed as a stifling and arbitrary set of intellectual constraints. An education that offered the endless rebellion of memory, the chance to listen to the supreme minds of western civilisation and to continue their great conversation, and that promised liberation through discipline was incomprehensible to those who wished to start the world anew and who believed that personal license was the royal road to freedom. With the closing of the grammars and the comprehensivisation of almost all of Britain's state schools, the tradition came to a stop. Elements only would survive, in a few brave holdouts, mostly among schools independent of state funding.

Chapter XII

Losing Battles

(a) Sir Winston Churchill: Never Surrender

World War II brought forth new champions for the Western tradition, and it is appropriate that Sir Winston Churchill, as prime minister, should have delivered one of the last great defences of liberal education in Britain. On 11 March 1953, taking a form letter written for him by civil servants responding to a TUC resolution complaining against a reduction of the adult education grant by ten per cent, Churchill inserted a paragraph that, in a characteristic burst of rhetorical brilliance, defines the case for upholding the tradition and issues a defiant cry for its support against all odds. The letter was included as Appendix 8 in the Ashby Report of 1954, which quashed the plans of Florence Horsburgh, then Minister of Education, for cutting the grant, at least in part due to Churchill's intervention. And yet Churchill only deferred the inevitable. The Ashby Report preserved the classic 1919 report that emerged from the First World War's Ministry of Reconstruction, but by the 1970s, with the Russell Report of 1973 and funding changes brought in during the late 1970s, state support for further education in the liberal mould fell away. Churchill's words had bought twenty-five years of respite, but did nothing to renew the faltering energy of the movement itself.

Extract from a letter from the Prime Minister to Sir Vincent Tewson, responding to a resolution passed by the Education Committee of the Trades Union Congress about grants for adult education, written at 10 Downing Street, 11 March 1953.

There is, perhaps, no branch of our vast educational system which should more attract within its particular sphere the aid and encouragement of the State than adult education. How many must there be in Britain, after the disturbance of two destructive wars, who thirst in later life to learn about the humanities, the history of their country, the philosophies of the human race, and the arts and letters which sustain and are borne forward by the ever-conquering English language? This ranks in my opinion far above science and technical instruction, which are well sustained and not without their rewards in our present system. The mental and moral outlook of free men studying the past with free minds in order to discern the future demands the highest measures which our hard pressed finances can sustain. I have no doubt myself that a man or a woman earnestly seeking in grown-up life to be guided to wide and suggestive knowledge in its largest and most uplifted sphere will make the best of all the pupils in this age of clatter and buzz, of gape and gloat. The appetite of adults to be shown the foundations and processes of thought will never be denied by a British Administration cherishing the continuity of our Island life.

(b) Gilbert Highet: We Cannot Progress Without the Classics

Churchill's battle was for adult education. Thanks to the new grammars, British secondary education was now providing an excellent liberal education, if limited in terms of how many it could reach. But by the late 1970s all that would change. Today, while just over 160 grammar schools remain, it is primarily Britain's private, fee-paying schools that perpetuate an educational model close to the old liberal ideal.[1] Yet even in the independent sector today, apart from a few dissenting voices, the liberal fragments persist largely as an unmoored tradition, rarely consciously linked to the centuries of effort that precede them. The few schools where the British still hand down elements of a liberal education too rarely justify it in those terms and, as such, remain vulnerable to new fashions and the deformation and corruption that any tradition must suffer without renewal in the light of its original principles. If aspects of the practice survive, the tradition that men like Coleridge, Mill, Ruskin and Mansbridge were so conscious of handing on has been decisively broken.

It began in the decline of the classics, which in 1960 were removed as a requirement for entry to the universities of Oxford and Cambridge. By 2003, the British Education Secretary Charles Clarke could publicly ques-

---

[1] Although too rarely acknowledged, this philosophical division between progressive and liberal approaches to education is the major difference, on a national scale if not always on the level of individual schools, between state and independent sectors—and not social class or generosity of funding. The difference is visible in the far greater emphasis in independent schools on developing character and leadership potential and on encouraging competitive sport and music alongside academic lessons—music and games being distinctive features of the original Athenian model. Moreover the academic, subject-specific teaching common to most independent schools is in stark contrast to the child-centred suspicion of didacticism and hostility to subject boundaries prevalent in the state sector. The state has effectively restricted what remains of liberal education to a wealthy elite. This is doubtless one major reason—for parents are harder to fool than politicians—why private education remains remarkably popular in Britain.

tion liberal education's ideals, calling education for its own sake "a bit dodgy" and observing he was "less occupied by classics". In that year, 0.2% of the GCSE examinations sat nationwide were for Latin, while ancient Greek papers accounted for less than 0.1%. By 2006, 183 candidates sat ancient Greek at A-level and just 927 took Latin; the higher education minister, Bill Rammell, said that the falling numbers of Classics students at university was "not necessarily a bad thing". In 2007, the exam board OCR, the last board still setting dedicated Latin and Greek A-level papers, announced that Latin, Greek, and ancient history A-levels were to be merged into a single qualification. Only spirited protests against the move, led by independent school pupils, at which the shadow higher education minister Boris Johnson donned a toga to publicise his personal dismay, saved the ancient history qualification.[2]

Gilbert Highet warned that it would come to this. He was a great Scottish classicist, but found success across the Atlantic in the United States, where he participated in the revival of liberal education enjoyed there throughout this period (on which see the book's final section). Highet wrote of the impending loss of classical knowledge in stark terms in 1954 in *The Migration of Ideas*. He pointed out that Milton, Shakespeare, Keats, Tennyson, Whitman and TS Eliot were all classically trained to a degree already unimaginable by the second half of the twentieth century.

> Now, some misguided educators, both in the United States and in a few other countries, believe that all change is necessarily progress, and that to abolish what is durable is a sure way to improve society.
>
> [...]
>
> I do not believe that the classics and good literature are dying. But I am certain that they have suffered a series of determined attacks from people who profess themselves to be teachers, and that these attacks, as ruthless as they are ill judged, are continuing today.

What would be the result, he asked, of this campaign to kill off the traditional literary education of the West?

Under the constant denigration of good literature—of course not only Greek and Latin but good literature in all languages, including our own—we may expect fewer and fewer good poets, playwrights,

---

2 The Iris Project has been encouraging Latin in UK state schools since 2006 under the visionary leadership of Lorna Robinson. In October 2008, Scotland's Education Secretary Fiona Hyslop also announced her support for returning Latin to the classroom, and in December 2008 Baroness Delyth Morgan, Parliamentary Under Secretary of State for Children, Young People and Families announced a consultation on the place of Latin within the new languages diploma, which could give it some increase in status. But the arguments advanced in Scotland and in the House of Lords with regard to slightly reversing Latin's decline were made only in vocational terms: its value in a science career, or to the learning of modern languages. Some 85% of Britain's state schools offer no Latin courses at all.

198 The School of Freedom

philosophers, storytellers, critics, and teachers to appear among us. One of my most admired colleagues, first my teacher and later my friend, once told me that he was convinced the aim of the educational revolutionaries was "to make everyone else as ignorant as they are themselves." Could that be true? If it were true, do you believe that they might possibly succeed?

(c) CP Snow and FR Leavis: Science Trumps Culture[3]

Science was also gaining new levels of assertiveness. When, between 1956 and 1962, CP Snow and FR Leavis reprised the Huxley-Arnold debate on the centrality of science in education, it was now Snow who stood in Arnold's place, delivering the prestigious Rede Lecture.

Snow was a scientist by training and a novel-writer by profession, and saw himself as able to stand between both worlds and comment on their differences.[4] He protested against the tragic vision of the humanities, arguing that it resisted the potential for social engineering as a means to a better future.

> There is a moral trap which comes through the insight into man's loneliness: it tempts one to sit back, complacent in one's unique tragedy, and let the others go without a meal.
>
> As a group, the scientists fall into that trap less than others. They are inclined to be impatient to see if something can be done: and inclined to think that it can be done, until it's proved otherwise. That is their real optimism, and it's an optimism that the rest of us badly need.

Snow wrote at the height of the Cold War—Khrushchev would proclaim "We will bury you," in November 1956, and in 1959 the crisis over the status of West Berlin, long-simmering, was beginning to come to the boil — and Snow's comments must be seen in the light of his admiration for aspects of the Soviet system, and his naïve disregard for its worst atrocities. He observes in his lecture's peroration that 'We [...] have a good deal to learn from the Russians, if we are not too proud.'

---

3   Sir Charles Percy Snow gave his Rede Lecture, 'The Two Cultures and the Scientific Revolution', in 1959, although an article by him prefiguring the argument, also called 'The Two Cultures', had appeared in the *New Statesman* on 6 October 1956. The lecture was published in 1959 and became much-celebrated. Professor Frank Raymond Leavis's response, the Richmond Lecture, 'Two Cultures? The Significance of CP Snow', was delivered and published in 1962 and later republished in Leavis's final collection of critical essays *Nor Shall My Sword* (1972).

4   His novels, famous at the time, are now scarcely-read; Snow popularised, but did not coin, the phrase 'corridors of power', using it as the title of a 1964 novel, and earlier in *Homecomings* (1954): 'The official world, the corridors of power'. This persistent cliché is now his main literary legacy.

In 1962, the year of Leavis's response, the prominent American conservative William F Buckley would use his magazine, *National Review*, to excoriate Snow for such glib relativism. Referring to an interview Snow gave in February 1962, observing that he could live happily in a Communist society and would find it difficult to choose between living in the America or the Russia of the 1960s, Buckley's elegant phrasing cannot conceal his contempt at what he heard:

> the voice of CP Snow, secure in a BBC studio, informing a subject people whose martyrs are slaughtered every day on their stomachs, stopped by machine gun bullets from crawling on their hands and knees to the West—the voice of Sir Charles telling them that they should not have troubled themselves, since the West is no different from what they are fleeing from, dying of. The voice of the machine, in the age of Science.[5]

Buckley, no one can now deny, was on the right side of this argument. Yet Leavis, sharing Buckley's assessment of Snow's nugatory intellect, although on different grounds, was generally condemned for his oratorically compelling, powerfully-argued but also often *ad hominem* demolition of Snow's case against an education centred on the humanities.

> The peculiar quality of Snow's assurance expresses itself in a pervasive tone; a tone of which one can say that, while only genius could justify it, one cannot readily think of genius adopting it.
>
> [...]
>
> [N]ot only is he not a genius; he is intellectually as undistinguished as it is possible to be. [...] he doesn't know what he means, and doesn't know he doesn't know.
>
> [...]
>
> Snow's argument proceeds with so extreme a naïveté of unconsciousness and irresponsibility that to call it a movement of thought is to flatter it.

However, it would be mistaken to portray Leavis as offering nothing more than character assassination. Nor is he reactionary or backward-looking in his lecture. It is because Leavis sees the enduring necessity of the liberal education tradition and its unique capacity to humanise our science-framed future, much as Matthew Arnold had before him, that he stands up for its importance, even at the cost of his own public reputation.

> I haven't chosen to say that mankind will need all its traditional wisdom; that might suggest a kind of conservatism that, so far as I am concerned, is the enemy. What we need, and shall continue to need not

5   'The Voice of Sir Charles', *National Review*, May 22, 1962, p. 358. Reprinted in *Cultures in Conflict: Perspectives on the Snow-Leavis controversy* (1964), ed. Cornelius and Saint Vincent.

less, is something with the livingness of the deepest vital instinct; as intelligence, a power—rooted, strong in experience, and supremely human—of creative response to the new challenges of time; something that is alien to either of Snow's cultures.

[...]

[T]here is a prior human achievement of collaborative creation, a more basic work of the mind of man (and more than the mind), one without which the triumphant erection of the scientific edifice would not have been possible: that is, the creation of the human world, including language. It is one we cannot rest on as something done in the past. It lives in the living creative response to change in the present.

If Leavis's devastating response lacks moderation, it was perhaps because he felt himself on the losing side, a man throwing all he had onto the battlefield in the hope of snatching victory from the jaws of defeat.

[H]ow mild a statement it is to say that *The Two Cultures* exhibits an utter lack of intellectual distinction and an embarrassing vulgarity of style.

[...]

Snow is, of course, a—no, I can't say that; he isn't; Snow thinks of himself as a novelist. [...] [A]s a novelist he doesn't exist; he doesn't begin to exist. He can't be said to know what a novel is.

Leavis, over-reaching in his invective and out of step with an intellectual mood dangerously sympathetic to the enemies of Western civilisation, failed to make his case. The man once described by GH Bantock as 'the last of the great renaissance humanists'[6] went down fighting, but the battle went against him, as it soon would against the tradition he represented.

(d) GH Bantock:
The Closing of the Grammars is the Closing of Minds

The system of state grammar schools and secondary modern schools instituted in Britain after 1944 had been imperfect; in many ways it had reinstated the divisions criticised by Tawney, marking out the liberal arts as the professional school of the brain-working classes. But in the reaction against this inequality, rather than looking back to Mansbridge and Tawney and offering a liberal education to all, comprehensivisation in the 1970s consolidated a new theory of education in British schools, rooted in the romanticism of Jean-Jacques Rousseau and laid out for British educators in the Plowden Report of 1967.

6   *Studies in the History of Educational Theory*, II, 'The Minds and the Masses' (1984), p. 342.

The school sets out deliberately to devise the right environment for children, to allow them to be themselves and to develop in the way and at the pace appropriate to them. It tries to equalise opportunities and to compensate for handicaps. It lays special stress on individual discovery, on first hand experience and on opportunities for creative work. It insists that knowledge does not fall into neatly separate compartments and that work and play are not opposite but complementary.[7]

Education towards a liberal ideal and without reference to utility, centred on a shared canon and the skills of thought, language and number, seeking the creation of harmonious character was replaced by a focus on career preparation, social utility and equality of respect for all courses that ultimately echoed CS Lewis's warning of modern education as a kind of farming in which pupils were dehumanised. Instead of preparing men and women for freedom, economic production units were to be processed for maximal utility to the state, made productive, right-thinking, psychologically "healthy" in the sense of being docile. In the words that Jean-Jacques Rousseau gives to his imaginary pupil Émile,

Conseillez-nous, gouvernez-nous, nous serons dociles: tant que je vivrai j'aurai besoin de vous.[8]

In search of equality, education was levelled — and, as Quintilian would have argued, and the worker's education movement had more recently proven — without need. Socialisation, psychotherapeutic introspection and self-maintenance and vocational training became mainstream goals for schooling; the new democratic age did not seek to produce orators, but well-trained consumers.

Black Paper 1975: The Fight for Education is a collection of essays that protest against the destruction of the grammars. They come from both sides of the political spectrum, including such luminaries as Iris Murdoch, still then a self-identifying socialist and nevertheless resisting the supposedly progressive reform: 'Why should socialist policy, of all things, be so grossly unjust to the underprivileged clever child, avid to learn, able to learn, and under non-selective education likely to pass in relaxed idle boredom those precious years when strenuous learning is a joy and when the whole intellectual and moral future of the human being is at stake?'

GH Bantock's essay in the same volume, 'Progressivism and the Content of Education', sees that the triumph of the comprehensive effectively ends a tradition of grammar schooling dating back more than a thousand years.

---

7   Volume I, Part 5, Chapter 15, Paragraph 505.
8   'Advise us, govern us, we shall be docile: I shall need you for as long as I am alive.' *Émile, ou, De L'Éducation*, (1762), Book V.

The essential contrast between the old and the new education can be expressed in this way. The old, which, granted, has evolved over the centuries since the time when Erasmus exclaimed that everything worth knowing was contained in the literature of Greece and Rome, has been based on the autonomy of the culture as something to be come to terms with, submitted to and grappled with in its own terms; the new, whether at the behest of 'Nature' or the collectivity, implies all the restrictiveness of immediate relevance [...]. [...] What has taken place is a shift in man's metaphysical image of himself—from a self that has to be made, to a self that simply has to be expressed. Rousseau's assertion of the importance of childhood as a state in its own right rather than as a potential for actualization marks—paradoxical!—a diminution in childhood itself.

From now on, 'Liberal' had different, politicised connotations. The parties of Westminster concerned themselves with pragmatic questions of how to improve educational outputs, and did not worry enough that the theory under which they laboured might be unworthy of their efforts, however skilful. The defense of grammar schools would now be made in terms of social mobility, and not the forgotten educational model that they had championed, a model that should have been widened, as had happened in the past, and not discarded in the rush to tear down what could not be granted immediately to all.

Chapter XIII

Returning to First Principles

Since the closure of the state grammar schools, several serious attempts have been made to mount a theoretically-based counter-attack to the rejection of the tradition. Given the role of rationalism in ending the reign of liberal education, which has always been defined more by praxis than theory, this amounts to an ingenious attempt to use the strength of the opponent against itself, and such justifications help to bolster the case for a revival of the tradition, such as occurred in Cicero's Rome, in Alcuin's Carolingian age, and throughout Renaissance Europe. Reprinted here in full are two significant philosophical arguments that support the restoration of our lost tradition of education. Also deserving of attention is another of Michael Oakeshott's essays, 'Education: The Engagement and its Frustration' (1971), as well as Roger Scruton's essay 'Modern Philosophy and the Neglect of Æsthetics' (1987), arguing that æsthetics must have a central place in philosophical thought.[1] Maurice Cowling's Mill and Liberalism *(1963) remains a powerful attack on Mill's philosophy and the reaction against tradition that it has led to – although, as we have seen, Mill himself spoke out in favour of preserving liberal education at least on one occasion.*

(a) Michael Oakeshott

A Place of Learning (1974)[2]

Un début dans la vie humaine. Paul Valéry

I have crossed half the world to find myself in familiar surroundings: a place of learning. The occasion is a cheerful one: the celebration of the centenary of your foundation. And I hope you will not think me patronising if

---

1   Oakeshott's essay was reprinted in *Education and the Development of Reason*, ed. Dearden, Hearst and Peters (1972) and in *The Voice of Liberal Learning*, ed. Timothy Fuller (1989; 2001). Scruton's essay was first published in the *Times Literary Supplement*, 5 June 1987 and reprinted in *The Philosopher on Dover Beach* (1990).

2   Presented as the Abbott Memorial lecture in the Social Sciences at Colorado College, September 1974. Reproduced in *Colorado College Studies 12*, 1975 and reprinted in *The Voice of Liberal Learning*, ed. Timothy Fuller (1989; 2001).

I first express my admiration for you and all others who, through the centuries, sailing under the flag of the Liberal Arts, have, with becoming humility, summoned succeeding generations to the enjoyment of their human inheritance. But it is an occasion also for reflection. And I have been honoured with an invitation to say something about the educational engagement which you and others have undertaken and to reconsider this adventure in relation to present circumstances. This is a large order, and you will forgive me if I respond to it only in part. Education is a transaction between teachers and learners, but I shall be concerned only with learners, with what there is to be learned and (in the first place) with learning as the distinguishing mark of a human being. A man is what he learns to become: this is the human condition.

1.

We are concerned, then, with ourselves and what we may be said to know about ourselves. This comes to us, first, in what purports to be information of various sorts. We are informed, for example, that human beings are the most intricate of living organisms, that they have evolved over millions of years from less complicated organisations of chemical constituents, that each is endowed with an inherited genetic character, subject to modification, which by means of complex processes governs its movements, and that these movements are continuously directed to the self-maintenance of the organism and to the survival of the species. Alternatively, human beings are alleged to be sentient creatures all of whose movements and utterances are expressions of a desire for pleasure and an aversion from pain. We are told, further, that Man was created by God, bidden to people the earth, endowed into an unlimited right to exploit its resources and directed not to be idle. And a human being has been said to be an immortal soul of unknown destiny lodged for a time in a mortal body. And so on.

Now, each of these statements about human beings is capable of elaboration in which its meaning may become clearer, thus allowing us to consider it from the point of view of whatever truth or error it may contain. They may all turn out to be (in some sense) true, or they may all be convicted of some error or obscurity. But with conclusions of this sort we are not now concerned. What concerns us is that each is itself a human utterance expressing a human understanding of the character of a human being, and that the capacity to make such utterances, whether they be true or false, itself postulates a man who is something besides what these, or any other such statements, allege him to be. They postulate what I shall call a 'free' man.

A human being may become 'free' in many different respects, and I shall suggest later that becoming educated is itself an emancipation; and human beings may also achieve various other degrees of what may be 'autonomy'; but I am concerned now with the 'freedom' (so to call it) of which a human being cannot divest himself or be deprived without temporarily or permanently ceasing to be human.

What, then, are we to understand by this 'freedom' inherent in being human and postulated in his capacity to make statements about himself? It is often identified with his having what is called a 'free will'. This is usually the case when what is being considered is the kind of utterance we call an action. But it is not a very satisfactory way of speaking. It is difficult to imagine what an 'unfree' will would be. And if what is being said is that human actions and utterances, properly speaking, are 'free' because they are willed (that is, because they are the outcomes of desires and are understandable only in terms of wants), then we are left with the question, in virtue of what must desiring be considered necessarily to be a 'free' activity? But this inherent human 'freedom', exhibited when a man makes or entertains statements about himself, is perhaps better identified in terms of his ability to understand, or (of course) misunderstand, himself. And he is sometimes said to have this ability in virtue of having, or being, a mind as well as a body. We must, however, be careful how we construe this distinction. What it distinguishes is not two things but, on the one hand, a process or organisation of processes the outcome of which is, for example, blue eyes or genetic resistance to malaria, and on the other hand the ability to understand such a process in terms of its regularities, to identify the substances involved and to discern how they are related to one another. In short, the distinction being noticed here is between a chemical process and a biochemist understanding and explaining (well or ill) what is going on in a chemical process. For mind is not itself a chemical process, nor is it a mysterious x left over, unexplained, after the biochemist has reached the end of his chemical explanation; it is what does the explaining. A geneticist, for example, cannot be merely a clerk who records the utterances of his own genes; such a record would not constitute a contribution to a science of genetics, and in any case genes are incapable of such utterances about themselves, they can make only blue eyes or a propensity to live a long time. Mind, here, is the intelligent activity in which a man may understand and explain processes which cannot understand and explain themselves.

But this is only one aspect of the matter. Intelligence is not merely concerned to understand physiological processes. Mind is made of perceptions, recognitions, thoughts of all kinds; of emotions, sentiments, affections, deliberations and purposes, and of actions which are responses to what is understood to be going on. It is the author not only of the intelligible world in which a human being lives but also of his self-conscious relationship to that world, a self-consciousness which may rise to the condition of a self-understanding. And this inherent 'freedom' of a human being lies not only in his ability to make statements expressing his understanding of himself and in the world being for him what he understands it to be, but in his being what he understands himself to be. A human being is 'free', not because he has 'free will', but because he is *in* himself what he is *for* himself.

Now, this reading of the human condition is familiar enough. It is embedded in the epic and dramatic literatures of the western world and in the writings of historians: this is how human beings appear in Homer, in the Sagas of Scandinavia, in Shakespeare and Racine, in Livy and in Gibbon. And not even the driest of modern behaviourists or the most blinkered neurobiologist is able wholly to reject it without rejecting himself. There have been times when this reading of human character was not only accepted but was embraced with enthusiasm. It was recognised as a glorious distinction to be welcomed, to be explored, cultivated and enjoyed; it was said to constitute the dignity of man. But, even then, this condition of being intelligent was seen to carry with it a penalty: the possibility of being wise entails the possibility of being stupid. Moreover, such a man is unavoidably responsible for his thoughts, utterances and actions. He cannot plead that his thoughts are caused by his inherited genetic character because thoughts have reasons and not causes and these reasons are other thoughts. He cannot plead that his utterances are not his own but are words put into his mouth by a god or that they are merely electrical discharges of his brain; they have meanings for which he is responsible and are judged in terms of whether or not they make sense. He cannot plead that his actions are not his own but are merely the outcomes of irrepressible biological urges, like the branches thrown out by a tree: these actions also have meanings and are chosen responses to understood situations.

But further, because this 'freedom' inherent in the human condition is not gratuitous and has to be paid for in responsibility, it has been viewed with misgivings and even counted a misery to be escaped, if only escape were possible. How much less burdensome to be incapable of error, of stupidity, of hatred and of wrong doing, even if this meant the surrender of truth, wisdom, love and virtue. But it is impossible. The very contemplation of such an escape announces its impossibility; only mind can regret having to think. And instead of deploring our condition we would be better employed considering exactly what is the price we pay for our unsought and inescapable 'freedom'.

I have called this price 'responsibility'. But the word has an inappropriate moral overtone. It suggests that we might refuse to pay for the freedom inherent in intelligent activity and that this refusal would somehow be a dereliction of duty; whereas (in the first place) it would be merely a failure to recognise a necessary condition. What distinguishes a human being, indeed what constitutes a human being, is not merely his having to think, but his thoughts, his beliefs, doubts, understandings, his awareness of his own ignorance, his wants, preferences, choices, sentiments, emotions, purposes and his expression of them in utterances or actions which have meanings; and the necessary condition of all or any of this is that he must have *learned* it. The price of the intelligent activity which constitutes being human is learning. When the human condition is said to be burdensome what is being pointed to is not having to think, to speak and to act (instead of merely *being* like a stone, or growing like a tree) but the impossibility of thinking or feeling without having slowly and often painfully learned to think something. And the inherent freedom of a human being lies in his thoughts and his emotions having had to be learned; for learning is something which each man does and can only do for himself.

Now, this inseparability of learning and being human is central to our understanding of ourselves. It means that none of us is born human; each is what he learns to become. It means that what characterises a man is what he has actually learned to perceive, to think and to do, and that the important differences between human beings are differences in respect of what they have actually learned. There is little doubt that our ability to learn has increased during the last million years or so, and that this ability is greater at some periods of our individual lives than at others, and perhaps also there are some genetic differences in our several abilities to learn; but the human significances of these changes and differences lies only in their reflection in what a man has actually learned to think, to imagine and to do; for this is what he is. And it means, also, that these differences are not merely those of more or of less success in learning, of better or worse achievements in becoming human, but are also incommensurable differences of human individuality. In short, this connection between learning and being human means that each man is his own self-enacted history; and the expression 'human nature' stands only for our common and inescapable engagement: to become by learning.

But what is this engagement I have called 'learning' in which alone we may become human? Let me notice, first, an account of the matter which, whatever its shortcomings, is at least clear. A biologist will tell us that a living organism (an octopus, for example) exists in relation to its environment. The organism is a continuously changing chemical structure sensitive to its circumstances and equipped to react to the stimulus of its surroundings. Its reactions are movements, not always successful, favouring its survival. But the inputs it receives from its environment are not uniform or necessarily themselves favourable, and in order to survive, the organism must be versatile in its reactions. Indeed, it is equipped with mechanisms which favour and record for future use successful or 'correct' reactions and suppress or disfavour those which have been unsuccessful or 'incorrect'. This process in which an organism adapts itself and records its reactions to its environment is called 'learning'; indeed, it is spoken of as a process of acquiring, storing and retrieving useful information and in a man it is said to be only more versatile than it is in an octopus.

Now, there is no need to question this account of metabolic and evolutionary change, rich in anthropomorphic analogy though it be. Nor need we doubt that some such process goes on in the early days of our post-natal existence. But clearly the learning in which we may become human is very different from this process of organic adaptation to circumstances. Indeed, this is not a recognisable description of the learning in which the biologist came to discern and to understand this organic process. Is Dr. Watson's discovery of the helical structure of DNA molecules properly to be described as itself a chemical reaction to an environmental input which promoted his biological survival?

The learning we are concerned with is a self-conscious engagement. It is not an induced reaction to a fortuitous environmental pressure but a self-imposed task inspired by the intimations of what there is to learn (that is, by awareness of our own ignorance) and by a wish to understand. Human learning is a reflective engagement in which what is learned is not merely a detached fragment of information but is understood or misunderstood and is expressed in words which have meanings. It has nothing to do with organic survival and much of it has little to do even with that selective 'getting on in the world' which is the human counterpart of organic homeostasis; it is concerned with perceptions, ideas, beliefs, emotions, sensibilities, recognitions, discriminations, theorems, with all (in short) which goes to constitute a human condition.

And in these respects human learning is distinguished also from some other experiences, or alleged experiences, with which it is sometimes confused. It is not acquiring habits or being trained to perform tricks or functions; it is acquiring something that you can use because you understand it. Further, the feelings of euphoria, of illumination or of depression which are induced by drugs, by flashing lights or electrical currents are no more learned than the unconsciousness induced by an anæsthetic, and they are no more significant; they make no contribution whatever to the achievement of a human condition. Indeed, in so far as they suggest that this condition can be acquired by chemical stimulus or by magic they obstruct the arduous self-conscious engagement of learning in which alone we may become human. Being bewitched is not learning. Nor is learning a teleological process in which a suppositious seed of *humanitas* in each of us grows and realises or develops what is already potential in it. The nearest we can get to what may be called a distinguishing 'natural' human equipment is self-consciousness; but that also is learned, although it begins to be learned very early in our individual lives. And while self-consciousness is the condition of all human intellectual and imaginative achievement, the vast variety of this achievement cannot be said to be potential in it.

Let me sum up this part of what I have to say. A human life is not a process in which a living organism grows to maturity, succeeds in accommodating itself to its surroundings or perishes. It is, in the first place, an adventure in which an individual consciousness confronts the world he inhabits, responds to what Henry James called 'the ordeal of consciousness'[3], and thus enacts and discloses himself. This engagement is an adventure in a precise sense. It has no preordained course to follow: with every thought and action a human being lets go a mooring and puts out to sea on a self-chosen but largely unforeseeable course. And it has no preordained destination: there is no substantive perfect man or human life upon which he may model his conduct. It is a predicament, not a journey. A human being is a 'history' and he makes this 'history' for himself out of his responses to the vicissitudes he encounters. The world he inhabits is composed, not of 'things', but of occurrences which he is aware of in terms of what they mean to him and to which he must respond in terms of what he understands them to be.[4] Some of these occurrences he learns to recognise as expressions of human thoughts and emotions — stories, poems, works of art, musical compositions, landscapes, human actions, utterances and gestures, religious beliefs, enquiries, sciences, procedures, practices and other artifacts of all sorts, which again, he is aware of only in terms of his understanding of them. Others, he learns to recognise as intelligent persons whom he is aware of in terms of who and what he understands them to be and to whom he is related in terms of transactions and utterances

3   [Editors' note] See for instance James's preface to *The Wings of the Dove*: 'a sick young woman, at the whole course of whose disintegration and the whole ordeal of whose consciousness one would have quite honestly to assist.' See also Dorothea Krook-Gilead's *The Ordeal of Consciousness in Henry James* (1962).

4   [Author's original note] Moreover, human beings (although they do not have the god-like power to confer self-consciousness where it is absent) do have the power to individualise and endow into historical life things and creatures which are not themselves historical: horses, dogs, trees.

which have meanings and may be understood or misunderstood. In short, he inhabits a wholly human world, not because it contains nothing but human beings and their artifacts, but because everything in it is known to him in terms of what it means to him. And he is condemned to be a learner because meanings have to be learned. Whatever a man thinks or says or does is unavoidably what he has learned (well or ill) to think, to say or to do. Even a human death is something learned.

2.

For a human being, then, learning is a life-long engagement; the world he inhabits is a place of learning. But, further, human beings, in so far as they have understood their condition, have always recognised special places, occasions and circumstances deliberately designed for and devoted to learning, the most notable of which are the human family, school and university. The human family (whatever form it may take) is a practice devised, not for the procreation of children, nor merely for their protection, but for the early education of newcomers to the human scene: it recognises that learning begins slowly and takes time. School and university are unmistakable; they are successive stages in this deliberate engagement to learn, and it is with these we are concerned.

Now, the distinctive feature of such a special place of learning is, first, that those who occupy it are recognised and recognise themselves preeminently as learners; although they may be much else besides. Secondly in it learning is a declared engagement to learn something in particular. Those who occupy it are not merely 'growing up', and they are not there merely to 'improve their minds' or to 'learn to think'; such unspecified activities are as impossible as an orchestra which plays no music in particular. Further, what is to be learned in such a place does not present itself by chance or arise circumstantially out of whatever may happen to be going on; it is recognised as a specified task to be undertaken and pursued with attention, patience and determination, the learner being aware of what he is doing. And thirdly, learning here is not a limited undertaking in which what is learned is learned merely up to the point where it can be put to some extrinsic use; learning itself is the engagement and it has its own standards of achievement and excellence. Consequently, what is special about such a place or circumstances is its seclusion, its detachment from what Hegel called the *hic et nunc*, the here and now, of current living.[5] Each of us is born in a corner of the earth and at a particular moment in historic

5   [Editors' note] See also Alexandre Kojève's lectures, in *Introduction to the Reading of Hegel* (1980; from lectures given 1934-1939), Chapter 5, 'A Note on Eternity, Time and the Concept', p. 111: 'even while existing in space-time, the being endowed with freedom must be able to *detach* itself from the *hic et nunc*, to rise *above* it, to take up a *position* in relation to it.'

time, lapped round with locality. But school and university are places apart where a declared learner is emancipated from the limitations of his local circumstances and from the wants he may happen to have acquired and is moved by intimations of what he has never yet dreamed. He finds himself invited to pursue satisfactions he has never yet imagined or wished for. They are, then, sheltered places where excellences may be heard because the din of local partialities is no more than a distant rumble. They are places where a learner is initiated into what there is to be learned.

But what is there for a human being to learn? A large part of human conduct is, and always has been, concerned with exploiting the resources of the earth for the satisfaction of human wants, and much of human learning is concerned, directly or indirectly, with this endlessly proliferating intelligent engagement. And it is genuine learning. An otter may be equipped with what for want of a better word we call an instinct which enables it to catch fish, a beaver in response to some biological urge may build a dam and an eagle may swoop down and carry off a lamb; but a fisherman must learn to catch fish and he learns to do so well or ill and with a variety of techniques, the engineers who designed and built the Boulder Dam were equipped with something more than a biological urge, and to breed sheep for meat or wool is an art that has to be learned. In respect of being concerned to exploit the resources of the earth a current human being is, then, an inheritor of a vast variety of instrumental skills and practices which have to be learned if they are to yield the satisfactions they are designed to yield. Moreover, the inventor and the user of these skills and practices is not Man or Society; each is the discovery or invention of assignable men, a Prometheus, a Vulcan, a Bessemer or an Edison. It is not Man or some abstraction called 'medical science' which cures the sick; it is an individual doctor who has himself learned his art from some assignable teachers. There is no such thing as 'social learning' or 'collective understanding'. The arts and practices we share with one another are nowhere to be found save in the understandings of living, individual adepts who have learned them.

And further, the satisfaction of human wants is pursued in transactions between human beings in which they compete or cooperate with one another. To seek the satisfaction of a want is to enter into relationships with other human beings. This human association is not the interaction of the components of a process, nor is it an unspecified gregariousness or sociability; it is made up of a variety of different kinds of relationships, each a specific practice whose conditions must be learned and understood if its advantages are to be enjoyed. And incomparably the most useful of these relationships is that which subsists between those who speak a common language in which to communicate their wants and to conduct the bargains in which they may be satisfied. Such a language, like all other conditions of human association, has to be learned.

To be human, to have wants and to try to satisfy them, is, then, to have the use of particular skills, instrumental practices and relationships. There is no action which is not a subscription to some art, and utterance is impossible without a language. These skills, practices and relationships have to be learned. And since this learning, so far as it goes, is genuine and may be extensive it is no surprise that there should be special places devoted to it, each concerned to initiate learners into some particular instrumental art or practice and often equipped with the opportunity of 'learning on the job', as it is called: Medical schools, Law schools, language schools, schools of journalism or photography, schools where one may learn to cook, to drive an automobile or run a bassoon factory, and even polytechnics where a variety of such instrumental skills may be learned.

There is much more that might be said about this activity of exploiting the resources of the earth, of the arts and relationships used in the satisfaction of human wants and the learning these entail. It is certainly genuine learning, although the special places devoted to it are appropriately limited in their aims and in their seclusion from considerations of utility. To learn an instrumental art is not merely being trained to perform a trick; it entails understanding what you are doing. And learning a practice is not merely acquiring a mechanical contrivance and knowing how to work it. A human art is never fixed and finished; it has to be used and it is continuously modified in use. Even using a language to communicate wants is itself an inventive engagement. But I do not propose to explore further this engagement in learning; there is something more important for us to consider. We catch a glimpse of it when we recognise that choosing wants to satisfy is also something that has to be learned and that the conditions to be subscribed to in making such choices are not the terms of the instrumental arts and practices in which chosen wants may be conveniently satisfied. It is never enough to say of a human want: 'I know how to satisfy it and I have the power to do so'. There is always something else to consider. But what thus comes into view is not merely an extension of the field of instrumental learning but an altogether different engagement of critical self-understanding in which we relate ourselves, not to our inheritance of instrumental arts, but to the continuous intellectual adventure in which human beings have sought to identify and to understand themselves.

Now, to recognise oneself in terms of one's wants, to recognise the world as material to be shaped and used in satisfying wants, to recognise others as competitors or cooperators in this enterprise and to recognise our inheritance of arts and practices, including a common language, as valuable instruments for satisfying wants—all this is, unquestionably, a self-understanding. It gives *an* answer to the question, Who am I? And indeed there are some who would persuade us that this is all we know or can know about ourselves and that all other thoughts human beings have had about themselves and the world are idle fancies and all other relationships are shadowy reflections of this relationship. But they refute themselves. In purporting to make a true statement about human beings and their relationships they identify themselves as something other than mere seekers after contingent satisfactions; they assume a relationship between themselves and those whom they address which is not that of exploiters of the resources of the earth but that of persons capable of considering the truth or falsehood of a theorem.[6]

But be that how it may, it is unquestionable that human beings, without denying their identities as exploiters of the resources of the earth, have always thought of themselves as something other than this and that they have been tireless in their explorations of these other identities. They have engaged in manifold activities other than this—adventures of intellectual enquiry, of moral discrimination and of emotional and imaginative insight; they have explored a vast variety of relationships other than this—moral, intellectual, emotional, civil; and they have perceived, dimly or clearly, that this identity as exploiters of the resources of the earth is not only evanescent and insubstantial when set beside these others but is itself conditional upon them. They have recognised that these understandings of themselves, and these valuations of occurrences (like everything else human) are themselves human inventions and can be enjoyed only in learning. Even in the most difficult circumstances, overwhelmed by the exigencies of the moment (life in the covered wagon, for example), they have carried these identities with them and imparted them to their children if only in songs and stories. Whenever opportunity has occurred they have set aside special places and occasions devoted to this learning, and until recently schools and universities were just such places of learning, sheltered enough from the demands of utility to be undistracted in their concern with these adventures and expressions of human self-understanding.

---

6   [Author's original note] When Francis Bacon identified human beings as exploiters of the resources of the earth and language as a means of communicating information about wants he added that this identity had been imposed upon us by God—thus identifying human beings *also* in relation to God. And even Karl Marx (inconsistently) recognised something called 'scientific' enquiry independent of the current conditions of productive undertaking.

3.

This, then, is what we are concerned with: adventures in human self-understanding. Not the bare protestation that a human being is a self-conscious, reflective intelligence and that he does not live by bread alone, but the actual enquiries, utterances and actions in which human beings have expressed their understanding of the human condition. This is the stuff of what has come to be called a 'liberal' education—'liberal' because it is liberated from the distracting business of satisfying contingent wants.

But why should we be concerned with it? If it purported to provide reliable information about 'human nature' our concern would be intelligible. But it does not. There is no such thing as 'human nature'; there are only men, women, and children responding gaily or reluctantly, reflectively or not so reflectively, to the ordeal of consciousness, who exist only in terms of their self-understandings. Nor is being human itself a special instrumental skill like that of an electrical engineer. And if our concern is with human self-understanding, why all this paraphernalia of learning? Is this not something we each do for ourselves? Yes, humanly each of us is self-made; but not out of nothing, and not by the light of nature. The world is full of home-made human beings, but they are rickety constructions of impulses ready to fall apart in what is called an 'identity crisis'. Being human is an historic adventure which has been going on since the earth rose out of the sea, and we are concerned with this paraphernalia of learning because it is the only way we have of participating in this adventure. The ancient Greek exhortation, Know Thyself, meant learn to know thyself. But it was not an exhortation to buy a book on psychology and study it; it meant, contemplate and learn from what men, from time to time, have made of this engagement of learning to be a man.

Human self-understanding is, then, inseparable from learning to participate in what is called a 'culture'. It is useful to have a word which stands for the whole of what an associated set of human beings have created for themselves beyond the evanescent satisfaction of their wants, but we must not be misled by it. A culture is not a doctrine or a set of consistent teachings or conclusions about a human life. It is not something we can set before ourselves as the subject of learning, any more than we can set self-understanding before ourselves as something to be learned; it is that which is learned in everything we may learn. A culture, particularly one such as ours, is a continuity of feelings, perceptions, ideas, engagements, attitudes etc. pulling in different directions, often critical of one another and contingently related to one another so as to compose, not a doctrine, but what I shall call a conversational encounter. Ours, for example, accommodates not only the lyre of Apollo but also the pipes of Pan, the call of the wild; not only the poet but also the physicist; not only the majestic metropolis of Augustinian theology but also the 'greenwood' of Franciscan Christianity. A culture comprises unfinished intellectual and emotional journeyings, expeditions now abandoned but known to us in the tattered maps left behind by the explorers; it is composed of lighthearted adventures, of relationships invented and explored in exploit or in drama, of myths and stories and poems expressing fragments of human self-understanding, of gods worshipped, of responses to the mutability of the world and of encounters with death. And it reaches us, as it reached generations before ours, neither as long-ago terminated specimens of human adventure, nor as an accumulation of human achievements we are called upon to accept, but as a manifold of invitations to look, to listen and to reflect. Learning here is not merely acquiring information (*that* produces only what Nietzsche called a 'culture philistine'), nor is it merely 'improving one's mind'; it is learning to recognise some specific invitations to encounter particular adventures in human self-understanding.

A man's culture is an historic contingency, but since it is all he has he would be foolish to ignore it because it is not composed of eternal verities. And it is itself a contingent flow of intellectual and emotional adventures, a mixture of old and new where the new is often a backward swerve to pick up what has been temporarily forgotten; a mixture of the emergent and the recessive; of the substantial and the somewhat flimsy, of the commonplace, the refined and the magnificent. And since learning here is not merely becoming aware of a so-called cultural inheritance but encountering and seeking to understand some of its specific invitations, a special place devoted to such learning is constituted only in terms of what it is believed there is to learn. And, of course, this belief is itself a response to what may be called the 'educational' invitations of the culture. To talk of being 'culturally conditioned' is rubbish; a man is his culture, and what he is he has had to learn to become.

4.

The wandering scholars who, in the twelfth century, took the road to Paris, to Bologna, to Chartres or to Toulouse were, often unknown to themselves, seeking within the notions of the time, a 'liberal' education; they are our forebears in this adventure. You and I were born in the twelfth century and although we have travelled far we still bear the marks of our birth-time. But when two centuries later the expression 'liberal studies' acquired a specific meaning it stood for an encounter with a somewhat remote culture which was slowly being retrieved from neglect — the Greek and Latin culture of antiquity. Some of the achievements of this ancient civilisation had never been lost: the Latin language as a medium of communication, some useful information (mostly legal and medical) and some notable pieces of writing. But the educational adventure of the fourteenth century sprang from an ever more extended recovery of this almost lost culture which revealed itself not only to have been one of great intellectual splendour, variety and reflective energy but also to be one in which a man of the fourteenth century could identify himself and which offered him a wealth of hitherto unheard of invitations to explore and to understand himself: languages recognised as investments in thought; epic, dramatic, lyric and historical literatures which gave a new dimension to human relationships, emotions, aspirations and conduct; enquiries (including those of the early theologians of Christianity) which suggested new directions for human reflection. Thus, 'learning' was identified with coming to understand the intimations of a human life displayed in an historic culture of remarkable splendour and lucidity and with the invitation to recognise oneself in terms of this culture. This was an education which promised and afforded liberation from the here and now of current engagements, from the muddle, the crudity, the sentimentality, the intellectual poverty and the emotional morass of ordinary life. And so it continues to this day. This education has had often to be rescued from the formalism into which it degenerated. Its centre of gravity moved from the culture of antiquity but without any firm settlement elsewhere. We have seen, sometimes regretfully, bits of this education fall away, having lost their compelling interest. It has been extended to include new and substantial vernacular languages and literatures. It has accommodated, somewhat reluctantly, the novel and still inadequately self-understood enquiry which has absorbed so much of the intellectual energy of modern times, namely the natural sciences. And it has had to resist the seductive advances of enemies dressed up as friends. And what now of its present condition?

The engagement has survived. We do not yet live in the ashes of a great adventure which has burnt itself out. Its self-understanding is not at present very conspicuous, its self-confidence is fluctuating and often misplaced, its credit is stretched and it has borrowed when it would have been better to economise, but it has not been lacking in serious self-examination. The torch is still alight and there are still some hands to grasp it. But I shall not dwell upon its present vitality, such as it is; our concern is with its infirmities and with those which may be counted as self-betrayals — not to censure them but to try to understand them.

Its most naïve self-betrayal is merely to have listened to the seductive voice of the world urging it, in the name of 'relevance' to take up with extraneous concerns and even to alter course. When, like Ulysses, we should have stopped our ears with wax and bound ourselves to the mast of our own identity, we have been beguiled, not only by words but by inducements. To open a School of Business, to undertake the training of journalists or corporation lawyers seem harmless enough concessions to modernity; they may be defended by the specious argument that they certainly entail learning, they give a place of liberal learning an attractive image of 'relevance' and the corruption involved may be written off as negligible. Events, however, hardly confirm this optimism. Having no proper part in liberal learning, these appealing divergencies are difficult to contain; they undermine rather than assail the engagement. Their virtue is to be evanescent and contemporary; if they are not up-to-date they are worthless. And this unqualified modernity rubs off on the proper concern with languages, with literatures and with histories which are thus edged into the study of only what is current in a culture. History is contracted into what is called contemporary history, languages come to be recognised as means of contemporary communication, and in literature the book which 'verbalises what everyone is thinking now' comes to be preferred, on that account, to anything else.

But the real assault upon liberal learning comes from another direction; not in the risky undertaking to equip learners for some, often prematurely chosen, profession, but in the belief that 'relevance' demands that every learner should be recognised as nothing but a role-performer in a so-called 'social system' and the consequent surrender of learning (which is the concern of individual persons) to 'socialisation': the doctrine that because the current here and now is very much more uniform than it used to be, education should recognise and promote this uniformity. This is not a recent self-betrayal; it is the theme of those wonderful lectures of Nietzsche on the *Future of our Educational Institutions* delivered in Basel a century ago in which he foresaw the collapse which now threatens us. And although this may seem to be very much a matter of doctrine, of merely how education is thought about and spoken of, and to have very little to do with what may actually go on in a place of learning, it is the most insidious of all corruptions. It not only strikes at the heart of liberal learning, it portends the abolition of man.[7]

But if these are the cruder subversions of liberal learning there are others, more subtle but hardly less damaging. It has come to be thought of as a 'general' education; that is, as learning not only liberated from the here and now of current engagements but liberated also from an immediate concern with anything specific to be learned. Learning here is said to be 'learning to think for oneself' or to be the cultivation of 'intelligence' or of

7   [Editors' note] CS Lewis's *The Abolition of Man* qv.

certain intellectual and moral aptitudes — the ability to 'think logically' or 'deliberatively', the ability not to be deceived by irrelevance in argument, to be courageous, patient, careful, accurate or determined; the ability to read attentively and to speak lucidly, and so on.

And, of course, all these and more are aptitudes and virtues that a learner may hope to acquire or to improve. But neither they, nor self-understanding itself, can be made the subject of learning. A culture is not a set of abstract aptitudes; it is composed of substantive expressions of thought, emotion, belief, opinion, approval and disapproval, of moral and intellectual discriminations, of enquiries and investigations, and learning is coming to understand and respond to these substantive expressions of thought as invitations to think and to believe. Or, this word 'general' is used to identify and to recommend an education concerned, indeed, with the substance of a culture, but so anxious that everything shall receive mention that it can afford no more than a fleeting glimpse of anything in particular. Here learning amounts to little more than recognition; it never achieves the level of an encounter, It is the vague and fragmentary equipment of the 'culture philistine'.

Nevertheless, a place of liberal learning is rarely without a shape which purports to specify what there is to be learned. And its present shape in most such places bears witness both to the ancient lineage of the engagement and to the changes our culture has undergone in recent centuries. The natural sciences, mathematics, the humanities and the social sciences — these are the lineaments of this education as it comes to us now. Let us briefly consider these constituents.

Liberal learning is learning to respond to the invitations of the great intellectual adventures in which human beings have come to display their various understandings of the world and of themselves. And before the natural sciences could be recognised in this character they had not only to offer something specific capable of being learned but also to present themselves as a distinctive enquiry or mode of human understanding. That is to say, they had to appear as very much more than somewhat mysterious information about the natural world which no educated man should be without, and something very much less than an unconditional or definitive understanding of the world. In respect of the first they have amply succeeded: every natural science now presents itself to the learner as a related set of theorems which invites critical understanding. In respect of the second they have been hindered, not by any inherent self-deception, but by two unfortunate circumstances. The first of these is the relic of a disposition to value themselves in terms of the use which may be made of the conclusions of their enquiries. This, in a place of liberal learning, has sometimes led to a proliferation of what may be called semi-sciences — organisations of information in terms of the use which may be made of it. But this is not a very important hindrance. The more serious encumbrance comes in some absurd claims made by others on their behalf: the claim that they themselves compose a distinctive culture (the silly doctrine of the 'two cultures'[8]); the claim that they represent 'the truth' (so far as it has been ascertained) about the world; and the claim that they constitute the model of all valid human understanding — a claim which has had disastrous consequences elsewhere. But in spite of these hindrances, the natural sciences have unquestionably earned a proper place for themselves in the design of liberal learning and know how to occupy it. No doubt, for example, a biological identity is not itself a human identity, but one of the significant self-understandings which human beings have come upon and explored is that of persons concerned with a specifically 'scientific' understanding of themselves and the world.

Of the humanities I need say little. They are directly concerned with expressions of human self-understanding and their place in liberal learning is assured and central: languages recognised, not as the means of contemporary communication but as investments in thought and records of perceptions and analogical understandings; literatures recognised as the contemplative exploration of beliefs, emotions, human characters and relationships in imagined situations, liberated from the confused, cliché-ridden, generalised conditions of commonplace life and constituting a world of ideal human expressions inviting neither approval nor disapproval but the exact attention and understanding of those who read; histories recognised, not as accounts of the past focused upon our contemporary selves purporting to tell us how we have become what we are and containing messages of warning or encouragement, but as stories in which human actions and utterances are rescued from mystery and made intelligible in terms of their contingent relationships; and philosophy, the reflective undertaking in which every purported achievement of human understanding becomes the subject of an enquiry into its conditions. And if any of this has got driven off its course it is by the winds which forever blow around the engagement of liberal learning, menacing its seclusion from the here and now or driving it upon the rocks of abstract aptitudes or socialisation.

But what of the latest born component of liberal learning: the social sciences? They are a mixed lot. Among them we may expect to find sociology, anthropology, psychology, economics, perhaps jurisprudence and something called 'politics'. They purport to be directly concerned with human

8 [Editors' note] CP Snow's 'Two Cultures' lecture and FR Leavis's response qv.

conduct. These are what used to be called the 'human sciences' — *geisteswissenschaften,* in order to make clear that their concern is with human beings as self-conscious, intelligent persons who are what they understand themselves to be and not with human beings in the loose and indistinct sense of highly evolved organisms or processes of chemical change, the concern of natural sciences. And insofar as these human sciences are what they purport to be (which is not so in every case) it would seem that they belong properly to the 'humanities'. But distinguished they now are; and if the project of distinguishing them from the 'humanities' was an unfortunate mistake, the terms of the distinction are nothing less than a disaster. These terms are specified in the words 'social' and 'science'.

'Social', of course, is a cant word. It is used here to denote an enquiry about human conduct concerned, not with substantive actions and utterances but with the relationships, the associations and the practices in which human beings are joined. This focus of attention is not, in itself, corrupting. It is that upon which most histories of law are centred; and it is the focus, for example, of Maitland's *Constitutional History of England* which, he tells us, is designed to be an account, not of human struggles, but of the results of human struggles in constitutional change. But it is chosen here, and is labeled 'social', in order to allege (or to suggest) that human beings and their performances are what they are in terms of these relationships, associations and practices; and to suggest, further, that these relationships and practices are not human devices, autonomous manners of being associated, each with its own specified conditions of relationship but are the components of an unspecified, unconditional interdependence or 'social' relationship, sometimes called a 'society' or 'Society'. In short, the contention is that this unspecified 'social' relationship is the condition, perhaps the determinant, of all human conduct and that to which human actions and utterances must be referred in order to be understood. But this substitution of the word 'social' for the word 'human' is a surrender to confusion: human conduct is never merely a subscription to a practice or to a relationship, and there is no such thing as an unconditional 'social' relationship. And this confusion is partnered by a commonplace corruption of our language in which the word 'social' has become the centre of endless equivocation. Selden in the seventeenth century said of the cant expression *scrutamini scripturas,* 'these two words have undone the world': a single word has sufficed to undo our cruder twentieth century.

It might, however, be supposed that in connecting the word 'science' with the word 'social' something has been done to restore exactness. But the outcome of this conjunction has been to add a ruinous categorical confusion to what need not have been more than a permissible partiality in considering human conduct. For the word 'science' here is intended to denote a natural science of human conduct; that is, to mean the investigation of human actions and utterances and the practices and relationships to which they may subscribe as if they were non-intelligent components of a 'process' or the functional constituents of a 'system' which do not have to learn their parts in order to play them. The design here is to remove human action and utterance from the category of intelligent goings-on (that is, chosen responses of self-conscious agents to their understood situations which have reasons but not causes and may be understood only in terms of dispositions, beliefs, meanings, intentions, and motives), and to place them in the category of examples of the operation of regularities which do not have to be learned in order to be observed; and to remove human practices, relationships, associations etc. from the category of procedures whose conditions have to be learned and understood in order to be subscribed to and can be subscribed to only in self-chosen actions and utterances, and to put them into the category of 'processes'. Rules are misidentified as regularities, intelligent winks as physiological blinks, conduct as 'behaviour' and contingent relationships as causal or systematic connections.

This project of collecting together a number of respectable enquiries under the head of 'the social sciences' and the attempt to impose this equivocal character upon them has not met with universal acceptance but it has gone far enough to have deeply damaged liberal learning; no other failure of self-understanding in the humanities has generated such confusion. And it is all the more damaging because in putting on the mask of 'science' some of these departments of learning have succumbed to the temptation to understand and to value themselves in terms of the use which may be made of the conclusions of their enquiries. Their recognition as the appropriate equipment for new technological enterprises and for the new and proliferating profession of 'social worker' has corrupted liberal learning. But this does not mean that, individually, and when properly recognised as *Geisteswissenschaften*, they have no proper place in liberal learning; it means only that they have been misidentified. Jurisprudence, until it was confused with a vapid concern for so-called social and psychological needs and become part of the equipment of 'social engineers', was a profound philosophical enquiry, one of the most ancient and respected components of liberal learning. Sociology and anthropology are respectable and somewhat attenuated engagements in historical understanding; they are concerned with human practices, procedures, associations etc. and their contingent relations, and with human actions and utterances in terms of their subscriptions to the conditions of practices. And psychology has long ago declared itself a 'natural', not a 'human' science. It is not concerned with substantive human thoughts, beliefs, emotions, recollections, actions and utterances but with so-called 'mental processes' which are vulnerable to reduction to genetic and chemical processes.

5.

Putting on one side engagements in learning which have no proper place in a liberal education, there are, then, departments of liberal learning in which self-consciousness has not yet been transformed into the self-understanding upon which authentic enquiry and utterance depends. But the more serious consideration for anyone who undertakes to review the present condition of liberal learning is the terms of the self-understanding of the engagement itself.

As it emerged in Western Europe liberal learning was understood to be a concern to explore the invitations of the culture of antiquity, to hold before learners the mirror of this culture so that, seeing themselves reflected in it, they might extend the range and the depth of their understanding of themselves. This idiom of the self-understanding of liberal learning was never very satisfactory; it was substantial, not formal, and it has long since passed away. It has been succeeded by other, similarly substantial, self-identifications. For example, when I was young it was thought (or at least suggested) that the whole of liberal learning might properly be understood in terms of a somewhat extended study of Geography: liberal learning was urged to find the focus of its attention in 'geographical man'. And we have since become familiar with a claim of this sort made on behalf of Sociology; if every department of liberal learning is not itself to be turned into sociology (philosophy into the sociology of knowledge, jurisprudence into the sociology of law etc.) then, at least, none is as it should be unless sociology were added to it. These, of course, are fanciful notions, but they are not unconvincing merely on account of their contingent implausibility. They are unacceptable because the identification of liberal learning they suggest is of the wrong kind. The self-understanding of liberal learning must, I think, be sought in the recognition that its component enquiries, in spite of their substantial differences, have a common formal character and that they are related to one another in a manner agreeable with that formal character.

I have already suggested that the components of a liberal education are united and distinguished from what does not properly belong to it in terms of their 'liberality'; that is, in terms of their concern with what Valéry calls *le prix de la vie humaine*[9], and their emancipation from the here and now of current engagements. But beyond this general consideration, these components may be resolved into and understood as so many different *languages*: the language of the natural sciences, for example, the language of history, the language of philosophy, or the language of poetic imagination.

Languages in a more commonplace sense are organisations of grammatical and syntactical considerations or rules to be taken account of and subscribed to in making utterances. These considerations do not determine the utterances made or even exactly how they shall be subscribed to; that is left to the speaker who not only has something of his own to say but may also have a style of his own. And, of course, no such language is ever settled beyond the reach of modification; to speak it is a linguistically inventive engagement. But here, the conditions imposed upon utterance by these languages of understanding constitute, not merely linguistic idioms, but particular conditional modes of understanding. Learning here is learning to recognise and discriminate between these languages of understanding, is becoming familiar with the conditions each imposes upon utterance, and is learning to make utterances whose virtue is not that they express original ideas (that can only be a rare achievement) but that they display genuine understanding of the language spoken. It is on this account that a learner may be recognised to understand a language such as that of philosophical or historical understanding and yet not be a philosopher or an historian; and also that a teacher may be recognised to have something into which he may initiate a learner which is not itself a doctrine. But since none of these languages of understanding was invented yesterday and each is the continuous exploration of its own possibilities, a learner cannot expect to find what he seeks if he attends only to contemporary utterances. These languages of understanding like other languages are known only in literatures.

What I am suggesting, then, is that from the standpoint of liberal learning, a culture is not a miscellany of beliefs, perceptions, ideas, sentiments, engagements etc. but may be recognised as a variety of distinct languages of understanding, and its inducements are invitations to become acquainted with these languages, to learn to discriminate between them, and to recognise them not merely as diverse modes of understanding the world but as the most substantial expressions we have of human self-understanding.

9

[Author's original note] *Tout ce qui fait le prix de la vie est curieusement inutile.* [Editors' note] From *Mauvaises Pensées et Autres* (1942), p. 217.

But the identity of a culture and of liberal learning remains obscure until we have some conception of the relationship of its components. Now, each of these languages constitutes the terms of a distinct, conditional understanding of the world and a similarly distinct idiom of human self-understanding. Their virtue is to be different from one another and this difference is intrinsic. Each is secure in its autonomy so long as it knows and remains faithful to itself. Any of them may fail, but such failure is always self-defeat arising from imperfect understanding of itself or from the non-observance of its own conditions. They may not all be equally interesting and they may compete for our attention, but they are not inherently contentious and they are incapable of refuting one another. Hence, their relationship cannot be that of parties in a debate; they do not together compose an argument. Further, they are not different degrees of divergence from some suppositious unconditional understanding of the world: their relationship is not hierarchical. Nor is it either a cooperative or a transactional relationship. They are not partners in a common undertaking each with a role to perform, nor are they suppliers of one another's wants. What then is left?

Perhaps we may think of these components of a culture as voices, each the expression of a distinct and conditional understanding of the world and a distinct idiom of human self-understanding, and of the culture itself as these voices joined, as such voices could only be joined, in a conversation — an endless unrehearsed intellectual adventure in which, in imagination, we enter into a variety of modes of understanding the world and ourselves and are not disconcerted by the differences or dismayed by the inconclusiveness of it all. And perhaps we may recognise liberal learning as, above all else, an education in imagination, an initiation into the art of this conversation in which we learn to recognise the voices; to distinguish their different modes of utterance, to acquire the intellectual and moral habits appropriate to this conversational relationship and thus to make our *début dans la vie humaine.*

6.

Liberal learning is a difficult engagement. It depends upon an understanding of itself which is always imperfect; even those who presided over its emergence hardly knew what they were doing. And it depends upon a self-confidence which is easily shaken and not least by continual self-examination. It is a somewhat unexpected invitation to disentangle oneself from the here and now of current happenings and engagements, to detach oneself from the urgencies of the local and the contemporary, to explore and enjoy a release from having to consider things in terms of their contingent features, beliefs in terms of their applications to contingent sit-

uations and persons in terms of their contingent usefulness; an invitation
to be concerned not with the employment of what is familiar but with
understanding what is not yet understood. And a university as a place of
liberal learning can prosper only if those who come are disposed to recognise and acknowledge its particular invitation to learn. Its present predicament lies in the circumstance that there is now so much to obstruct this
disposition.

There was a time, not so long ago, when liberal learning was, not better
understood, but more generally recognised than it now is and when the
obtrusive circumstances of the early upbringing of many (and not merely
of the better off) were such that they did not positively stand in the way of
the recognition of its invitation. They were, indeed, circumstances where
the localities in which one was born and grew up were more enclosed than
they now are and certainly less superficially exciting. Memorable experiences were fewer and smaller, there was change but it moved at a slower
pace; life could be hard but the rat-race as we know it now was in its
infancy. They were also somewhat narrow circumstances which bred little
concern with what might be going on outside the locality and none at all
with world affairs. But they were intellectually innocent rather than positively dull, uncrowded rather than vacant. For there was in these circumstances a notable absence of the ready-made or of oppressive uniformities
of thought or attitude or conduct. If experiences were fewer, they were
made to go further; if they were smaller they invoked imaginative enlargement. And the natural world was never so far distant as it now often is and
the response to it was allowed to be naïve and uncluttered, a response of
wonder and delight. In all this School was important; but it was a place of
its own. I often recollect that memorable sentence from the autobiography
of Sir Ernest Barker: 'Outside the cottage, I had nothing but my school; but
having my school I had everything.' There, in school, the narrow boundaries of the local and the contemporary were swept aside to reveal, not
what might be going on in the next town or village, in Parliament or in the
United Nations, but a world of things and persons and happenings, of languages and beliefs, of utterances and sights and sounds past all imagination and to which even the dullest could not be wholly indifferent. The
going was hard; there was nothing to be got without learning how to get it,
and it was understood that nobody went to school in order to enjoy the sort
of happiness he might get from lying in the sun. And when with inky fingers a schoolboy unpacked his satchel to do his homework he unpacked
three thousand years of the fortunes and misfortunes of human intellectual adventure. Nor would it easily have occurred to him to ask what the
sufferings of Job, the silent ships moving out of Tenedos in the moonlight,

the terror, the complication and the pity of the human condition revealed in a drama of Shakespeare or Racine, or even the chemical composition of water, had to do with *him*, born upon the banks of the Wabash, in the hills of Cumberland, in a Dresden suburb or a Neapolitan slum. Either he never considered the question at all, or he dimly recognised them as images of a human self-understanding which was to be his for the learning. All very innocent, perhaps even credulous; and in many cases soon overlaid by the urgencies of current engagements. But however superficially they might be appreciated, these were not circumstances which generated a positive resistance to the invitation of liberal learning in a university. Indeed, their very innocence nurtured a disposition to recognise it.

But these circumstances are no longer with us. The way we live now, even though it may contain notable relics of the earlier condition, is somewhat different. The world in which many children now grow up is crowded, not necessarily with occupants and not at all with memorable experiences, but with happenings; it is a ceaseless flow of seductive trivialities which invoke neither reflection nor choice but instant participation. A child quickly becomes aware that he cannot too soon plunge into this flow or immerse himself in it too quickly; to pause is to be swept with the chilling fear of never having lived at all. There is little chance that his perceptions, his emotions, his admirations and his ready indignations might become learned responses or be even innocent fancies of his own; they come to him prefabricated, generalised and uniform. He lurches from one modish conformity to the next, or from one fashionable guru to his successor, seeking to lose himself in a solidarity composed of exact replicas of himself. From an early age children now believe themselves to be well-informed about the world, but they know it only at secondhand in the pictures and voices which surround them. It holds no puzzles or mysteries for them; it invites neither careful attention nor understanding. As like as not they know the moon as something to be shot-at or occupied before ever they have had the chance to marvel at it. This world has but one language, soon learned: the language of appetite. The idiom may be that of the exploitation of the resources of the earth, or it may be that of seeking something for nothing; but this is a distinction without a difference. It is a language composed of meaningless clichés. It allows only the expression of 'points of view' and the ceaseless repetition of slogans which are embraced as prophetic utterances. Their ears are filled with the babel of invitations to instant and unspecified reactions and their utterance reproduces only what they have heard said. Such discourse as there is resembles the barking of a dog at the echo of its own yelp. School in these circumstances is notably unimportant. To a large extent it has surrendered its character as a place apart where utterances of another sort may be heard and languages other than the language of appetite may be learned. It affords no seclusion, it offers no release. Its furnishings are the toys with which those who come are already familiar. Its virtues and its vices are those of the surrounding world.

These, then, are circumstances hostile to a disposition to recognise the invitation of liberal learning; that is, the invitation to disentangle oneself, for a time, from the urgencies of the here and now and to listen to the conversation in which human beings forever seek to understand themselves. How shall a university respond to the current aversion from seclusion, to the now common belief that there are other and better ways of becoming human than by learning to do so, and to the impulsive longing to be given a doctrine or to be socialised according to a formula rather than to be initiated into a conversation? Not, I think, by seeking excuses for what sometimes seem unavoidable surrenders, nor in any grand gesture of defiance, but in a quiet refusal to compromise which comes only in self-understanding. We must remember who we are: inhabitants of a place of liberal learning.

(b) Anthony O'Hear:
The Good is not Reducible to Human Choice

Education, Value and the Sense of Awe (1992)[10]

Human beings are undoubtedly part of nature. Our existence is dependent in many complex ways on the balance of nature, obviously on conditions on our planet, perhaps less obviously on the state of the sun and the solar system, and doubtless too, on things which happened right at the start of the universe.

We can look in detail at aspects of our make-up and experience. We can, for example, examine just how our perception of colour works, showing how a coincidence between certain wavelengths of light and properties of our sense organs yields us this experience. We can also tell stories about the survival value of our having colour vision. Colour vision allowed our remote ancestors to pick out berries, fruits, predators, etc., better than their competitors in the struggle for existence, which is why we have it now. In principle, it seems that a combination of the physiological and the evolutionary could give explanations of much of our physical and mental make-up, showing us to be products of nature and part of nature.

---

10   Presented as the first of two Victor Cook Memorial Lectures. Reprinted in *Values, Education and the Human World*, ed. John Haldane, Imprint Academic, Exeter, 2004, pp. 68–84. This book also includes a companion piece by the same author, 'The Pursuit of Excellence'.

It is true that human beings, unlike other species in nature, are not purely Darwinian in their mode of development. Human parents can and do systematically transmit what they have learned in life to their off-spring. In Darwinian natural selection the gene is the means by which parents transmit faculties, abilities and dispositions to their offspring. The key point about the genetic transmission of characteristics is that the experience of parents normally has no effect on their genes, and so can't be genetically handed on. A man might have acquired a calloused hand in decades of hard manual work, but this has no bearing on the likelihood of his son being born more horny-handed than had the father not laboured.

Unlike other animals, however, we have developed symbol systems, of which language is the most important. In learning their native language, children pick up all sorts of habits of thought and behaviour, way beyond their genetic inheritance. They learn classifications, meanings and evaluations, many of which could hardly be envisaged in the absence of a community and some of which are peculiar to a particular community. Without language a creature would be hard put to distinguish shame from guilt, let us say, or either emotion from a whole range of other negative feelings and reactions. And as we learn from anthropology and literature, the precise meaning of shame is rather different in England now from the associated emotion in Homeric Greece or modern Japan.

In learning a language, we learn a form of life, as Wittgenstein emphasized. And in so doing, we learn in all sorts of ways from the *experience* not just of our parents, but also of other forebears both close and remote. Does anything follow from the Lamarckian nature of human culture about why cultural forms, our forms of knowledge and our forms of life, survive and develop in the way they do?

Let us suppose for a moment that the Cartesian project of refuting scepticism about our most basic beliefs and values is adjudged a failure; and that it proves impossible to base what we know and believe on any foundation unassailable by sceptical doubt. We might then explain the persistence of our basic beliefs and customs in terms of their usefulness to our survival — in Darwinian terms, that is — rather than in terms of their rationality. We believe, say, that most of us have never been on the moon, that the world has existed for a long time, that I have a hand in front of me, or that causing wanton injury is wrong, not because, without begging the question, we can prove any of these things to be true, but rather because these are beliefs and values presupposed in our form of life, a form of life which has proved its mettle in assuring the success and survival of those who are part of it. In this way there is a form of natural selection operating on beliefs and values: those which belong to successful groups and (perhaps) help their survival are thus selected for in so far as the group itself survives.

Naturalistic accounts of the survival of beliefs and values are not without some plausibility; nevertheless there is no difficulty in envisaging that a society or group might derive its very success from its adherence to a *false* belief or a *distorted* value. Precisely because a false belief or distorted value is likely to distinguish the group which possesses it from other groups, it forms the focus around which the group identifies itself, and from which it gains its cohesion and strength in face of what it sees as infidels. Few non-Muslims, for example, would regard the central claim of the Koran to be true or approve of the Muslim treatment of women; yet in the early centuries of Islam and arguably again today, it is from their adherence to the — at best — questionable claim about Allah, Mohammed, the Koran and the associated ethos, that the followers of Islam derive their power (and an Islamic anthropologist might well make similar remarks about Christ being the Second Person of the Blessed Trinity and Christian attitudes to sexuality).

Thus, even though we can give naturalistic accounts of our faculties and beliefs, we can also raise questions about the truth and epistemological status of what they tell us. The naturalistic analysis of colour perception to which I referred earlier does pose for us the question as to whether something (colour) which *seems* to be a fundamental property of the universe really is so. In other words, even while giving a naturalistic account of a part of our experience, we are led to question the validity of certain initially unquestioned beliefs or attitudes associated with that experience.

What I conclude from this ability we have to question and think about our genetic and cultural inheritance is that as human beings we are not simply passive elements in a wider, more inclusive process of nature, subject only to the pushes and pulls exerted on us by those processes. At the very least we are capable of standing back from our engagement in what Newman called the flow of life. One potential result of this reflectiveness is that people disengage from their existing perceptions and practices, regarding them as products of physiological or social factors which may lead to distorted or partial perspectives on the whole of which they are a part. (So colours are not part of the stuff of reality; one's natural adherence to the values of the culture in which one is brought up owes as much to one's upbringing as to any strongly grounded sense that they are right.)

Because of our possession of symbol systems, particularly language, we do not just act, feel and react in the world. We are able to formulate for ourselves beliefs about the principles on which we act, to theorise about them and to criticise and improve them, and also imaginatively to construct new ones. Our Lamarckian nature is not just a matter of our being able to transmit information non-genetically. What makes that possible also makes possible our ability to reflect on and, as a result, modify our beliefs and values. A world of meanings, then, of explicitly formulated beliefs and attitudes and other cultural products stands between us human beings and the world of raw, uninterpreted fact.

In reflecting on particular beliefs and values we hold, we can, as I have said, view them naturalistically, as the result of various causal factors, natural and social. Looking at them in this way, we may regard them as what might be called projections of aspects of our make-up on to the world. Thus, our sense that the world is coloured, along with our sense of some actions being right and others wrong, comes to be seen as a matter of neurophysiological activities and emotional feelings, which have their origins within us, being diffused over a world in which there are really no colours, no moral properties. Hume, who held this view both of colour and of morality, also held that seeing an object as beautiful or deformed is a matter of 'gilding' or 'staining' it with the colours borrowed from internal sentiment.[11]

Without denying that aspects of our perception, and many of our beliefs and our attributions of value, both moral and æsthetic, are due in part to features of our own make up, I now want to suggest that in the case of judgments of truth and value, it is impossible for us to regard our best considered efforts as simply projections. In the case of our beliefs about the surrounding world and its contents, it is — as I have shown — possible to discount some, seeing them as products of an idiosyncratic interaction with reality. But the reason we can do this is because we regard the larger story — the causal story — as sufficiently true for the purpose. In telling this larger story, we are assuming, and have to assume, that at certain points our beliefs *are* attuned to the world.

Indeed, it is hard to see how we could do otherwise while continuing to act and make our way through the world. A thoroughgoing scepticism on our part regarding beliefs about the world is not possible so long as we continue to act in the world; part of our acting indeed involves discriminating between true and false beliefs, and acting on those we believe to be *true*; beliefs we take to be true we cannot see as simply an effect of some idiosyncratic interaction of ours with the world which leads us to project on to the world features which it does not really possess.

---

11   See *An Enquiry Concerning the Principles of Morals* (1751), Appendix I, 'Concerning Moral Sentiment'.

For analogous reasons which have been elaborated by Charles Taylor[12] it is equally hard to see our value judgments as simply projections of feeling, as just some gilding and staining of the world on our part, or as manifestations of a Nietzschean will-to-power. As part of being what Taylor calls a 'functioning self', deliberating, judging and acting in the world, we cannot help but have recourse to notions like courage, generosity, kindness, dignity, fairness and their opposites. We need such concepts to make sense of our own lives, and to understand the lives of others. The use of evaluative notions such as the ones I have mentioned in a life-guiding way presupposes that the user accepts these terms as indicative of virtues which are good in themselves, and good not simply because they serve certain interests of his. Maybe the virtues do serve human interests in a general sense, but to do a generous or a noble or a courageous act implies that the agent is seeing what he is doing as generous, noble or courageous – and hence as good in itself – and good not just because it serves certain interests, individual or collective.

The Nietzschean or other moral sceptic may claim that all we ever do in our valuing is to serve self-interest, more or less openly, more or less widely conceived. But this is to overlook the obvious fact that even in seeking our own interest or self-fulfilment, we have to regard some things as worth being interested in, as worthwhile in themselves, as goods in themselves in which the self might find fulfilment. And, in practice, even the most thoroughgoing proponents of reductive views of value usually end up advocating some value as ultimately worthwhile in itself, as we see in various ways in the cases of Nietzsche himself (will-to-power), EO Wilson (knowledge) and Michel Foucault (liberation). And [...] for most of us power and liberation, at least, are valued as means to the attainment of other ends which are valuable in themselves and to which they are but means. [...]

Reflectiveness, then, which might at an earlier stage in our argument have seemed to be on the point of destroying morality, by interpreting our morality naturalistically, may now come to the aid of morality, when we begin to think about the actual fabric of our moral life. For if someone were to say that the only things worth being interested in for themselves – the only constitutive goods for us – were selfish pleasure and riches, we could remind him of the saying in the Gospels about the profit of gaining the whole world when one suffers the loss of one's own soul, or of the Socratic adage that the good man cannot be harmed. That on some level we all understand these and similar sayings, as well as everyday talk about such virtues as compassion, courage, kindness and justice, and that we feel our-

12 *Sources of the Self* (1989).

selves bound unconditionally by some of what is implied in such talk shows that untempered hedonism is not in practice the only value in our lives (and similar objections could also be made to the monistic re-valuations of Nietzsche, Wilson and Foucault).

As Taylor puts it, moral scepticism of a Humean or a Nietzschean type thinking that 'we do not speak from a moral orientation which we take to be right' is 'a form of self-delusion'

> incompatible with the way we cannot but understand ourselves in the actual practices which constitute holding that (orientation): our deliberations, our serious assessments of ourselves and others. They are not constructs you could actually make of your life while living it... [but are] only kept aloft by a certain lack of self-lucidity, which keeps the relevant meta-construal from connecting with the terms in which we cannot but live our actual moral experience.[13]

Scepticism about truth and about value, particularly scepticism motivated by naturalistic accounts of our perceptions, beliefs and practices, involves detaching ourselves from our actual existence as agents, as believers, as participants in a world natural and social. Our reflectiveness can lead to a sort of moral and epistemological disengagement, disembodiment even, given that our existence as agents is intimately connected with our being embodied in a world; but this stance is at odds with our experience and participation in our practices — scientific, moral and æsthetic. Reflectiveness about our beliefs and values can straightforwardly improve them, as when one realises that some apparently bent sticks are not bent, or perhaps, more complicatedly, that a prevalent conception of justice is fuelled more by resentment for some of one's fellows rather than by genuine concern for others. But at another level, reflectiveness ceases to improve and begins to undermine. The two examples I have just given have historically been powerful in setting thinkers off in the direction of scepticism about *all* appearances, about *all* values. But then further reflection can reveal that global scepticism itself is unsustainable, at least as a doctrine to live by: that as reflective agents we are creatures with a natural orientation to the true and to the good, and that as we conceive it in our lives, the good is something more than individual self-interest.

In saying that we have an orientation to the good and the true, am I also claiming that there is anything outside of us to which this orientation is directed? In the case of truth, we can, of course, say that the world itself forms the objective correlate of our drive to truth. Some would doubtless follow CS Peirce in seeing the sometimes uncertain harmony between our theories and the world underwritten by both us and the world being

---

13   *Sources of the Self,* pp. 99–100.

moved by the love of God. But perhaps we do not need any metaphysical claim of this sort to make sense of our need to distinguish between what is and is not true, the need being something built into our self-consciousness and its object and immediate satisfier being the world itself.

Things, though, get more difficult when we come to consider what I am calling our orientation to the good. Although the structure of our experience as self-conscious agents is the basis of our ability to make a distinction between what is good and what is merely useful to us individually or collectively, the problem is to know what the object might be to which our orientation to the good is directed. What, in other words, can we regard as the source of our moral goods, goods which have the command they have over us because we do not see them simply in terms of projections of human desires or needs? What we see as *just* a projection of our desires or needs, individual or collective, can, in virtue of that very fact, equally be seen as provisional, cancellable, dispensable; replaceable by some new willing of mine, as against the willing of the rest. This, at least, is what I learn from Nietzsche. But from my own experience and from what I see of life around me, I learn that, for example, the imperatives against wanton cruelty or in favour of certain types of moral and physical courage are not provisional, cancellable or dispensable. I learn this particularly on the occasions when I see that I and others do dispense with them, and when it is forcefully borne in on me that a form of human life without such values would be a bad form of life. I can say this even while admitting that my precise conception of the good life and its virtues may be mistaken. What, in the light of any valuations and the role that they play in my life, I cannot admit is that the whole conception is wrong, and that there could be a good form of human life which did not in some large measure contain virtues continuous with and intelligible in the light of my conception.

There is doubtless a considerable embarrassment today in saying *anything* about objective values, or about the background needed for such talk. As Iris Murdoch put it in her essay 'Against Dryness':

> We no longer see man against a background of values, of realities which transcend him. We picture man as a brave naked well surrounded by an easily comprehended empirical world. For the hard idea of truth, we have substituted a facile idea of sincerity. What we have never had, of course, is a satisfactory Liberal theory of personality, a theory of man as free and separate and related to a rich and complicated world from which, as a moral being, he has much to learn. We have bought the Liberal theory as it stands, because we have wished to encourage people to think of themselves as free, at the cost of surrendering the background.[14]

14   *Encounter*, Vol. XVI, No. 1, January 1961, p. 18.

The problem I have been skirting round is the question as to whether that orientation to the good — which I find embedded in our form of life and moral discourse — can survive an ethic based on some notion of human choice, sincere or not. My conclusion has been that it cannot. We have to see ourselves as subservient to a good which cannot, as things stand, be seen as reducible to human choice, individual or collective. The good and the virtuous are what we *ought* to choose, they are not constituted as such by our choices. That in the absence of a shared symbolic order, such as was at one time provided by dogmatic religion, it may be hard to justify this sense, or, in the face of a certain type of questioning, to keep it alive, is true, but not necessarily an occasion for despair. After all, not everything about dogmatic religion was or is conducive to human flourishing, or even to the exercise of a reasonably generous conception of the virtues. In any case, apart from our lived sense of the sacredness of human life and of something approaching awe in matters to do with the creation, beginning, nurturing, and ending of specifically human life, we do have other non-religious intimations of the transcendent:

> Good art, thought of as symbolic force rather than statement, provides a stirring image of a pure transcendent value, a steadily visible enduring higher good, and perhaps provides for many people, in an unreligious age without prayer or sacraments, their clearest *experience* of something grasped as separate and precious and beneficial and held quietly and unpossessively in the attention.[15]

One thinks in this context of such emblematic figures in twentieth century art as Proust, Cézanne, Rilke and Henry Moore: Proust, with his painstaking *récherche* of experience, and the sense that our lives and hopes and experiences can be redeemed when they are expressed, contemplated and articulated æsthetically; Cézanne painting Mont Sainte-Victoire for the three dozenth time, and proclaiming '*le paysage se pense en moi et j'en suis la conscience*';[16] Henry Moore embarking on a similar exploration of the complex correspondences between landscape and human form; and Rilke's enterprise in his *Neue Gedichte* of bringing the unexpressed to expression, of transforming what is outer and visible into inwardness and feeling, an enterprise encapsulated in his letter of November 13th 1925:

> our task is to impress this preliminary, transient earth upon ourselves with so much suffering and so passionately that its nature rises up again 'invisibly' within us. We are the bees of the invisible.

---

15   Iris Murdoch, *The Fire and the Sun* (1977), pp. 76–7.
16   See Merleau-Ponty, *Sens et non-sens* (1965) p. 30.

We drink ceaselessly the honey of the visible, so as to gather it into the great golden beehive of the invisible.[17]

And again in the words of the *Ninth Duino Elegy*:

> Are we perhaps *here* to say: House,
> Bridge, Fountain, Gate, Jug, Fruit Tree, Window —
> possible Pillar, Tower ... but to say — do you see —
> oh to say in such a way, as the things themselves never
> within intended to be?

There is then a task, a value that comes to be only in and through human existence, including human desire and choice, but once the task and the value exist, they are entitled to command desire and choice.

I find it significant that it is hard to think about our moral experience without being drawn to think of the transcendent, particularly when I contemplate the work of the artists I have mentioned, and I am sympathetic to the attempt to provide some such context for human life. Nevertheless my argument up to this point strictly speaking requires only that what Taylor calls the best account of our lives and moral experience rests on the recognition of value sources regarded as independent of and, as things stand, as irreducible to our desires, individual or collective. On pain of distorting our understanding of value and of our lives, we cannot see our values as projections of our desires or as no more than devices for the smooth running of society. Whether that sense of the autonomy of moral value reflects something metaphysical about us, or whether it is a feature of human life which — like language and self-consciousness — has emerged during the course of our evolution, or whether both are true, can be left open for my current purpose. For that it is sufficient to assert that there are values, including moral values, which spring into existence (along with human desire, passion and choice), but that once the values exist, they are entitled to command our desires, passions and choices.

As I believe that the nurturing of this sense of the objectivity of value is a crucial part of civilised life, and essential to the order which sustains civilised life, I now want to consider how best children might be brought up or educated to possess it. In one sense, of course, the question is easy to answer. They should be brought up to use the concepts and make the judgments whose pervasive role in our form of life founds the basis of the sense that value is objective. Nevertheless, something more interesting should be said, if only because there are currents of educational thinking which are likely to undermine that sense of awe on which any idea of the objectivity and transcendence of value depends.

---

17   *Collected Letters* (1936) p. 355.

The characteristic terms of our moral vocabulary are terms such as generosity, honour, honesty, dignity, kindness, justice and compassion. Endowed with virtues such as these, individuals come to act in a de-centred way, and to regard the world and their fellows as they are, rather than as means to one's own ends. To have these attitudes and virtues is to be imbued with respect for others and a sense of awe towards the imperatives thus incumbent on us.

By contrast, in his essay 'Inside the Whale' [1940], George Orwell wrote

> Patriotism, religion, the Empire, the family, the sanctity of marriage, the Old School Tie, birth, breeding, honour, discipline — anyone of ordinary education could turn the whole lot of them inside out in three minutes.

It does not, of course, follow from this that 'anyone of ordinary education' would be right to do this; my concern, though, is that there might be something about 'ordinary education' which disposes young people to engage in superficial re-valuations of the sort Orwell mentions, and that engaging in them will be enough to destroy the penumbra of awe which ought to attach to at least some of the things he mentions.

While I [...] would like to see education as a transmitter of culture and an inculcator of value, there is currently a somewhat different conception of education, that by which individuals are led to question received opinion and values and to take it on themselves to decide what they will regard as valuable or not.

The view I am referring to has obvious roots in seventeenth century and Enlightenment philosophy. Its most influential British exponent is the JS Mill of *On Liberty*, in Chapter Two of which we are told that all beliefs and values, including and especially true beliefs and correct values, prove their mettle only by being submitted to rigorous and systematic criticism. A consistently Millian approach suggests that all purported values, all proposed goods are always up for critical examination, that, for example, sadism or genocide are things we have to find *reasons* to reject on pain of not understanding the meaning of the prohibitions, and that those values which do not accord with what seems to us to be rational are to be rejected.

The Millian approach did not, of course, originate with Mill. We can remember the words of Francis Bacon, the prophet of much that even now characterises the scientific method (with which the view of education I am now discussing is often closely linked):

> What happiness it would be to throw myself into the River Lethe, to erase completely from my soul the memory of all knowledge, all art,

all poetry; what happiness it would be to reach the opposite shore, naked like the first man.[18]

— the same Bacon who, as Oakeshott tells us, tried to prevent Charterhouse being founded, on the grounds that its curriculum was centred on the ancient classics. Diderot, similarly, was insistent that a true philosopher would 'trample underfoot prejudice, tradition, venerability, universal assent, authority — in a word, everything that overawes the crowd' and dare 'to think for himself' and 'to admit nothing save on the testimony of his own reason and experience'.[19] And what if the philosopher's 'reason and experience', as in the case of Diderot himself and even more in the case of Holbach, told him that it is natural for men to be moved only by pleasure and pain? Does this not in the end lead — as Taylor argues — to a blurring of the distinction between moral and non-moral evaluation: we just do what we are programmed by nature to do — i.e. seek pleasure and avoid pain — and that is also what we ought to do. But this 'ought' is no longer the clearly autonomous ought of morality. In this perspective there seems little room for any 'ought' of a moral as opposed to a causal sort, any ought which will furnish us with a sense of goods other than those of pleasure and pain, which are hardly moral goods at all, and which do not require any sense of awe to sustain. Moral thinking thus reduces either to a Californian plea to 'be natural' or, for those who realise that such a plea may lead to logistical difficulties at least, to a device for permitting the simultaneous satisfaction of as many human preferences as possible. (This, I take it, is the essence of the utilitarian position from Bentham to Hare.) But, once the sense of the moral ought has been naturalised by utilitarianism, why should any individual feel bound to obey the dictates of the device? Why should each man not just do what seems to him most pleasant and least painful in the light of his reason and experience? Why should I as an autonomous individual obey the rules which lead to the smooth running of society, and not just seek my own pleasure? My argument is that this is the point at which the individual needs allegiance to constitutive moral goods and virtues beyond his 'natural' search for pleasure.

It will be said that the elevation of individual reason and experience to be the arbiter of moral judgment does not necessarily lead to a collapse of autonomous moral authority or value in this way. Might not one conclude even for oneself that, say, the traditional moral values of Christianity are the right ones? This is precisely the situation envisaged by Kant in the

18   As quoted by Michael Oakeshott in 'Education: The Engagement and its Frustration', *Journal of the Philosophy of Education*, V (1), January 1971.
19   *Sources of the Self*, p. 323.

Grundlegung, where the man confronted with the Holy One of God (Christ) turns away to consider the dictates of his own conscience and reason. But, as Iris Murdoch has urged, the man envisaged by Kant—'free, independent, lonely, powerful, rational, responsible, brave', the 'ideal citizen of the liberal state' and 'offspring of the age of science', confidently rational and yet increasingly alienated from the world his discoveries reveal—this man actually embodies the notion of the will, of my will, albeit universalised, as the creator of value.

> Values which were previously in some sense inscribed in the heavens and guaranteed by God collapse into the human will. There is no transcendent reality. The idea of the good remains indefinable and empty so that human choice may fill it. The sovereign moral concept is freedom.[20]

I do not want to deny the Kantian insight that morality has to do with the finding of reasons for actions of an interpersonal sort. Morality *is* to do with de-centring one's world and one's motivation. But the de-centring involved in morality requires more than the purely formal demand for the universalisation of one's principles. It requires also, in the jargon, some 'thick' conception of the good and the virtuous, some notion of what true virtue and true goodness consist in beyond rationality in a formal sense, and this is a conception which each one of us inherits first in our culture and tradition, and which we then learn the meaning of in experience.

Particularly in philosophy, the area in which reason is held to be central, we need to remind ourselves at this point of one very basic fact. Despite the claims of Mill in *On Liberty* there is no guarantee that the sort of systematic critical examination of principles which he envisages will lead to an improvement of the principles, behaviour, or of a culture more generally. As Maurice Cowling has pointed out:

> æsthetic and intellectual achievement depend on persistent development of requisite sensibilities, on traditions of professional competence and on patrons and audiences who are willing to be interested, not on the pervading commitment to make men scrutinise their consciences.[21]

And, this is where what I have to say bears on education. Mill wanted just such a systematic scrutiny of even the best-founded beliefs and values to be conducted by the young. On pain of our and their losing 'living apprehension' of a truth, he urged the 'teachers of mankind' to find

20   *The Sovereignty of Good* (1970), p. 80.
21   *Mill and Liberalism* (1963; 1990), p. 157.

> some contrivance for making the difficulties of the question as present
> to the learner's consciousness, as if they were pressed upon him by a
> dissentient champion, eager for his conversion[22]

particularly where there is general agreement on a truth. Yet this kind of
rationalistic and dialectical approach to value, encouraging as it will the
setting of uneducated preference on the same level as mature wisdom, is
likely actually to undermine the sense of value as autonomous, on which
both morality and culture depend. Such indeed was the view of Nietzsche,
who was more aware than most philosophers of the subtle inter-relation-
ships that exist between value, culture, reason *and* education. In his essay
'On the future of our educational institutions', he wrote

> It is a crime to have incited someone to 'autonomy' at an age when sub-
> jection to a great guide is to be cultivated.
>
> Correct and strong education is above all obedience and custom.
>
> Indulgence of the so-called 'free personality' (by teachers) is nothing
> but a sign of barbarism.[23]

I will leave it to you to decide the extent to which contemporary educational practice is, in Nietzsche's terms, indulgent and barbaric, and to
what extent it is permeated by notions of greatness and of obedience and
custom, though I will just say that part of the motivation and attraction of
phenomena such as political correctness and the contemporary clamour
for what is called equal opportunities in education is that they promise to
indulge those who, rightly or wrongly, feel themselves excluded from the
customs and culture which prevail (feelings which are often simply a consequence of an educational philosophy which, not stressing obedience and
custom, might almost have been designed to induce a sense of exclusion).[24]

Nietzsche's remarks are partly psychological, but not exclusively so. They
are of a piece with the ethical criticisms he made of Socrates in *The Birth of*

---

22   *On Liberty* (1859), Chapter 2, Part 2.

23   Quoted by Cooper in *Authenticity and Learning: Nietzsche's Educational Philosophy* (1983), p. 38.

24   [Author's original note] I should point out that the highly influential system of moral
education known as values clarification is predicated on the twin assumptions that 1) the
teacher must not impose his or her values on pupils and 2) pupils must be encouraged to
explore and express what they think about moral matters. In our own country these
assumptions have been embodied in the well-known Schools Council projects on the
Humanities Curriculum and Moral Education, and permeate much that goes under the name
of Personal and Social Education. It is the combination of assumed relativism on the part of
teachers and rationalisation on the part of pupils which I am objecting to, as it is likely to
undermine in pupils any robust sense of the objectivity of value. (I am indebted to Fred Naylor
for this information.) [Editors' *addendum*] The *Times* recently reported (David Charter, 'Schools
told it's no longer necessary to teach right from wrong', 31/7/06) that under a rewritten
National Curriculum, schools would only encourage children to develop their own 'secure
values and beliefs'.

Tragedy and elsewhere. The objection to Socrates is that by his quibbling, his cleverness and his relentless and ultimately fruitless search for definition, he destroyed the confidence of the best in what was best. In this, of course, Nietzsche is following Aristophanes:

> They sit at the feet of Socrates
> Till they can't distinguish the wood from the trees
> And tragedy goes to POT;
> They don't care whether their plays are art
> But only whether their words are smart
> They waste our time with quibbles and quarrels
> Destroying our patience as well as our morals
> And teaching us all to talk rot.[25]

Why might Socratic questioning and Socratic education destroy morals? Not everything in morals, or anything else, can be given an explicit verbal formulation or, even less, a verbal justification. But the presumption of Socratic questioning as demonstrated in the *Euthyphro* is that what can't be so expounded and justified should be rejected. It is significant that Mill holds up for our admiration the
Socratic principle that those who had merely adopted the commonplaces of received opinion did not understand the subject. My feeling, to the contrary, is that morality is better served by people who are content to grow into holding certain commonplaces, and in whom the development of this experience is not held up by the premature exercise of what Mill himself calls 'a negative discussion'.[26]
Even more important, we have to recognise that, particularly in the realm of value, abstracted from a grounding in experience and tradition, 'reasoning' is likely to mislead in the way Nietzsche and Orwell feared. In other words, contrary to the Millian spirit, self-critical examination of principles ungrounded in moral experience can threaten morality, rather than preserve or strengthen it.

Practical reasoning is not just intellectual cleverness. It requires on the part of the reasoner a disposition towards the good and the virtuous and, as I argued earlier, that requires on the part of the agent a sense that in being so moved he—or even more, those whose principles he is examining—are not merely projecting sentiments of their own on the world, or at least, are not necessarily doing that.

Aristotle is very clear about the need for the right dispositions on the part of the man who is to discuss morality successfully. As far as practical reasoning goes, he says:

---

25 *The Frogs*, lines 1491–9.
26 *On Liberty*, Chapter 2.

it makes no small difference, then, whether we form habits of one kind or of another from our very youth: it makes a very great difference, or rather all the difference.[27]

The point is that we can reason well about value if we have been brought up so as to acquire habits of respect for the good and the virtuous, a respect which assumes both that certain values are not in any serious sense open to question and that the right values have gradually emerged in the experience and discourse of the many and the wise. It is in its tendency to discount the way in which the experience and knowledge of the many and the wise has helped to delineate the forms of goods we discover as much as we create, that I find the Bacon-Diderot stress on individual instant reason unfortunate. This is especially so in education, where the reasoners are likely to lack the experience and wisdom necessary to judge which things are good and virtuous.

The contrary Aristotelian expectation—or hope—is that once young people have been encouraged to do what is good and virtuous, they will feel attracted to it. In their subsequent reasoning they will both see the reasons for it and have such a respect for it that they will not find basic moral virtues and principles seriously open to question. That they will (and should) subsequently reason about values is taken for granted by Aristotle (and by me) for two reasons. The first is because in life, situations never repeat themselves exactly; so intelligence and flexibility of mind will be required to know just what the good thing to do is in a given situation. And secondly, as rational beings, it is incumbent on us to understand the reason for things, including the reasons for our conduct. Nothing I am saying is intended to suggest that morality is either inflexible or not to be reasoned about; what I am concerned to establish is the motivational and dispositional basis on which good reasoning about morality can proceed.

What I have been suggesting in this lecture is that although we, as human beings, are in a general sense part of nature, we do have orientations towards the good and the true which take us out of the purely natural, and invite us to think of our beliefs and values as subject to demands of truth and goodness in some absolute sense. Reflection on our moral life shows that we do indeed find ourselves obliged and moved by values which we cannot regard purely as mere projections of human feeling. Education has a key role in transmitting such values to the young, but this role is likely to be subverted if the educational process is conceived in narrowly rationalistic terms, encouraging young people to rationalise or criticise values whose proper understanding depends on the precritical acquisition of certain moral dispositions. Educators ought then to be more con-

27 *Nicomachean Ethics*, 1103b 24–5.

cerned with inculcating in the young a sense of awe and respect for the virtues of civilised life than with encouraging their pupils to regard these virtues as open to choice or simply a reification of preferences. A rationalistic approach to values and to education is likely to foster the latter attitude, whereas an education stressing custom and respect is likely to encourage the former.

I have been speaking of education as a process in which children ought to be inspired by the notion of an autonomous and existing order of value. This is an order, not of their making and not of ours as teachers either; but it is one to which some human deeds aspire and which some human works reflect. In formal education, the existence of an autonomous objective realm of value is best initially pointed to by immersion on the part of pupils in those works which—in the Wittgensteinian distinction—show its existence; that is, not in works of philosophy or the social sciences, which talk about it and on occasion talk it out of existence, but in works of literature and the arts more generally, in which its fabric is articulated and illustrated.

In emphasizing the objectivity of value and the centrality of literature to its understanding, I would, though, not want to underestimate the importance of the study of the natural sciences here. Indeed, the pursuit of science itself does give us direct experience of truths independent of us, direct experience of objectivity. In recognizing the independent existence of the natural world, and in studying this world, we learn what it means to submit ourselves to a reality outside of us, and that itself does involve a certain type of virtue and submission to something authoritative over us. Where science is conceived in more than technological or instrumentalist terms, its pursuit actually makes sense only against the background of a concern for truth and knowledge for its own sake, a concern which is hard to justify or explain so long as we conceive human life in utilitarian terms. Science then is part of our existence in a world of interest-free value and certainly has its place alongside literature in an education which recognises the objectivity of value.

The realm of value of which I have been speaking in this lecture has largely been that of moral value. Morality, as I conceive it, is part of the fabric of everyday life, and much of what I have said about it derives from its central place in our everyday lives. So, in dealing with morality, although they will be taking their pupils beyond self-interest, teachers will not be taking them beyond the everyday, even if they may intimate that the everyday has implications beyond the everyday.

But, in human life there are realms with their own objectivity and autonomy other than the moral. The realms I particularly have in mind are those of developed cultural forms, the sciences, the arts and the humanities, and I see their study as having much to contribute to the awakening in children of a sense of higher value and therefore as reinforcing that decentring of desire and impulse which is implicit in morality.

In my second lecture, I will speak about education as a process of initiation into worthwhile forms of knowledge and experience beyond those of daily life. On education seen in these terms, Nietzsche had this to say in *Human, all too Human* [1878]:

> The value of the grammar school is seldom sought in the things that are actually learned ... The reading of the classics — every educated person admits this — is ... a monstrous procedure: before young people who are in no way whatever ripe for it, by teachers whose every word, often whose mere appearance, lays a blight on a good writer. But herein lies the value that usually goes unrecognised — that these teachers speak the abstract language of higher culture, ponderous and hard to understand but nonetheless a higher gymnastics for the head: that concepts, technical terms, methods, allusions continually occur in their language such as young people almost never hear in the conversation of their relations or in the street. If the pupils merely listen, their intellect will be involuntarily prepared for a scientific mode of thinking. It is not possible for them to emerge from this discipline as a pure child of nature quite untouched by the power of abstraction.[28]

Unfashionable it may be, but I like the 'hidden curriculum' of children listening, of their being captivated by the forms and meanings of words they cannot criticise and which, at first anyway, they barely apprehend. Such a hidden curriculum is far more apt to make children receptive to the objectivity of value and to the existence of higher values than is the classroom filled with pupil reaction and the scepticism of the not-yet-educated, the classroom the Enlightenment has bequeathed us via Dewey. I realise, though, that Nietzsche's words, along which much of what I have been saying, especially in the closing sections of my lecture, raise the question of which or whose culture we are to use to inspire our children with notions of value beyond the everyday. They also raise the question of what we should do educationally if it turns out that some or many of our children are unable to get very far with the abstract language of higher culture. But these are questions for another occasion.[29]

28   Volume I, Section 266.
29   On which see the companion lecture, 'The Pursuit of Excellence', also reprinted in *Values, Education and the Human World* (2004).

SECTION FOUR

Liberal Education *Redux*

In recent decades, Britain has largely only thought about the enduring value of the liberal education tradition. Across the Atlantic, throughout the twentieth century, groups of Americans set to work to restore liberal education's impact. From John Erskine's pioneering work at Columbia in the early decades of the twentieth century (work inspired by his experience teaching soldiers in Europe after World War I) to the Catholic colleges living out Cardinal Newman's dream, America became, and remains, the latest haven for the liberal education tradition. Perhaps in the twenty-first century, as when Alcuin brought liberal learning back to Carolingian Europe from the School of York, this pragmatic, American spirit will prove a resource for a new British revival.

Chapter XIV

Revival in America
From World War I to
Christian Classical Schooling

> To put an end to the spirit of inquiry that has characterized the West it
> is not necessary to burn the books. All we have to do is to leave them
> unread for a few generations. On the other hand, the revival of interest
> in these books from time to time throughout history has provided the
> West with new drive and creativeness. Great books have salvaged,
> preserved, and transmitted the tradition on many occasions similar to
> our own.[1]

(a) American Lessons: Rereading the Great Books

Ever since liberal education left the shores of Greece, it has shown its
capacity for revival by those committed to its principles. As Robert Ralph
Bolgar writes in *The Classical History and its Beneficiaries*, the Venerable
Bede and Alcuin of York had to read the antique sources and deliberately
bring them back into the mediæval classroom: 'They moulded their teaching on the information these records [St. Augustine's *De Doctrina*, the
grammars of Donatus and Priscian, etc.] gave them about what had been
done in the past. They put into practice what they read, and found that it
worked.'[2]

In the twentieth century, it was America's turn to follow this path. If the
reformers did not ultimately succeed on the grand scale, America, large
enough to contain many contradictions, remains the home of a number of
separate, conscious attempts to preserve and reinvigorate the tradition of
liberal education for modern students, both in their early schooling and at
university level. In researching the latter years of the British tradition, it
becomes quite striking how often the speakers are recorded addressing

1 Robert Maynard Hutchins, Great Books of the Western World, volume I, *The Great
Conversation: The Substance of a Liberal Education*, 'The Tradition of the West' (1952).
2 (1954), p. 27.

American audiences (Albert Mansbridge's commencement address 'The Waters of Learning'; Oakeshott's 'A Place of Learning'; even back to Matthew Arnold's 'Literature and Science' lecture, in its revised form), or how the American reception of a British proposal gave that work its afterlife (Sayer's *Lost Tools of Learning*; Lewis's *Abolition of Man*). The Thomas More College of the Liberal Arts appreciates its debt to Europe, and sends all its sophomore students to Rome for a semester, but its campus is in Merrimack, New Hampshire, and not in the country that once educated St. Thomas.

The revival grew from a longstanding culture that valued self-education. A notable example is the tradition of Chautauqua assemblies, an adult education movement beginning in 1874 and popular into the mid-1920s in rural America. President Theodore Roosevelt called it 'the most American thing in America' and certainly these grand, multi-day assemblages of speakers and entertainers featuring lectures, music and classic plays attested to the national hunger for knowledge and self-improvement that continues to be one vital aspect of the American Dream. Nor was Chautauqua alone. The generosity of Andrew Carnegie (who thought Matthew Arnold the most charming man he ever knew) established libraries for self-improvement across the nation. In New York, workers took their education seriously. The 'Lectors' hired to read to Puerto Rican and Cuban cigar makers in New York provided material for passionate intellectual discussions and their listeners also became discriminating opera and theatregoers. The New York Public Library's incorporation of the Astor (1848), Lenox (1880) and Tilden (1886) bequests created one magnificent free and public collection. In 1895, Charles Sprague Smith founded The People's Institute to provide intellectual lectures to the city's recent immigrants, and the Institute was later led by Scott Buchanan, who introduced the Great Books curriculum at St. John's College.[3] New York's Cooper Union was established in 1859 as a full-scholarship college, together with a public reading room and a library, by Peter Cooper, who believed the best education should be 'free as air and water'.

Out of this background came America's twentieth-century liberal education revival, centred on the reading of the Western canon: the Great Books. Today, the Great Books Foundation (www.greatbooks.org), established in 1947 to promote liberal education for the general population, still

---

3   Tim Lacy has recently contended that The People's Institute offers the true origin of the Great Books curriculum, rather than John Erskine's work at Columbia. Those interested in examining his research in detail should consult his doctoral thesis with Loyola University, Chicago: 'Making a Democratic Culture: The Great Books Idea, Mortimer J Adler, and Twentieth-century America'.

supplies extracts from the canon and related resources for reading groups of all ages. A century ago, in 1909, the modern American revival laid its cornerstone with the publication of the first volume of the Harvard Classics, edited by Charles W Eliot.

Eliot, the President of Harvard from 1869 to 1909, had transformed that university into a world-class research institution. In his career, he had been a bold spokesman for, *inter alia*, downgrading the prominence of classical languages in education. But it was his much-repeated claim that anyone could educate themselves in the liberal sense by reading for ten or fifteen minutes a day from a five-foot (originally just three-foot) shelf of books that inspired the Harvard Classics. They were not the first-ever effort in this vein. John Lubbock's Hundred Best Books had been put forward in 1886, and the Everyman's Library series was conceived in 1905 by JM Dent in London; Bohn's Libraries (possibly the source of the idiom 'to bone up' on a subject) began appearing in 1846, and the Tauchnitz reprint editions of British and American authors had been published since 1841. Nonetheless, Eliot's Five Foot Shelf was perhaps the first American attempt, and important for its combination of deliberate concision with a uniform edition. It has been called the most comprehensive and well-researched anthology of all time. It aimed, for those who read their way along the shelf, 'to present so ample and characteristic a record of the stream of the world's thought that the observant reader's mind shall be enriched, refined and fertilized'.[4]

The Harvard Classics were a spectacular success. When Eliot died in 1926, nearly three hundred thousand complete sets of the fifty-one volume library had been sold. By 1930, some seventeen and a half million volumes had been sold by monthly subscription, and a number of imitators had also entered the market, increasing the sale of canonical works to the general population even further.[5]

But if the Harvard Shelf provided the essential tools for revival, the educational movement itself really began with the creation of courses based around these books. Despite Eliot's instrumental role in driving the classical curriculum out of Harvard, others were bringing the canon, with the classical authors now often read only in translation, back into the undergraduate classroom. On 15 January 1901, a Great Books course began at the University of California in Berkeley, under Charles Mills Gayley, who was also instrumental in establishing debating as an important part of the campus culture there. Gayley seems to have been a brilliant lecturer. By 1909,

---

4   Taken from Eliot's preface.
5   To coincide with the Five Foot Shelf's centenary, Christopher R. Beha's memoir of reading the entire collection, *The Whole Five Feet*, was published in May 2009.

when the first volume of the Harvard Classics was published, Gayley's one hour introductory lectures on the Great Books could draw audiences of more than a thousand, and were reported at length in the student newspaper, *The Daily Californian*. More significantly, at New York's Columbia University George Woodberry had inspired one of his pupils to a similar passion for the canon. John Erskine would go on to create America's most influential great books course, beginning in 1920.

Erskine marks the real beginning of a lasting liberal education revival in America, and for him the impetus seems to have come from Woodberry's influence, combined with his own experience in Europe. In the immediate aftermath of World War I, he was involved in providing education for the American troops on their way back to civilian life. In the ruins left by that confrontation, at the American Expeditionary Forces University at Beaune, Erskine saw education with a new urgency. Transmitting the best that had been thought and said became a passion. On his return to America, Erskine founded the general honours course in classic texts at Columbia that was eventually known as 'Humanities A' and today 'Literature Humanities', part of the Core Curriculum for all undergraduates at the college. The course would go on to have considerable influence, and Columbia would also later become the home to the much-loved classicist Gilbert Highet, whose radio broadcasts in the 1950s discussing classic literature with a general audience were carried by over 300 stations in the US and Canada.

Out of Columbia's example, related courses developed across American universities, including the St. John's College Great Books program, founded in 1937 by Scott Buchanan and Stringfellow Barr and still taught on the twin campuses of Santa Fe and Annapolis. Sister Miriam Joseph's primer to the core of the mediæval liberal arts curriculum, *The Trivium*, was also first published in 1937. Demand continued, and it was reissued in 1940, 1948 and most recently in 2002.

Perhaps the most important student of the Columbia Core was Mortimer Adler, who studied there with Erskine himself. Adler had also befriended Robert Maynard Hutchins, who became President of the University of Chicago in 1929 and invited Adler to join the Law School there as a philosopher of law, the Philosophy faculty itself being apparently resistant to Adler's candidacy. With Adler's help, Hutchins brought some of the ideas represented by the Columbia Core to Chicago, but more importantly, Adler and Hutchins re-energised the Great Books movement in America, creating the Great Books Foundation in 1947 and ultimately bringing together the resources for a new attempt at the Five Foot Shelf in *Great Books of the Western World* (1952), this time hoping to produce not just a uniform edition of masterworks, but also a detailed concordance by which related passages could be contrasted and compared.

Those two projects began in the immediate aftermath of the Second World War, even as Erskine's project had come from the 1914-1918 conflict. Just as in the UK, this renewed battle for civilised values gave fresh impetus to the cause of liberal education, but in the United States the calls for revival had more influence. In 1940, Mortimer Adler published *How to Read a Book*, which, revised with Charles Van Doren in 1972, has become a staple introduction to disciplined reading for American students. Robert Maynard Hutchins published *Education for Freedom* in 1943, the same year that Mark Van Doren, Charles Van Doren's father and a Pulitzer Prize-winning poet and critic, published *Liberal Education*, not as one who was liberally-educated but as someone who hoped to be.

> My book is not by one who considers himself educated. It is by one who still wishes to be, and who has set out to discover if he can of what the experience would consist.[6]

Nevertheless, *Great Books of the Western World* did not sell in such prodigious quantities as the Harvard Classics, even after door-to-door encyclopædia salesmen took up the cause. In part, this may have been the fault of the series format, with unwieldy, rather ugly volumes, content in columns of small print and out-of-copyright translations, out-of-tune in twentieth-century ears. A second edition, in 1990, dealt with some of the worst translations, but walked into the crossfire of the canon wars, criticised for insufficient revisions to reflect contemporary concerns at under-representation of women and of non-European or even non-Anglophone authors.[7]

The popularising of philosophy and great works by Will Durant and his wife Ariel had more currency in the post-war years, perhaps because the Durants were more open to discussing non-western philosophers. Durant received a joint Pulitzer Prize with his wife in 1967 and the Presidential Medal of Freedom from President Ford in 1977, but the couple died within two weeks of each other in 1981, as the canon wars began heating up. Allan Bloom's 1987 *Closing of the American Mind*, a hymn to what he saw as a dying vision of education on the American university campus, was a bestseller, but the stinging reviews it received from America's intellectual elite were a more accurate guide to the times. Harold Bloom's 1994 attempt to define *The Western Canon* along broadly traditional lines became notori-

---

6   Van Doren (1943), p. 11. Mark Van Doren also taught at Columbia, beginning in the same year as Erskine's Great Books course, 1920-1959.
7   Alex Beam offers an up-to-date, though slightly flippant history of the project in *A Great Idea at the Time: The Rise, Fall and Curious Afterlife of the Great Books* (2008).

ous, but largely as a lone reaction against the new schools of literary criticism that had become dominant. The New York Times reviewed the book under the title 'Bloom at Thermopylæ', to indicate that this was a doomed, if heroic, last-ditch stand for the Great Books.

In the limited success of the *Great Books of the Western World* (although it must be acknowledged that the seond edition is still in print) and the other popularising guides to the canon that followed, the limited success of America's Great Books movement over the twentieth century can be measured. Popular sympathy for the ideal remained quite high, but the intelligentsia, education's gatekeepers, were less and less convinced. Unsurprisingly, with the suspicions of authority and official culture that marked the years after 1960, such a project, despite the traditionally revolutionary nature of much of the material, came to seem a dead-end. While the Great Books Foundation continues, it work now includes supplying materials to school reading groups, something not part of its original mission.

In America's schools, the Great Books movement has also been supplemented by a broader concept—the transmission of core knowledge. The Core Knowledge Foundation was founded by ED Hirsch Jr in 1986, in response to a problem he had noted as early as 1978: some students, especially those from poorer backgrounds, were strangers to commonly-accepted items of cultural knowledge regarding, for instance, American history. The idea that an educated civic conversation on great issues demands at least some common vocabulary and knowledge, and that fairness demands that this be provided to all citizens, produced the Core Knowledge curriculum, which is designed to build solid, specific, shared knowledge in sequence throughout school years education.[8]

Such supplementary work is also carried out at American universities. The Symposium Readings at Lynchburg College, Virginia, begun in 1976, have been suggested as a model of their kind: encouraging cross-curricular engagement with the Great Books. The conservative Intercollegiate Studies Institute, founded in 1953 to 'educate for liberty' operates as an umbrella organisation across American colleges, providing students with resources that support liberal learning. In 2007, the ISI published *The Great Tradition*, its own comprehensive collection of original sources on liberal

---

8   This idea may be gaining currency in Britain as well. Even Michael Young, once the author of *Knowledge and Control* (1971), a revolutionary manifesto for restructuring the school curriculum to increase pupil engagement, uses his 2008 book *Bringing Knowledge Back In* to warn that schools must not forget their role in transmitting difficult-to-acquire knowledge. Michael Gove, the Shadow Education spokesman for the Conservative party, used the 2008 Aske's Education Lecture to stress the progressive nature of demanding that knowledge-acquisition remain central to national education.

education, and in February 2009 published Anthony O'Hear's *The Great Books* — an introduction to the high points of the Western canon.

In general, then, it is in courses at schools and universities that the American liberal education revival now continues, not as a shelf of great books for the adult autodidact, but in liberally-conceived courses or course supplements built upon those books and the idea of essential knowledge, and standing in counterpoint to what has become the mainstream of American education — making John Erskine, rather than Charles W Eliot, the more visionary of the revival's founders, and Mortimer Adler, who created the Paideia schools movement,[9] more successful in retrospect than Robert Maynard Hutchins, although Shimer College, the Great Books College of Chicago, could be said to be the inheritor of Hutchins's curriculum.

Hutchins himself might not have minded being marked down by history as a man with a limited legacy. There is no doubt that his tireless and stirring promotion of the value of a liberal education did much to keep the ideal alive and to energise those who would take it forward in new ways. And he was in any case fond of quoting words that have been attributed to William the Silent or Charles the Bold:

> It is not necessary to hope in order to undertake, nor to succeed in order to persevere.

(b) Why America?
US Exceptionalism versus Models for Britain's Future

For Britain, the larger question may be not how, but simply why America has proved more enthusiastic, certainly more practically committed, to the defence of liberal education. In some respects, this was quite surprising: American educators from the days of Emerson possessed a pragmatic streak and a desire to challenge tradition that resisted education for its own sake, particularly in ancient languages — as witness the work at Harvard of Charles Eliot before he devoted his retirement to the Five Foot Shelf. Was it only a British lack of American "can-do" spirit that made the difference?

America did have certain advantages that helped to make it the natural setting for such a revival. Here, small liberal arts colleges were a long-established fact. Even a more narrowly vocational higher education never replaced that tradition. Here too, the emphasis in America on looking back to their founding for inspiration proved influential. America's Declaration of Independence may have been a product of the Enlighten-

---

9   See *The Paideia Proposal* (1982).

ment, but it was also a neoclassical uprising, adopting appellations such as 'Senate' and 'Capitol' and ultimately constructing Washington DC as a second Rome, dominated by white marble columns and pediments and with all quadrants of the District of Columbia designated in relation to the Capitol's Pantheon-inspired Rotunda. The founding fathers of America were men raised on liberal learning and inspired by the democratic message of its originators in ancient Greece and Rome, and whenever their inheritors look back to these great statesmen and their debates, they also discover the educational tradition that produced them, and their common debt to Europe's cultural heritage. So, for instance, the Thomas Jefferson Classical Academy in Mooresboro, NC, chooses to follow a modern interpretation of the mediæval curriculum advocated by Dorothy Sayers to honour Jefferson's memory. More widely, Dr. Oliver DeMille's influential Thomas Jefferson Education books and courses show the synergy between the American founding and a restored liberal education.[10]

America also had a newcomer's respect for European culture and an awareness that the cultural legacy inherited from so far away could easily be lost. This sense of fragility readily translated into a preservationist movement, including the Harvard Classics, even as it also produced counterforces that sought to break from the past, particularly with the politically-correct canon controversies that raged over the privileging of "Dead White European Males" in the 1980s and 1990s, on which William Casement's 1996 history, *The Great Canon Controversy*, provides an overview, while David Denby's 1996 account of attending a Great Books course in middle age, *Great Books: My Adventures with Homer, Rousseau, Woolf, and Other Indestructible Writers of the Western World*, offers a useful corrective.

It is also probably true that America was more open to a liberal education revival because of the strongly religious character of its civic life. A liberal education does not have to follow any religious doctrine. Indeed within the United States the twin campuses of St. John's College in Santa Fe and Annapolis demonstrate, despite their name, a Great Books curriculum without a religious foundation. The Paideia Schools inspired by Mortimer Adler also continue to work in the tradition without necessarily instructing their pupils into any faith, focusing instead on combining factual instruction, skill acquisition and Socratic discussions. Yet it is also true that the liberal education tradition was intimately bound up with the fortunes of Christianity for many centuries, as discussed in the introduction and as the main body of the book bears out. It is then no surprise to

---

10   DeMille is also the Chancellor of George Wythe College in Utah. George Wythe taught law and read the Great Books with Thomas Jefferson, who referred to him as "my second father".

find that America, the most religiously-observant Western nation, should boast first-rate Catholic liberal arts colleges. Thirty years ago, an Englishman, Christopher Derrick, had to come to America to see the work of Thomas Aquinas College. His subsequent book, *Escape from Scepticism: Liberal Education as if Truth Mattered* (1977) is still worth reading and celebrates a modern place of learning where faith and reason coexist harmoniously.

> What kind of image will most aptly suggest the distinctive happiness which I observe in these rather unusual students? An image (I think) of liberation; and I have titled this book accordingly. Most colleges and universities today provide excellent education of the servile kind; but along with this, most of them provide also an indoctrination in scepticism, and this is something which paralyzes and imprisons the mind. But these particular young people have been set free.

Today, Thomas Aquinas College continues to thrive, ranked in 2009 by the Princeton Review as one of the nation's 50 "Best Value" private colleges. Since its establishment in 1971, a number of new Catholic colleges have joined it in the USA. Meanwhile, the *Vitale* Supreme Court ruling of 1962 and the *Schempp* and *Murray* decisions of 1963 effectively outlawed schooling with a religious character from America's public classrooms. The response has been the growth of Christian homeschooling and new, private school foundations in America, and both have turned to the liberal education tradition for guidance. The Christian Classical School movement is large and various but supports a strong academic education. While the emphasis on religious instruction and a characteristic rejection of evolution are startling by British standards (although Britain is not without its creationist academies, and all UK state schools are legally obliged to provide 'daily collective worship for all registered pupils'), they sit alongside an education that is genuinely liberal. Patrick Henry College (motto: for Christ and for Liberty), founded in 2000, offers homeschoolers a college where they can continue to pursue a liberal education within the Christian ethos of their early education. Their legal debate team is already recognised as possessing some of the nation's foremost young orators.[11]

The USA is bigger and much less centralised than Britain, thus allowing for a much greater degree of genuine diversity in education. The situation in Britain is further exacerbated because in 1989 the state nationalised both exams and the curriculum, through the national curriculum and state licensing of the examinations permitted in state schools. As was utterly predictable at the time (and was predicted in print by one of the editors of this anthology), the state curriculum in the UK has been increasingly cap-

---

11 For an overview and discussion of the movement, see 'The New Classical Schooling' by Peter J Leithart in *The Intercollegiate Review*, 43 (1), Spring 2008.

tured and moulded in their image by the progressives and utilitarians of the political and educational establishments, with the dire results for classical study in particular we have already mentioned.

A revival of liberal education in Britain such as exists in parts of the USA seems increasingly remote in our time, not least because of the moral weakness of the independent sector. Terrified of losing charitable status and of appearing elitist, some notable and recent exceptions notwithstanding, all too often even our historic public schools are content to follow lamely in the footsteps of their colleagues in the maintained sector, and to implement what the state decrees on syllabuses and exams (and on much else besides). It is fair to say, though, that liberal educators in British schools have had very little support from the universities. Individual academics complain constantly about the levels of knowledge and understanding of incoming students, but those leading the universities are notable for their silence on what is happening. One can only conclude that this is an almost inevitable consequence of the fact that all but one of Britain's universities are funded by the very same state whose policies have contributed so markedly to the erosion of liberal learning in our country. In delivering 'A Place of Learning' at Colorado College (see the section 'After Tradition' above) Michael Oakeshott charmingly observed that he had crossed half the world to find himself in familiar surroundings: a place of learning. Without correction, the time may be approaching when we Britons will have to cross half the world to find ourselves in a very unfamiliar place: a place of learning — as, indeed, Christopher Derrick was already discovering some thirty years ago.

By contrast to Britain's crushing reliance on central control, the American revival has been rooted in freedom, and has survived by demonstrating those elements of liberal education that accord so well with its own national tradition: its democratic character, aiming to liberate all who wish to submit to its disciplines; and its supra-political status, offering a form of learning whose value partisans of both right and left can agree upon. America in the twentieth century made Allan Bloom's erudite and conservative *Closing of the American Mind* a bestseller in 1987. It found Leo Strauss, the godfather of neo-conservatism, proclaiming 'liberal education is the counter-poison to mass culture' in 1959. And yet it also produced the St. John's campuses, Clemente courses in the humanities and Paideia schools, all of which leaned politically away from Strauss and Bloom.

America revived liberal education most successfully by re-emphasising it as a mass endeavour that transcended party lines, and there is food for thought here for Britain, where issues of class and ideology have helped to keep such a generous education a matter of suspicion, from one side or the other. After World War II in America, the GI Bill brought men from the army into college who might never have anticipated such an education, with great success. Robert Maynard Hutchins used to argue, "the best education for the best is the best education for all", and Mortimer Adler's *Paideia Proposal* and the ongoing Paideia Schools movement derived from it, centred on the National Paideia Center, remains the most comprehensive attempt to develop a truly modern, universal, faith-neutral, non-ideological liberal education.[12] Those involved began with the assumption that 'All children can learn', and went on to combine liberal studies with a number of other elements, some progressive, adapting themselves to the exigencies of a system that had to prepare students for earning their living as well as using their minds. The result may not be the final word, but it is a living experiment in revival with many creditable results, often in areas of socioeconomic deprivation.

Another attempt to bring liberal education to those traditionally excluded from the humanities curriculum was the Clemente Course of Earl Shorris, founded in 1994 and since extended around the United States and overseas. Resembling the workers' education movement in Britain, Shorris provided university-level liberal arts courses to the socially marginalised. He hoped to encourage them into personal liberation and the capacity to live the political life as understood by Pericles, Aristotle and Cicero, engaging with the world through reasoned argument and personal control. The course took Socrates as its model and proved very successful, demonstrating once again that those long considered unsuitable for the liberal arts can indeed benefit from their power. Shorris's memoir, *Riches for the Poor* (2000), details a highly original, modern remaking of the generous education devised by the ancient Greeks.

> "You've been cheated," I said. "Rich people learn the humanities; you didn't. The humanities are a foundation for getting along in the world, for thinking, for learning to reflect on the world instead of just reacting

12   That said, America still grapples with the limits that natural ability places on access to a liberal education at the highest level. The approach, derived from Plato, of concentrating on liberally educating a cadre of future leaders was taken up most notoriously by Leo Strauss and is evident today in Oliver DeMille's George Wythe College, which proudly claims to be 'Building Statesmen', and the exclusive and secluded Deep Springs with its 'education for service'. Charles Murray's 2008 book *Real Education* addresses this topic in some depth. See also his *Wall Street Journal* articles 16-18 January 2007, 'Intelligence in the Classroom', 'What's Wrong with Vocational School?' and 'Aztecs vs. Greeks'. In the last of these, Murray writes, 'In short, I am calling for a revival of the classical definition of a liberal education, serving its classic purpose: to prepare an elite to do its duty.' However, even Murray does not discount the value of a humanities-led education for all, he merely questions how far it can go. Following ED Hirsch and the Core Knowledge movement, he argues that 'More people should be getting the basics of a liberal education. But for most students, the places to provide those basics are elementary and middle school.' (Charles Murray, 'Are Too Many People Going to College?' *The American*, 8/9/08).

to whatever force is turned against you. I think the humanities are one of the ways to become political, and I don't mean political in the sense of voting in an election, but political in the broad sense: The way Pericles, a man who lived in ancient Athens, used the word 'politics' to mean activity with other people at every level, from the family to the neighbourhood to the broader community to the city/state in which he lived.

"Rich people know about politics in that sense. They know how to negotiate instead of using force. They know how to use politics to get along, to get power. It doesn't mean rich people are good and poor people are bad. It simply means that rich people know a more effective method for living in this society.

"Do all rich people or people who are in the middle know the humanities? Not a chance. But some do. And it helps. It helps to live better and enjoy life more. Will the humanities make you rich? Yes, absolutely. But not in terms of money. In terms of life.

[...]

"It is generally accepted in America that the liberal arts and the humanities in particular belong to the elite. I think you're the elite."[13]

Shorris developed a course that, with slight alterations, could be offered with success in the Yucatán, Mexico, demonstrating that liberal education still transcends boundaries, reaching across the divisions that cultural identity politics can emphasise too much. In an increasingly culturally-fragmented Britain, there are surely again lessons here worth learning, about finding potential among the disregarded, and about refusing to allow accidents of birth and background to deprive individuals of the best education possible.

Here is a suitable moment to leave the tradition, which is endlessly in the process of becoming, even as it looks back to its roots to remember where its origins lie. The story of liberal education in America is by no means an unmitigated success, but it continues, and shows that a practical revival of such an education is possible. Our broken tradition can still be mended, by many routes. The ancient ideals of self-mastery, weighty reading and civilised debate remain as valuable as ever, worth journeying across an ocean to bring home once more, as Mark Van Doren once dreamt of seeking their distant origins by looking towards Europe.

> The liberal arts lie eastward of this shore.
> Choppy the waves at first. Then the long swells
> And the being lost. Oh, centuries of salt
> Till the surf booms again, and comes more land.
>
> Not even there, except that old men point
> At passes up the mountains. Over which,

13   Shorris (2000), pp. 127-8.

Oh, centuries of soil, with olive trees
For twisted shade, and helicons for sound.

Then eastward seas, boned with peninsulas.
Then, orient, the islands; and, at last,
The cave, the seven sleepers. Who will rise
And sing to you in numbers till you know

White magic. Which remember. Do you hear?
Oh, universe of sand that you must cross,
And animal the night. But do not rest.
The centuries are stars, and stud the way.[14]

It seems fitting to pair this with Goethe's lyric 'Kennst du das Land' (c.
1783). A dream of Italy (or of the Greece Goethe never actually got to) and
itself a palimpsest of James Thomson's 1746 English ballad 'Summer'
('Bear me, Pomona! To thy citron groves'), it is a reminder of one of the
times when the greatest spirits in European culture saw salvation in the
ancient worlds of Greece and Rome. Thomas Carlyle translated it, and
wrote to Goethe to say that his wife played it for him often on the piano-
forte. Louisa May Alcott's biographer, Madeleine Stern, imagined Alcott
singing it beneath Ralph Waldo Emerson's window, and Professor Bhaer
hums from it 'like a big bumblebee' in *Little Women*. It was set to music by
many of the great composers of the nineteenth century, including Schubert
and, most memorably, Hugo Wolf. No doubt echoing somewhere in Van
Doren's imagination when he wrote, here again the American, European
and British traditions meet with their classical antecedents: as Thomson
invokes the Roman goddess of the orchard, Pomona, and in Goethe's mel-
ancholy evocation of classical magnificence. All share freely in the great
and endless conversation that a liberal education is always ready to invite
new voices to join, whether men or women, whether of the old world or
the new. Goethe's poem stands as a passionate invitation to the world con-
jured up in liberal education and an urgent summons to know that world
really, for those with eyes to see, ears to hear and the heart to respond; and
as such offers a fitting conclusion to our work.

Do you know the land where the lemon trees bloom,
Where in dark foliage golden oranges glow,
A soft wind blowing from the azure heaven,
The myrtle standing still and the laurel tree high?
Do you know it, really?

Thither, thither,
May I with Thee, o my beloved, go.

14 'The Seven Sleepers', from *The Seven Sleepers and Other Poems* by Mark Van Doren (1944). The
collection's dedication is to St. John's College, 'where the Seven are awake'.

Do you know the house? Roof resting on columns,
The gleaming hall, the glittering rooms,
And marble statues standing, looking at me:
'What, my poor child, have they done to you?'
Do you know it, really?

Thither, thither,
May I with Thee, o my protector, go.

Do you know the mountain, and its cloud-wrapt path,
Where in mist the mule picks its way;
In its caverns dwell the dragons' ancient brood,
The cliff falls sheer, and over it the stream?
Do you know it, really?

Thither, thither
Lies our way. O Father, let us go!

Index